RELIGION, FAITH AND PHILOSOPHY

SCM AS/A2

Religion, Faith and Philosophy

P. J. Clarke

scm press

All rights reserved. No part of this publication may be reproduced,
stored in a retrieval system, or transmitted,
in any form or by any means, electronic, mechanical,
photocopying or otherwise, without the prior permission of
the publisher, SCM Press.

© P. J. Clarke 2008

The Author has asserted his right under the Copyright, Designs and
Patents Act, 1988, to be identified as the Author of this Work

British Library Cataloguing in Publication data

A catalogue record for this book is available
from the British Library

978 0 334 04170 2

First published in 2008 by SCM Press
13–17 Long Lane,
London EC1A 9PN

www.scm-canterburypress.co.uk

SCM Press is a division of
SCM-Canterbury Press Ltd

Typeset by Regent Typesetting, London
Printed in the UK by CPI William Clowes
Beccles NR34 7TL

Contents

Introduction ... 1

PART 1 GOD, FAITH AND PHILOSOPHY

1 The Existence of God ... 7
2 The Nature of God ... 52
3 The Knowledge of God ... 61
4 Religious Faith ... 77
5 The Language of Faith ... 91
6 Faith and Reason ... 104

PART 2 RELIGION AND HUMAN EXPERIENCE

7 The Meaning of Religion ... 113
8 Religious Experience ... 119
9 Religion and Spirituality ... 137
10 Religion and the Afterlife ... 145

PART 3 RELIGION AND THE CHALLENGE OF ATHEISM

11 God and Evil ... 165

12	Religion and Science	177
13	God, Science and Miracles	190
14	Religion and Atheism	201
15	The Challenge to Religious Language	215

PART 4 RELIGION AND HUMAN BEHAVIOUR

16	Religion and Ethics	235
17	Religion and Virtue	264
18	Religion and Conscience	276
19	Religion and Freewill	286

Profiles of Key Names Mentioned in the Text	296
Glossary	315
Select Bibliography	329
Index	331

For Brigitte, Virginie and Colleen

Introduction

Philosophy of religion as both an academic and personal study

Philosophy of religion is the investigation into the nature of religion, and of the arguments used either to defend or to challenge both the claims of religion, and various aspects of religious belief. The term 'religious studies', as used by the various examination boards for the GCE A level, incorporates philosophy of religion as understood in this way. It includes topics such as the basis and nature of religious belief, and how far religious beliefs stand up to, or stand vulnerable to, the attacks of those who may be variously described as non-believers, sceptics, rationalists, non-theists, or atheists. This book will therefore aim to cover those topics that form part of the standard diet of philosophy of religion, and which we can here summarize briefly (see box, p. 2).

> A scrap of knowledge about sublime things is worth more than any amount about trivialities.
> St Thomas Aquinas

> What is the use of studying philosophy if all that it does for you is to talk about some abstruse questions of logic etc., and if it does not improve your thinking about the important questions of everyday life?
> Wittgenstein

One of the recognized attractions of philosophy of religion is the relevance of its subject matter to the understanding of life, and life's problems. Such a study bears inevitably on the personal beliefs of those who engage in it, whether these be religious or non-religious. It would therefore be surprising if the study of religion in this way did not engage the student in more ways than one. For some, the primary aim of the study may be simply to gain a

INTRODUCTION

> **Philosophy of religion**
> - Arguments for the existence of God.
> - The concept of revelation.
> - The nature of religious faith.
> - The relationship between faith and reason.
> - The meaning of religious experience.
> - The relationship between science and religion.
> - The meaning of religious language.
> - The understanding of miracles.
> - Beliefs about death and the afterlife.
> - Arguments for the non-existence of God.
> - The problem of evil and suffering.
> - The relationship between religion and ethics.
> - Issues about the meaning and nature of ethical obligation.

> The unexamined life is not worth living.
> *Plato*

> The philosopher is not a disembodied mind but a man with prejudices and passions of his own which may influence his intellectual life.
> *Frederick Copleston*

respected academic qualification in a subject of interest. For another it may be to engage in the challenge of philosophical thinking, in the hope of expanding the mind in the way that philosophy does. For others it may be an opportunity to engage in a personal search for ways to understand the meaning of life, through the eyes of those who have taken this search seriously. If taken for the latter reason, Plato would be pleased!

Gaining academic merit through knowledge, understanding and evaluation

The natural concern of all students is to be successful in their studies, and to obtain the best grades possible in reward for their efforts. In this subject area there are two opposing views to be considered or compared within all the topics studied, namely the view of the believer or theist, and the view of the non-believer or atheist. The primary requirement for the student is to show a knowledge of both views. This means that the student must be informed and objective, but not necessarily impartial. Impartiality would be impossible, since nobody has an empty mind. Everyone brings to their studies their own prior beliefs, convictions and even prejudices. This

INTRODUCTION

is as true of the philosophers and authors being studied as of those who study them!

The understanding of different viewpoints provides the necessary basis for making an evaluation. But

> Philosophy should never be studied for its own sake, but for wisdom and virtue.
> *St Augustine*

evaluation does not necessarily involve taking sides. Many issues 'depend' on certain fixed convictions on the part of either the theist or the non-theist. Making an evaluation does not mean showing that one side has better reasons than the other (this is normally what is called the 'my own view' approach). Showing the difficulty of making a clear evaluation is itself an acceptable form of evaluation. This will often be the case.

Different world views: theism and non-theism

It may be useful at the beginning to understand how the theist differs from the non-theist. For the theist, religious faith is the belief that the world came about and is guided by a personal presence called God. To believe in God is to see life in the light of God's existence. This means accepting certain religious and moral values on the understanding that human destiny extends into an afterlife. Not to believe in God is to see life from a 'secular' or 'rationalist' perspective, one that rules out any belief in a transcendent realm, a personal God, or an afterlife. Theists hold that their beliefs are justified as being a reasonable interpretation of human experience. Non-theists deny that any beliefs can be reasonably held unless they are confirmed by clear empirical evidence.

The focus on Christianity as representative of religious issues in philosophy

Since a full treatment of all religions would be beyond the scope of this book, the religion of Christianity will be its particular focus. While this will owe something to the author's own background, education and experience in education, the focus on one religion should not prevent a balanced understanding of the philosophical issues faced by all. Thus, for instance, the issue of God's existence, the question of religious experience, the problem of evil, the

INTRODUCTION

nature of revelation, the meaning of faith, how God can be described and spoken about, whether religion can be reconciled with science, how belief in God affects our understanding of ethical issues, are all as relevant to Judaism and Islam as they are to Christianity.

While such questions will form the main themes of this book, it may be noted that a certain repetition of themes and ideas will occur. This is quite inevitable since many separate topics raise issues that are interrelated with others. For instance, while the existence of God is covered in a specific chapter, most other areas of thought also bear on the question of God's existence or non-existence. I might also point out that the term 'man' will be used for convenience in an all-inclusive way, to stand for humans, humankind, human beings, and mankind.

Finally, while this book will aim to cover various topics for A level, it will often go beyond a mere curriculum-oriented approach in order, hopefully, to enable students to have some useful additional background for the understanding of the various topics from which questions will arise.

For all their help and support in seeing it through to publication I would like to thank sincerely Barbara Laing, Natalie Watson, Mary Matthews and Andrew Moore of SCM Press in London.

PJC, July 2008

I would advise all in general that they would take into serious consideration the true and genuine ends of knowledge; that they seek it not either for pleasure or contention, or contempt for others, or for profit or for fame, or for honour or promotion, or such-like adulterate or inferior ends; but for merit and emolument of life, that they may regulate and perfect the same in charity.

Francis Bacon

Part 1 God, Faith and Philosophy

1 The Existence of God

- The nature of the arguments.
- The ontological proof.
- The cosmological argument.
- The teleological argument.
- The moral argument.
- The strengths and weaknesses of the arguments.
- The arguments in relation to religious faith.

Demonstrating the existence of God by intellectual argument

Traditionally there have been two main approaches to demonstrating the existence of God. One is the deductive, logical or a priori approach represented by **Anselm** in his Ontological Argument, and later by **Descartes**. Here philosophy is used to argue God's existence from the concept of God. The other is the inductive, or a posteriori approach famously taken by **Thomas Aquinas,** based on existing data about the world and the experience of living in it. Later philosophers such as **Kant** used the a posteriori/inductive method and argued for God's existence from the inner experience of moral duty, and in the case of **Schleiermacher**, from the emotional sense of 'absolute dependence' which every human being encounters as part of conscious life in the world. Others again have claimed certitude about God's existence from what is called religious experience. But we begin with the so-called rational arguments for God's existence, and specifically with the ontological proof.

> **Methods of argument**
>
> **Premises** Statements of alleged, or presumed, truth or fact.
>
> **Deductive/a priori** Argument that involves no empirical evidence. The conclusion follows the premises necessarily, or logically. Best example: mathematics. This type of argument is also called analytical; for example, all spinsters are women. Conclusion: 'This is a spinster therefore . . .'. But is the ontological proof like this?
>
> **Inductive/a posteriori** Premises are based on empirical evidence. The conclusion follows from the premises, and claims to be an empirically true conclusion. Inductive conclusions in science usually go from the particular to the general, for example, the water I tested froze at zero degrees centigrade. Conclusion: 'All water will freeze at . . .' The teleological argument is like this; for example, this watch shows evidence of intelligent design. The universe is like a watch. Conclusion: 'The universe shows evidence of intelligent design.' But is the universe like a watch? If a premise is challenged the conclusion is unsound.

THE ONTOLOGICAL PROOF

The difference between proof, probability and possibility

Before looking at the ontological proof in more detail it may first be noted that it sets out to be a proof (whether valid or otherwise) as opposed to a mere argument that leads to something less than proof, such as probability or possibility. Probability is the claim that something may be the case. Possibility is the claim that something may or may not be the case, but could be the case. Proof is the demonstration of the claim that something is, or is not the case. In logic and mathematics proof lies in the necessity of the conclusion (2+2 = 4). In scientific circles the word proof means 'inductive' proof, and is used loosely to mean 'beyond reasonable doubt'. It requires the use of clear empirical evidence to establish a truth-claim, but all scientific claims are never more than probable!

THE EXISTENCE OF GOD

> ***The ontological proof*** God ***must*** exist in reality, not that he ***may***, ***might***, ***could*** or ***probably*** exists.

The ontological proof is unique in that it does not use empirical methods, yet it leads to a conclusion about what is the case in reality. This means that the proof operates on two levels, logical and factual, something that added enormously to its complexity. At one level it looks like a logical proof, but as we shall see it claims more than this. The ontological proof is the claim that God must exist in reality; not that he may exist, or probably exists. The proof either successfully demonstrates that God exists in reality, or fails to do this. It would therefore be absurd to say that this argument shows the 'probability' of God's existence. This makes it distinctively different from the other arguments – like the teleological argument, which is empirically based – and which are more about probability than proof.

> ***Logical proof*** As in mathematics and verbal analysis, the conclusion is logically necessary.
>
> ***Scientific (inductive) proof*** Based on empirical evidence and experimentation.
>
> ***Hypothetical proof*** A proof that follows conditionally. If I were married I would not be a bachelor.
>
> ***Probability*** Less than proof. A hypothesis supported by most, but not all, of the evidence.

Anselm's ontological proof: the idea of God means he must exist

One of the most renowned attempts to prove God's existence was that of **Anselm of Canterbury** with his so-called ontological (from the Greek *ontos* meaning being) argument. The argument is based on the notion of the being (or nature) of God, and proceeds to show that when the peculiar and unique being of God is properly understood it entails his existence in reality. The argument historically predates the other arguments and is different in kind from them. Both the cosmological and teleological arguments derive from empirical observations of the world. The cosmological argument derives from the observation that everything in the world needs a cause. The teleological argument proceeds from the observation that the world exhibits signs of organization, and argues to the existence of an intelligent designer. By contrast, the ontological argument is self-contained, and owes nothing to empirical observation. It analyses the notion of God, and concludes to his existence.

The first form of Anselm's proof: from the mind to reality

In the first form Anselm (*Proslogion*, chapter 2) sets out to show by a priori (logical) reasoning that God must exist. For Anselm, God is that 'than which nothing greater can be conceived'. The fool in the Bible who said 'there is no God' knew what he meant, and was a fool, said Anselm, because his denial of God was absurd and contradictory. Had the fool thought about what he had said, he would have realized that the God whose existence he denied was a Being whose greatness is such that he simply must exist. Thus to deny the existence of God is a logical absurdity. It is perhaps here that the main weakness of the argument lies. Many people are not impressed by logic even if they understand it. To deny God's existence may be a logical absurdity, but in reality it is not seen as an existential absurdity, that is, an absurdity that bears on real life.

> The fool hath said in his heart there is no God.
> *Psalm 14.1*

From this starting point at the level of pure thought Anselm argues that for God to be really God he must exist not only in the mind, as a concept, but in reality as well. In other words the 'concept' of God (as that than which nothing greater can be conceived) logically implies his existence in reality! Once God exists in the mind as a concept, it is simply a matter of seeing what the concept implies, namely a Being who is that than which nothing greater can be thought. To qualify for this definition God must exist in reality, because existing in reality is 'greater' than existing merely as a mental concept. Of only God can this be said. It may be noticed, however, that there is a certain ambiguity in Anselm's baffling reasoning. At one level the idea of God in the mind implies his logical existence. At another level the idea of God in the mind implies his real existence!

> **What Anselm means** If God exists **logically**, he must also exist **existentially** (in reality).

THE EXISTENCE OF GOD

It is this jump from the concept of God to the reality of God that has posed the greatest challenge to the argument. It is this jump that has made some critics accuse Anselm of 'defining God into existence'. Some writers assert that the reasoning would be acceptable if Anselm made the more cautious and (and perhaps more logical) claim that God exists 'by definition' rather than in reality. Anselm, however, claims that the idea of God, as that being than which nothing greater can be thought, implies his existence in reality, and this makes all the difference.

> **Summary of Anselm's first proof**
> 1 God is a being greater than which no being can be imagined.
> 2 The concept of God exists in human understanding.
> 3 The concept of God as existing in reality can be grasped by the understanding.
> 4 A being existing in reality is greater than a being only imagined to exist.
> 5 For God to be the greatest being imaginable he must exist in reality.
> 6 Therefore God exists in reality.

> *Anselm's tower* at Canterbury Cathedral is real, but does Anselm establish the reality of God?

Second form of the argument: the perception of God's necessary existence

In his second form of the proof Anselm (*Proslogion*, chapter 3) takes a negative approach, but essentially makes the same point. He starts with the impossibility of God not existing. Anselm here addresses God, and declares that he 'so truly exists' that he could not conceive of his non-existence. A being whose non-existence is impossible is truly great, said Anselm, so great that nothing greater can be conceived. Here Anselm appears to avoid some of the problems of his first formulation. Gone is the jump from the concept of God in the mind to his existence in reality. In this form of his proof Anselm introduces the notion of necessary existence, and claims that only God can possess this. But it is difficult to see how this is a new formulation of the first proof, rather than just a different way of putting it. In the first case he goes from the mind to reality; in the second case he seems to go from reality to the mind!

> **1st Form** God, existing in the mind, **must** exist in reality if he is TTWNGCBC.
>
> **2nd Form** God, existing in reality, **compels** the mind to see that he necessarily exists.

Necessary existence is a term (not accepted by many philosophers) to mean an existence that is categorically and essentially different from contingent existence. Necessary existence can have no beginning and no end. In this sense necessary existence becomes a predicate, a defining characteristic, and therefore a perfection, that can only uniquely be possessed by God. This restriction of the meaning of necessary existence to God, and God alone, might allow Anselm an 'escape route' from later criticisms of his reasoning.

> **Summary of Anselm's second proof**
> 1 God is that being than which no greater can be imagined.
> 2 It is greater to exist necessarily than not.
> 3 God must be a necessary being.
> 4 Therefore God necessarily exists.

Early criticisms of the proof

The earliest criticism came from a fellow monk, Gaunilo, who produced a parody of the argument, and something of a red herring in relation to what Anselm was trying to say. If God could be defined into existence then 'a most perfect island' should also be possible to define into existence. Anselm quickly spotted the fallacy of the argument, noting that no contingent thing could be confused with a being with necessary existence. No island could have 'maximal excellence' since it could always be added to, or improved, making it impossible for it to be 'that than which nothing greater can be conceived'. Theoretically an island could only be the best of its kind, while God is superior to and inclusive of all kinds and categories. Besides, maximal excellence can be achieved by a spiritual being in respect of knowledge, power and love. Hence God is said to be omnipotent, omniscient and omnibenevolent (meaning 'all loving' and morally perfect).

THE EXISTENCE OF GOD

> ***Contingent*** means being dependent on something else for its existence. No contingent thing could have ***perfection***, since being contingent is an imperfection. Only a non-contingent, or ***necessary*** being could have perfection (maximal excellence). Therefore 'a most perfect island' is absurd.

Aquinas, despite accepting Anselm's conclusion on other grounds, appears to have disagreed with Anselm for reasons that he must not have seen as very convincing. He held that God could never be adequately conceived in the mind since humans are incapable of doing so. The human mind, he believed, is incapable of conceiving so great a being as a transcendent God. If this is the case it is futile to go from a conception of God to claim his existence in reality. Yet Anselm is not saying this. All he is saying is that a most fundamental understanding of the concept of God is possible to the mind, one that anyone can understand. It is well known that Aquinas described God as that being whose essence (his nature) is to exist *a se esse* (by himself). This comes very close to Anselm's point, but Aquinas arrives at it by another route. Aquinas refused to accept that God's existence could be proven from the mere concept of his essence. As an empiricist he believed that God's existence could more convincingly be shown from the way things are in the world of creation. Hence his reliance on the cosmological and teleological arguments. Aquinas was probably also aware of the empirical fact that Anselm's proof cut little ice with unbelievers, and indeed ordinary people; for which reason he felt other approaches were necessary.

Descartes's argument: God is given in the mind as a perfect being

> ***Descartes*** held that necessary existence was a perfection, perceived as such in the mind, but many disagreed with his mental logic.

Descartes centuries later agreed with Anselm's ontology. But he arrived at Anselm's conclusion somewhat differently, and some say he may not have been familiar with Anselm's version at all. However, the versions of both are similar in respect to the fact that, first, both deal with ideas of God; second, both appeal to the impossibility of thinking of God as not existing;

and third, both were absolutely convinced of the power of their reasoning. In fact Descartes did not see his argument as a 'proof' of God's existence, merely a 'transparent truth' that could be seen by anyone who is free of 'philosophical prejudice'. By this casual admission Descartes shows a certain naivety in regard to the ontological proof. As **Leibniz** later noted, dryly, the argument unfortunately was not as clear to others as it was to Descartes!

> **Descartes** *believed (1) that he had a 'clear and distinct idea' of a 'most perfect being'; (2) that such an idea was already in the mind (**innate**). How far therefore could his approach be called **psychological** as much as **logical**?*

Unlike Anselm, at least in his first formulation, Descartes makes no use of a definition of God to argue his case. This makes his approach look more psychological than logical. This can be shown from the fact that his proof derives from two sources, both in the mind: the theory of innate ideas, and the theory of clear and distinct perception. Unlike Anselm, who began with the idea of 'that than which nothing greater can be conceived', he began with the idea of God as a supremely perfect being. He said that he had a 'clear and distinct idea' of 'a most perfect being', unlike contingent things (of which he had less clear ideas): he could only think of them as things whose existence was dependent.

Thinking about his clear and distinct idea of a most perfect being, Descartes concluded that to be a most perfect being God must also have, among other properties, existence. A most perfect being could never be dependent (contingent) on anything else. God was also an 'innate' idea (an idea you are already born with) in his mind. But, according to Descartes, innate ideas come from the 'substance' of that of which they are ideas. The idea of God as a supremely perfect being could never be produced by an imperfect being like himself. Therefore the idea of God must come from the real substance of God himself, thus confirming his necessary existence.

> My understanding that it belongs to his (God's) nature that he always exists is no less clear and distinct than is the case when I prove of any shape or number that some property belongs to its nature.
>
> *Descartes*

THE EXISTENCE OF GOD

The triangle and the mountain

Descartes famously used a geometric analogy to emphasize how God's existence was part of God's essence. He said that he could no more think of God without thinking of him existing eternally than he could think of a triangle without knowing that its angles amounted to 180 degrees. He also used the geographical image of a mountain and its surroundings, which he called a valley. He could no more think of God without thinking of him as necessarily existing, than he could think of a mountain without the existence of the valley that surrounds it. Existence was 'attached' to God as a necessary part of his essence like a mountain is 'attached' to its surrounding valley.

Kant's objections to the ontological proof

> ***Objection 1*** We could never ***know*** about a necessary being.
>
> ***Objection 2*** Existence can never be a ***predicate*** of a concept.

1 *A necessary being is beyond conception*

Later philosophers, but most notably **Kant**, disagreed with the ontological proof. He had two major objections. The first was the notion of necessary existence (see quote below). He said such a notion is merely a product of reason; we could never form any conception that it was real. Kant is arguing on *epistemological* grounds that our knowledge is necessarily confined to empirical realities: that we cannot go from the existing world to some supposed transcendent 'world' beyond the present. Both Anselm and Descartes would insist however that necessary existence can *only* belong to a transcendent world, and that the notion of a necessary being arises naturally from our experience of contingent things around us. Besides, even though we can have no clear conception of a necessary being as Kant pointed

> It is evident that the concept of an absolutely necessary being is a mere idea, the objective reality of which is far from being established by the mere fact that it is a need of reason ... the conditions of the understanding refuse to aid us in forming any conception of such a being.
>
> *Kant*

15

out, because it has no basis in experience, it does not mean that a necessary being cannot be thought to exist.

2 Existence is not a proper predicate of an existing thing

Kant's second objection was based on the difference between a predicate and its subject (example: the rose (subject) is red (predicate). He argued that existence can never be attached to anything as a predicate, that is, a defining characteristic. I can say that a spaceship is a vehicle for travelling in space. This is my understanding (concept) of a spaceship. But to go further and say that spaceships exist in reality is to say something additional. It is to make a claim that goes beyond the concept, and make a claim about what exists in reality. It is to say that spaceships actually exist, or more technically, are instantiated, that is, that there are instances of spaceships in reality. To imagine something existing is certainly to have the same concept of the thing as of that which does really exist, but the concept cannot imply its reality. As Kant said, I can imagine having money in the bank, or 'add noughts to my bank account', but that would not make me any wealthier! Therefore the concept of God in the mind is no proof that such a God exists in reality.

> ***Concept*** I can ***imagine*** what a unicorn 'is', with all its characteristics.
>
> ***Reality*** Imagining a unicorn '***existing***' adds nothing to my concept of a unicorn.
>
> But how far can Anselm claim (as he does) that the **concept** of God implies his **actual** existence?

Many, however, claim that Kant simply ignores the subtlety of Anselm's argument. Anselm would no doubt agree with Kant that it is indeed true of contingent things like spaceships and bank accounts, that the concept of them does not imply their reality. But this does not apply in the unique case of God. In the case of God we are dealing with a unique concept, one that logically implies the unique reality of God. Besides, Anselm might reply to Kant that he is not talking about the normal case of existence, but of necessary (that is, non-contingent) existence. But, as we have seen above, Kant refuses to grant Anselm the licence to go from the level of conceptual reasoning to assertions

THE EXISTENCE OF GOD

about what is the case in reality, and this does seem to create an impasse for the argument. Besides, many would say that the attempt to make God a logical exception, by way of necessary existence, is simply a case of special pleading, and as such would add no value to his argument.

> **Kant** Existence is not a predicate of any being.
>
> **Anselm** Existence is a predicate of necessary being.
>
> *How legitimate is it for Anselm to claim that* **logic** *demands that God* ***must*** *exist?*

To say instead that the 'concept' of God implies the concept of necessary existence is a much more modest claim than to claim the actual existence of God, as Anselm does. Others, like **Russell**, have charged Anselm with confusing the characteristics of a concept with the real existence of what the concept represents. Thus, although the concept of unicorns exists in the mind, it does not follow that there are unicorns existing in reality. This is a fairly straightforward point, but no doubt Anselm would reply that God is a unique being in virtue of having existence as a necessary part of his essence, and that the concept of God does imply his existence in reality. For both Anselm and Descartes necessary existence is a precondition for God to be perfect. Therefore to compare God's existence to something that might only have contingent existence in the world is simply to misunderstand the argument.

> **The ontological proof and the *concept* of God**
>
> - The *concept* of God is of TTWNGCBC.
> - The *concept* of a being TWNGCBC is a concept of God.
> - The *concept* of such a being exists in the mind.
> - The *concept* in the mind is of a being who is TTWNGCBC.
> - This *concept* implies the *concept* of a being existing in reality.
>
> *If Anselm had argued that the concept of God implied the concept of his necessary existence there would have been no problem. But Anselm was claiming that God exists at the level of* **reality***. Can Anselm get away with the jump from concept to reality? Anselm's reply is that the logic of his argument* ***implies*** *the real existence of God. Therefore there can be no 'ifs' about God's existence. But how convincing is this?*

Problems with Descartes' argument

Objections to Descartes' argument follow much the same path as those brought against Anselm's. **Kant**'s objection about existence being classed as a predicate of (an existing) thing holds for both. Yet **Descartes** would, no doubt, resist Kant's criticism by insisting that his clear and distinct idea of a necessary and eternal being is one with sound metaphysical foundations. Descartes may reply that he does not see existence as a predicate of God's nature, but a property which God, and only God, possesses, and one which he can clearly conceive, but to most people this would be hair-splitting. In medieval terminology God, and only God, is capable of being *a se esse*, that is, '*to be by himself*' existing unaided eternally. Thus it would appear that for both Descartes and **Anselm**, the concept of God is sufficient to yield an understanding that the concept is of some being that exists in reality, not just in the mind.

> For both **Anselm** and **Descartes** the *concept* of God is sufficient to establish his existence in reality, but for many people this does not work. Many would suspect that both are arguing from a knowledge of God obtained through other means. With this knowledge, it would be possible to 'define God into existence', but without it, impossible.
>
> *How far would already 'knowing' that God exists enable Anselm and Descartes to get away with their arguments?*

If Descartes (and Anselm in his second formulation) are both convinced that their psychological powers provide them with a clear concept (or intuition) of a being who possesses the perfection of necessary existence, this would appear to put them both in an unassailable position. In the end, however, the most obvious challenge to Descartes' proof is his claim that a clear and distinct idea of something yields knowledge of its essential properties. This may be true in mathematics and geometry but, as his critics would argue, cannot be convincingly established in relation to a supposed supreme being, as Descartes had claimed. This means that in the final analysis Descartes is left with his own convictions, which to him are intuitional and certain. To others they are merely a manifestation of Descartes' own faith in his own reasoning.

THE EXISTENCE OF GOD

Modern formulations of the ontological proof: Hartshorne and Plantinga

> **Charles Hartshorne** has made a major contribution to reviving the argument, focusing on the difference between contingent and necessary existence.

God is either impossible or necessary

Charles Hartshorne, a modern American philosopher, considers that Anselm's second formulation is the more convincing. He believes that the 'modal' distinction between existing contingently and existing necessarily is central to Anselm's proof. He accepts with **Kant** that contingent existence is not a predicate, but holds that this is not true of necessary existence. He believes that there is something significant about a being that cannot be thought not to exist. In this connection he believes that there are some necessary truths concerning existence in general, such as, for instance, that something exists to start with. Relying on the ontological argument, be believes the concept of a necessary being is required to justify the existence of the contingent things that make up the world. If contingent things exist, it is more than merely 'not impossible' that a necessary being, the only possible explanation that overcomes the problem of contingent things being the source of other contingent things, should exist.

> *Hartshorne* Things exist which are ***contingent*** and cannot explain themselves. This lights up the possibility of a ***necessary*** being that is able to explain itself. For God to have maximal greatness, or to be even ***possible***, he must be non-contingent on anything else.

Hartshorne's key notion is the distinction between possibility and impossibility in relation to God's existence. He takes two approaches here. If, for instance, God's existence were contingent it would be impossible. This follows from the fact that a contingent being depends on other beings in order to come into existence. Such a being would also be vulnerable to going out of existence. A being that was dependent in such ways could not be pre-eminent, or have maximal greatness, and therefore could not be God. For God's existence to be possible, therefore, it must be necessary, or non-contingent. This, he believes is the prime achievement of the ontological proof. His second approach is to claim that the existence of a possibly necessary being is a concept that can be held without contradiction. For such a being to be possible, such a being must necessarily exist. He argues that the burden rests with disbelievers to show why the concept of a necessary being is contradictory. He believes that no one has yet produced an argument to show this.

> **Hartshorne** believes it is **possible** that a necessary being exists, and that it is for disbelievers to show that a necessary being is **impossible**.

Alvin Plantinga has also provided a modern formulation of the ontological proof, one that is not too dissimilar from **Hartshorne**'s. He uses the notion commonly used in modal logic of 'possible worlds'. A necessary being, like a necessary truth, is one that must exist in all possible worlds. His argument goes like this. In some possible worlds some things are contingent (there are cars and trains for instance), and some are necessary (5+5 =10). A contingent being may possibly exist in one possible world, but not in all possible worlds. A necessary being, by contrast, would exist in all possible worlds. A necessary being would have to have the qualities of maximal excellence which are: omnipotence, omniscience and moral perfection. Such a being would also have to have maximal greatness, that is the unique capacity to exist in all possible worlds. But if such a possible being exists, then it necessarily exists. If it necessarily exists in all possible worlds, then it necessarily exists in any actual world. Therefore God necessarily exists in our world.

> **Plantinga**
> - If God exists in our world, he necessarily exists in our world.
> - If God necessarily exists, he necessarily exists in our world.
>
> *Can you spot the difference between these two, and how is this different from Anselm's formulation?*

It can be seen however that both Hartshorne and Plantinga are dealing with the logical implications of necessary existence. If God exists in our world, he

THE EXISTENCE OF GOD

(by the force of logic) necessarily exists, and vice versa. It does not follow, however, that God actually exists, and this makes all the difference. From this it appears that these two modern reformulations of the proof only work within the confines of logic. But many would argue that a purely logical proof of God's necessary existence would not establish the real existence of a necessary being. This unfortunately remains the real issue about Anselm's proof.

> ***Alvin Plantinga*** revived Anselm's argument that God is a necessary being. For God to be possible he must be necessary, and the idea of a necessary being can be held without contradiction to exist in our world.
>
> *But is this enough to prove that God actually exists?*

Where the ontological argument stands in relation to religious faith

A widely recognized problem with the argument concerns its relationship to religious faith. If it were so logically compelling, it is argued, where would it leave the morally and religiously free option which is faith? If faith of its nature is a free choice to believe in God, how can it be possible to show that God necessarily exists by rational means? An argument that could claim to establish God's existence as logically necessary would have the same logical force as showing that two plus two equals four. If the argument were patently successful nobody could claim exemption from the obligation to accept it. This would make faith a hostage to reason. But the proof has never been seen as an obstacle to faith in that sense.

> ***Faith*** God exists on the basis of revelation and the Bible.
>
> ***Reason*** The ontological proof shows why the biblical God must be TTWNGCBC.

For the believer at least Anselm's proof makes clear that no understanding of God can be arrived at without being consistent with Anselm's reasoning. Some say that Anselm was working backwards from an already existing faith in God whose existence he was merely reflecting on philosophically. In other words Anselm wanted to provide a clear vision of what belief in God implied at the philosophical level, the level of pure reason. Religious scholars like **Karl Barth** consider it more appropriate to see the argument as a sound exercise in logical reasoning that can usefully accompany faith, providing a vision of a unique being with the qualities of one who can be called the 'Almighty', and as uniquely worthy of worship. In particular it makes philosophically explicit what believers already know about God from revelation, namely, that he is that than which nothing greater can be conceived, an omnipotent, omniscient and morally perfect being.

> For the believer, ***Anselm***'s proof provides a philosophical insight into the ***uniqueness*** of God.

THE COSMOLOGICAL ARGUMENT

The cosmological argument is sometimes known as the argument from universal causation, or as the first-cause, or uncaused-cause, argument. While the argument does not claim to say anything about God, this is only partly true. It clearly echoes the ontological proof by its implication that God is that being which has necessary existence, without which God could not be the first cause, or uncaused cause of everything. However, it differs from the ontological proof in being a posteriori rather than a priori, and so arrives at the notion of God's necessary existence from a different angle. This can be seen from the way it proceeds from facts about the empirical world (such as that everything we experience needs a cause, or reason for its existence) to the conclusion that an uncaused cause is necessary to avoid an unsatisfactory *infinite regress*, which Aquinas rejected as impossible (see more on the reasons for this below).

> **Aquinas** rejected an infinite regress as ***logically*** impossible, but many would argue that the Big Bang also rules it out ***empirically***. With an infinite regress there would be no need for a first cause, and the cosmological argument collapses.

THE EXISTENCE OF GOD

Origins of the cosmological argument in Plato and Aristotle

Both Plato and Aristotle produced forms of the argument which point to the fact that the world to them was not considered capable of explaining itself. **Plato** held that pre-existing matter had existed from eternity, but needed a first cause in the form of some kind of 'self-originated motion' to impart organization and form to it. This he believed must be life, since only life is able to move itself. He called it the *World Soul*, to which he attributed wisdom and supreme intelligence. Likewise, **Aristotle** too argued for a first cause or *Prime Mover* to get the universe into its present form. Neither had any concept of *creatio ex nihilo*. They inherited the view of **Parmenides** that 'nothing can come from nothing', which led them to accept the concept of eternal matter. Medieval theologians like Aquinas would draw a theistic conclusion from Parmenides' *ex nihilo nihil fit*, to argue that God, and only God, can create from nothing.

Aquinas' cosmological argument

The most famous formulations of the argument were produced by the influential medieval philosopher and theologian **St Thomas Aquinas**, who taught in Paris, Naples and Cologne. His argument takes three forms: a prime-mover argument, a first-cause argument, and an argument from contingency. These were the first three of his famous 'Five Ways' for proving the existence of God. (The other two ways were an argument from *telos* in the universe to an intelligent designer, and an argument from the degrees of excellence in things to an ultimate standard of excellence.)

> **Aquinas**' arguments for God's existence were meant to show the philosophical soundness of religious belief.

His *first way* is based on the observation that things require other things to change or move them. There can be no infinite regress of things requiring to be changed or moved because in that case there could be no beginning to the sequence of changes, and then nothing would ever get started.

But things exist today, therefore there must have been a prime mover to

23

> **Aquinas' cosmological argument**
>
> *From motion*
> - Everything in the world is moving or changing.
> - Nothing can move by itself.
> - There cannot be an infinite regress of things being changed or moved.
> - Therefore there must be a prime mover.
> - This all men call God.
>
> *From causality*
> - Everything in the world has a cause.
> - Nothing is ever the cause of itself.
> - There cannot be an infinite regress of causes.
> - Therefore there must be a first cause to start the causal chain.
> - This all men call God.
>
> *From contingency*
> - Everything in the world is dependent on (or contingent on) something else.
> - Being contingent means that something need not exist.
> - If everything need not exist, at some time they did not exist.
> - If at one time nothing existed, nothing would exist today.
> - But things do exist today.
> - Therefore there must be a non-contingent or necessary being to explain this.
> - This is what all men call God.

initiate change. The *second way* is relatively similar, and argues from things and events in the world needing a cause, to an ultimate First Cause which is required for the series of cause and effect to get started at all. The *third way* argues from the fact of contingency to the need for necessity. If everything is contingent, that is, if it might or might not have existed except for something else causing it to exist, and if that cause is itself contingent on something else, then at some point in time nothing would be in existence. Since 'nothing can come from nothing' there would be nothing existing today, which is clearly false. This means that a series of contingent causes cannot be self-explanatory. This gives rise to the need for a necessary, or non-contingent, cause to account for all contingent causes and effects. This, said Aquinas, is what everyone calls God.

The Kalam cosmological argument

If the world had a beginning it was caused by God

Medieval Muslim scholars such as **al Kindi** and **al Ghazali** have also been prominent in attempting to

THE EXISTENCE OF GOD

prove God's existence, and it is known that Aquinas was aware of their work. The best-known argument from Muslim scholars is called the Kalam argument. What is distinctive about the Kalam argument is its assumption that the universe had a beginning in time. By 'universe' here is meant the whole of empirical reality. If the universe did have a beginning in time, then, the argument goes, it must have a cause to account for its coming to exist, and this cause is ultimately God.

The key premise of the argument is that 'everything that comes into existence must have a cause of its existence'. This is followed by the premise 'the universe once came into existence' followed by 'the universe must have a cause of its existence'. This is followed by the conclusion 'if the universe has a cause of its existence then that cause is God'. God is here understood philosophically as not belonging to the causal chain of empirical effects. The argument clearly resembles **Aquinas**' third way in which he argues that anything that itself needs a cause for its existence cannot be an ultimate cause. Since everything in the material world needs a cause for its existence, the ultimate cause of everything must be outside the material realm, and does not itself need a cause to explain its existence. That, as **Aquinas** put it (referring to the empirical fact of religious belief), is what people call God.

> **Summary of the Kalam argument**
> *Premise 1*: Everything that begins to exist needs a cause of its existence.
> *Premise 2*: The universe had a beginning to its existence.
> *Conclusion 1*: Therefore the universe must have a cause which is outside the universe.
> *Conclusion 2*: Such a cause is called God.

The Kalam argument exposes the problem of infinity

Defenders of the Kalam argument point to two sources to show that the universe did come into existence in time. The first source is science, which has confirmed the Big Bang as the moment of the beginning of the universe. Science, however, has only recently been used in support of the argument. The other source is mathematics, the original source used in the argument. According to mathematical reasoning the notion of infinite time is incoherent and contradictory. If this is the case then the Kalam argument is coherent and valid.

GOD, FAITH AND PHILOSOPHY

> ***Science*** Rules out an ***actual*** infinity in space or time. The Big Bang was the beginning.
>
> ***Mathematics*** Only accepts a ***notional*** infinity, that is, infinity is merely a 'concept'.

In the interests of brevity, the reasoning goes like this. There are two kinds of infinites, actual and conceptual. Conceptual infinites are only imaginary, bear no relation to reality, and are only used in mathematics. Actual infinites are impossible because we could never have experience of such things. First, if we take infinite time, it would have to include an infinite number of things, be infinitely long in duration, and again we could have no experience of such a thing. Second, an infinite past cannot be coherent because it could never be traversed, that is, its beginning could never be reached because, logically, it has no beginning! This can be seen by switching from the image of time to considering the notion of an infinitely distant point in space.

> ***Notional infinity*** Used in mathematics with the same 'notional reality' as the concept of nought.
>
> ***Actual infinity*** Impossible to conceive either in space or time. Has no starting point, and changes within it would also be impossible. Infinite regress presents the same problems.
>
> *But why did Russell either see no problem with this, or feel that the problem didn't matter?*

An infinitely distant point in space could never be reached because it would be infinitely far away. It would be like a receding horizon that is always ahead of the viewer, and can never be reached as a matter of logical necessity. Infinite space cannot therefore be traversed because, like infinite time, it could have no starting point. Likewise an infinite past time could never be traversed because it would always be infinitely past, and therefore the present could never arrive. In other words it would take an infinite time to reach the 'present', which is impossible. But the present has been reached, and the past has been traversed. The past therefore must have been finite, which means that everything must have had a beginning in time, which must have had a

THE EXISTENCE OF GOD

cause. The conclusion that the cause is God is resistant to all questions about his cause, since the idea of God having a cause is logically incoherent.

> **Russell**'s *'brute fact' dismissal of the problems of an infinite regress, shows that it can be easily ignored as 'too metaphysical' and 'irrelevant', but in the context of philosophical reasoning is this playing fair?*

But many would object, and say that however convincing this might be at a rational level, it is of little interest at the empirical level. We simply have no idea about any supposed reality beyond the range of what we can experience, and as far as we know the world as we have it is, in **Russell**'s words, a brute fact, and all metaphysical reasoning about what happened before is of little practical interest to anybody. The argument, however, challenges such reasoning.

> **Leibniz** produced his own argument, holding that everything must have a 'sufficient reason' for its existence. His argument converges with other cosmological arguments. He famously asked, 'Why is there something and not nothing?' suggesting, like **Aquinas**, that the question has an answer.

Copleston's cosmological argument

Frederick Copleston famously debated religious issues with **Bertrand Russell** in a BBC radio broadcast in 1947. When discussing the cosmological argument, Russell showed little interest in the argument's line of reasoning, claiming that 'we could never know' the answer to such a question, and 'for all we know the universe is just there'. Copleston expressed his exasperation with Russell by saying, 'If someone refuses to sit at the chess table and move, he cannot of course be checkmated!' This in a way exposes the weakness of the argument. If people refuse, or fail, to see its reasoning there is little more that can be said. Copleston, however, produced his own formulation of the argument, one mainly borrowed from **Aquinas**, based on the notion of contingency, which now follows (see box).

Criticisms of the cosmological argument

In the course of time the cosmological argument came under heavy criticism. Philosophers like Hume and Kant set out to undermine the reasoning behind such 'rational' type arguments. **Kant** showed that since all knowledge was a product of the mind working on the data of experience, no valid conclusions could be drawn about anything outside of our experience. The idea of invoking a supernatural being is purely speculative, and at best there is no way of knowing the existence of such a being. **Hume** took a similar, but more empirical approach, and argued that what applies within the world regarding cause and effect cannot be presumed to apply beyond the world. For all we know reality is different beyond the world of space and time, and what is valid within the world may cease to be valid beyond it. If both these objections stand, then the argument collapses. Both Hume and Kant also rejected the notion of a necessary being, and with it **Aquinas**'s idea that an infinite regress is impossible. If these objections are valid then again the argument collapses.

Russell attempted to add force to these criticisms by holding that the universe was a *brute fact*, and any attempt to find a cause for it was futile and

> **Copleston's cosmological argument**
> - All things in the world are contingent: they might or might not have existed.
> - Therefore everything in the world depends for its existence on something else.
> - There cannot be an infinite series of dependent contingent things.
> - Therefore there must be an original cause in the universe which is not contingent.
> - Therefore this cause must be a necessary being, which is the cause of itself.
> - This necessary being is what people call God.

> **Objections to the cosmological argument**
> - Our knowledge cannot extend beyond experience (Kant).
> - We cannot suppose causality operates beyond our experience (Hume).
> - Maybe matter is eternal and has its own powers of existence and development (Hume).
> - What happens outside our experience is of no practical interest (Russell).

unproductive. He believed that because things in the world needed a cause for their existence, there was no necessity that the universe as a whole needed a cause. Theists, however, have replied that such reasoning is not very convincing, as it supposes that the universe as a whole is different from its parts. The universe is clearly a contingent phenomenon; and just as its parts are contingent, so is the whole. Not only that, but science has confirmed that the 'parts' of the universe all originated in a common moment of singularity, the instant of the Big Bang. Therefore it is a contingent thing, and as such cannot be invoked as the cause of itself. Besides, Aquinas was not attempting to explain the universe as a ready-made, complete entity, something that needed to be explained in addition to its parts within the world. He was merely arguing that for the universe to come about, together with all its parts, there must have been a first cause to start the whole process (the chain of cause and effect).

> **Russell** ridiculed the idea of a first cause by saying, 'just because everyone needs a mother doesn't mean the human race needs a mother'. Such a remark shows a failure to understand the link between **all** caused realities (everything), and the need for a ***first*** cause, at some point, to begin the ***causal chain***.

Responses to the criticisms: the notion of personal agency

Swinburne takes up Russell's brute-fact argument and claims that this is unsatisfactory. Very few are content to accept that things are as they are because 'they just happen to be like that'. He believes the cosmological argument has important explanatory force in answering the question why there is a universe at all. He argues that if an explanation is sufficient, it leaves no room for further questions. This is clearly not true of the universe, which is a contingent thing no more able to provide a satisfactory explanation of itself than its contingent parts are able to explain themselves. For this reason we must appeal to something beyond the contingent for a satisfactory explanation of that which is contingent.

> According to **Swinburne** the most satisfactory explanation of anything should leave fewest questions to be answered.

Swinburne believes that the existence of God is more probable than any rival explanation because it invokes the notion of a personal being. The explanation of something in terms of personal agency, Swinburne believes, provides greater finality to a question than any other explanation. No scientific explanation for the existence of the universe is able to do this because every such explanation begs the question, 'Why should a mechanistic or blind-force explanation be satisfactory to questioning beings?' Therefore the notion of personal agency is in the end a more satisfactory explanation than any other. The fact that to believe this requires faith does not alter its candidacy as possible, if not probable, solution (see also Plato above, p. 23, on this).

> ***Swinburne*** The cosmological argument overcomes the limitations of contingent explanations, and introduces ***personal agency*** as a more satisfactory solution than ***blind material force***s, because it leaves fewer questions to be answered.

The question of the limitations of contingent explanations

Theists might respond to the criticisms already mentioned by making a few final points. **Kant**'s criticism that we can obtain no knowledge outside of our experience was effectively to condemn all metaphysical speculation as pointless. Such speculation, however, is inevitable, given the questions raised by certain aspects of our experience, such as the need for ultimate non-contingent causality. If the world as a contingent reality cannot explain itself, something else must be invoked to explain it. This was the central argument of **Aquinas**.

For this reason many insist today that the cosmological arguments cannot be ignored because they deal with areas of thought and speculation that demand an explanation. The scientist **W. L. Craig**, in defending the Kalam argument, sees it as confirmation of Aquinas' view that an infinite regress is impossible: Since, he says, we know from science that the world had a beginning in time, it must have had a divine cause of its beginning, because no contingent cause can be the cause of itself. According to Craig the implications of contingency, and the principle that nothing can come from nothing, continue to pose serious problems, unless God is invoked as the ultimate cause of everything.

THE EXISTENCE OF GOD

> The cosmological argument ultimately depends on whether *contingent* things are able to *explain* themselves.
>
> *Many think that chance is a 'less astonishing' explanation than personal agency, but how far is this a valid response?*

Theists would point out that the claim that an 'evil demon' created the world, or a 'committee of demi-gods', as suggested by **Hume**, only begs the question the argument sets out to answer: Why should contingent beings provide an ultimately satisfactory answer to the existence of all other contingent things?

The cosmological argument and religious faith

The criticism that the argument only establishes the existence of an uncaused cause, and that this cannot be identified with the God of theism, is seen by many as a trivial point. Theists have no difficulty in seeing that the postulate (claim) of an uncaused cause is a philosophically valid description of the God they believe in, not only on the basis of faith and revelation, but also in relation to the requirements of classical theism (see the nature of God, p. 31). A being with *aseity* (existing *a se*, or by himself) who is capable of creating the world *ex nihilo* (out of nothing) spells out enough about the nature of God to identify it as the God of theism. At the same time, however, it is unlikely that the argument would be of much interest to believers, either to support faith, or to allay doubts about God's existence. But how far it is capable of engaging rationalists in the questions it raises, is perhaps in the end more an empirical than a philosophical question.

> ***Faith*** God made the world (Genesis).
>
> ***Reason*** The world cannot be explained without a First Cause (God).
>
> *How far can the cosmological argument be seen to be relevant to religious faith?*

THE TELEOLOGICAL ARGUMENT

The argument that systematic order in the universe points to God

Deriving its name from the Greek *telos* (aim), the teleological argument is often called the argument to (not from) design. The important point here is that if design is established, the conclusion to a designer (which in turn implies intelligence) is established. The argument is based on the supposition that an ordered universe like ours points to an explanation, of which an intelligent designer is the most probable. Historically the argument drew its conclusions from a global perception of an ordered world that inspired awe and wonder. Theists point to the biblical text 'The heavens declare the glory of God, and the firmament reveals his handiwork' (Psalm 19) as indication that empirical observation of the universe raised questions, and that for many a theistic answer was the most appropriate.

> The **teleological** argument supposes that the evidence of **telos** (aim, purpose) in the way the world is, and how it works, points to an intelligent being that would best explain that *telos*.

More recent forms of the argument rely on spectacular observations from astrophysics that the conditions necessary to support life were so unlikely as to suggest an answer that could not be provided by science alone. Many suggest that the idea that an inanimate system of reality, arising from the existence of nuclear particles acting randomly from blind energy, could produce the conditions that make an understanding of their operation possible (human intelligence), suggests an answer that goes beyond science. In this view, if an answer goes beyond science it is reasonable to suppose the answer could be consistent with a religious viewpoint. For this reason **Aquinas** finds it reasonable to suppose that the phenomenon of *telos*, or purpose in the universe, something that cannot be supposed ultimately to come from a blind inanimate source, is best explained by an intelligent being, a being that corresponds to what 'all men call God'.

THE EXISTENCE OF GOD

Aquinas' teleological argument (twelfth century)

Aquinas' fourth of his 'Five Ways' argues from the apparent order and design in the world around us to an intelligent agent of design, called God. Everything appears guided and ordered to some end. The alternative, says Aquinas, would be an unpredictable, chaotic world without law, order or organization. Instead we can see that inanimate matter is governed by the predictable physical laws of nature, and the animal world in turn is governed by instinct, which is equally directed towards orderly aims and objectives. This suggests a hidden hand guiding all things to their proper end. This, says Aquinas, can be illustrated by an (intelligent) archer directing an (inanimate) arrow to its target. Here Aquinas argues for a source of reality that is personal and intelligent, as opposed to one that is blind and impersonal.

> We see that things which lack knowledge, such as natural bodies, act for an end, and this is evident from their acting always, or nearly always, in the same way, so as to achieve the best result. Hence it is plain that they achieve their end not fortuitously, but designedly. Now whatever lacks knowledge cannot move towards an end, unless it be directed by some being endowed with knowledge and intelligence; as the arrow is directed by the archer. Therefore, some intelligent being exists by whom all natural things are directed to their end; and this being we call God.
> *Thomas Aquinas*

> Aquinas used the image of a target and arrow to show that the arrow needed personal guidance to hit its target. In the same way, he suggests, many things in the world show signs of purpose, which suggests the hidden presence of an intelligent (personal) originating designer.

Paley's teleological argument (nineteenth century)

> *Paley used a watch as an image that suggests intelligence and purpose. How far have modern discoveries about the workings of nature undermined his argument?*

One of the most famous formulations of the teleological argument was produced by **William Paley.** The Oxford divine pointed to two apparently observable but interconnected aspects of the visible world, the appearance of purpose and order. Both aspects were illustrated in his famous analogy of a watch. Just as an intricate mechanism like a watch, which is purposely designed to record the time, points to an intelligent watchmaker, so does the universe, which (he claimed) resembles a watch in many respects, also point to an intelligent designer. Paley also appealed to more detailed workings of nature, such as the operation of the human eye, which also shows remarkable evidence of purpose and intelligent design, to argue for the existence of a hidden intelligent designer (God). To achieve purpose there must be order, something that Paley claimed could be seen in the universe at large, and in the detailed working of natural laws, and in nature as a whole.

Paley's argument revised

Old version In crossing a heath, suppose I pitched my foot against a stone . . . for all I knew it had lain there for ever . . . But suppose I found a watch upon the ground, I should hardly think of the answer I had given before . . . For this reason, that when we come to inspect the watch (we discover) that its several parts are framed and put together for a purpose . . . The inference we think is inevitable: the watch must have had a maker.

Revised version In crossing the universe suppose I come across a multiplicity of heavenly bodies all spinning in space . . . For all I knew they may have been there for ever . . . But suppose I come across the solar system, and then the planet earth, I would hardly think of the answer I had given before. For this reason, that when we come to inspect this part of the universe and especially its relationship to planet earth, and the planet itself, (we discover) evidence that its several parts are framed and put together for a purpose, the purpose being the evolution and sustenance of intelligent life. The inference, we think, is inevitable: all this could be no accident; it must have had a maker.

How far does this imaginary version of Paley's argument go towards overcoming the objections to the original argument?

The anthropic-principle form of the argument (twentieth century)

The so-called anthropic principle derives from the observation that the universe is remarkably geared to support human life. According to this principle the universe would be meaningless unless humans (anthropoids) were here to observe it. Some theists have used the 'strong anthropic principle' as a basis for arguing that the universe was ultimately created with the purpose of producing human life. A more 'moderate' anthropic principle has been put forward by **John Polkinghorne** as a serious basis for the supposition that something more than pure chance needs to be invoked to explain the existence of human life.

> The *anthropic principle* was coined as a response to the *Copernican principle*, which held that man is not the centre of the universe. The anthropic (from the Greek *anthropos*, man) principle arose from the observation that human conscious life is necessary to observe the universe at all. Non-theists (or naturalists) see this as a brute fact, while theists see it as an improbable fact, suggesting that the universe was 'designed' to produce self-conscious life.

Scientists agree that even an infinitesimal variation in the conditions that followed the Big Bang would have resulted in conditions impossible for the existence of life, let alone human life. More specifically, had the conditions been different, the universe would have expanded more quickly than it did, and would have contracted correspondingly faster, in either case making life impossible. (This has led to the use of the term 'fine tuning' to highlight the need for such precise conditions favourable for life.) Polkinghorne has given a corresponding image of cosmic unlikelihood with the concept of an inch-wide target lying on the farthest reaches of the universe being accurately hit from earth. On this basis it is proposed that something more than the operation of physical forces is necessary to explain the existence of a purposeful universe at the centre of which is human life.

Swinburne's form of the argument (twentieth century)

Swinburne's approach to the teleological argument is distinctly modern inasmuch at it takes into account the basic principles of scientific truth-searching, and offers reasons why the hypothesis of personal agency behind the existence of the world is worthy of serious attention. He therefore believes the argument is not a knock-down proof for the existence of God, but instead a good basis for believing in its probability. Probability, after all, is the most that science can offer, but science by itself, he believes, is unable to go beyond a certain point in any of its theories, and is therefore not the final stage of any explanation. The orderliness of the universe is a fundamental fact which, among other things, is crucial to the meaningfulness of human life. Either it is a brute fact and unexplainable, or it has an explanation. If it has an explanation, the explanation must be personal agency.

> ***Paley*** Stresses the spatial order (intricate positioning) of the universe; but this is something that is now explained by the Big Bang and evolution.
>
> ***Swinburne*** Stresses the temporal order of the universe, the way it operates through time by way of natural laws, suggesting design and purpose, rather than blind chance.
>
> *Paley, however, had already included the notion of intelligent purpose, which matches Swinburne's point about personal agency.*

Swinburne believes that Paley's argument appears to be too dependent on spatial order, the recognition of the intricate workings of things, and that this has been weakened by evolution. But he believes that the temporal order which the universe displays is a much more solid basis for the argument to design. Temporal order is the order that can be seen in the way things succeed each other by natural law. This is evident in the regularity of cause and effect which is the basis for the universe being an ordered whole, rather than a chaotic mass of matter. Throughout the universe, the physical laws of cause and effect appear to be constant and reliable. Either this is the result of chance, or part of the design of an intelligent being. In particular the precise nature of the Big Bang, the moment when cause and effect led to the destiny of a life-supporting universe, is of special significance. In Swinburne's view it is more probable to suppose that behind such a mysterious phenomenon lay the hand of a personal agent (God) than to suppose the whole thing was a chance occurrence.

> **Swinburne** has highlighted the two fundamental hypotheses that compete for credibility. Either the universe is the product of ***blind chance***, or it is the product of ***personal agency***. However, non-theists (naturalists) accept blind chance as an acceptable belief on the basis of it being a 'brute fact', and a mystery we cannot penetrate.

Swinburne uses the analogy of a box containing decks of cards to highlight the difference between blind mechanism and personal agency. If the cards in each deck are found to be packed in correct order by suit and value, it may be supposed that the least probable explanation is that they were all thrown together randomly and packed as they were. By contrast, the most probable explanation is that they were produced by a machine which put them in correct order. The machine in turn was the creation of an intelligent designer. In the same way, he argues, if the universe displays the conditions that enable us as humans to live in it, we should be more inclined to see that as a sign of some personal agency at work than mere blind chance.

> Richard Swinburne held that the constancy of the laws of physics over the whole universe is as unexpected as cards falling into place in remarkable order. In each case a personal agency is the most likely explanation.

Challenges to the teleological argument

The fundamental objection to the teleological argument resides in the conflict between supposed design and natural processes, among which the process of evolution plays a leading part. If evolution is accepted as something that can credibly explain both the existence and form of living beings, then the claims of the teleological argument about the involvement of an extrinsic designer cannot be sustained. At the factual, empirical level this appears to be the case, because naturalistic explanations look impressive. But defenders

GOD, FAITH AND PHILOSOPHY

of the argument insist that a natural process such as evolution itself needs an explanation that cannot be provided by appeal to natural processes alone. Hence the deadlock. We begin, however, with **Hume**'s objections.

Hume's objections to the argument

> **Summary of Hume's objections**
> - The world could have come about by accident (chance) rather than design.
> - Even if it was designed, there is no reason to suppose the designer was God.
> - The evidence of poor design (earthquakes, pain) suggests a poor designer.
> - Since the universe is unique, we cannot suppose universes need designers.
> - All signs of existing design can be explained naturalistically.

Hume's objections have two things in common. All reject the theistic assumption that the world was the product of an intelligent, omnipotent being called God. They also in each case suggest an alternative naturalistic explanation to a theistic one. In Hume's defence, he was providing a warning for believers about claiming too much on the strength of a teleological approach. In his view, whatever the arguments for theism, this was not one of them. But his objections have one noticeable weakness. They ignore the key problem raised by the other arguments: the problem of contingency. They therefore overlook the necessary connection between the cosmological and teleological arguments.

> **Hume**'s objections assume that contingent things can explain themselves, which highlights the dependence of the teleological argument on the cosmological argument.

There is such a connection because the assumption of teleology points to the need for a non-contingent being whose existence raises no further questions about that being's existence. To say, therefore, as Hume does that the world can effectively explain itself only begs the question of why anything contingent could do so. This shows how the teleological argument is dependent on the cosmological argument, and cannot be separated from it.

THE EXISTENCE OF GOD

> *Hume's critique of the teleological argument was a warning to theists that its foundations were weak, but what could be considered the main weaknesses of Hume's objections?*

Mill's objection to the argument

Mill's objection rests on Hume's empirical observation that the universe shows poor design. He agreed with Hume that evidence of poor design weakened the argument. He believed that the evil and suffering produced by nature goes unpunished, and that this suggested an unguided universe. 'Either there is no God or there exists an immoral and incompetent God.' While Mill's objection highlights a flaw in the argument, it is not original. It is really another form of the anti-theistic argument from evil and suffering which is answered by theodicy (see p. 166). Under the impact of theodicy the conclusion 'either God does not exist or he is immoral and incompetent' are not the only possibilities. Theodicy shows that evil and suffering are possibly inconsistent with a loving God.

> Both **Hume** and **Mill** argued that evidence of poor design undermined the argument. But many have replied that *poor* design is still *design*, and there may be *reasons* for it.

Dawkins' objection to the argument

The modern biologist **Richard Dawkins** adopts a standard post-evolutionary stance in objecting to the claim that religion has anything to say about the origins of life. Instead, he believes that natural selection and DNA can be shown to be the two driving forces in the development of all living things. Above all, he maintains, all the evidence shows that these processes operate by way of blind chance, apart from the internal dynamism present in each. Dawkins concentrates solely on **Aristotle**'s notion of 'efficient causality', clearly distancing himself from any possible religious theory which would postulate some personal agency working with aim and purpose, which Aristotle called 'final causality' (see p. 187). However, Dawkins has been challenged by **Plantinga** to face up to some of the implications of his naturalistic anti-religious theory that everything is ultimately a product of blind forces.

> **Dawkins** concentrates on the *efficient* causes of things. He rules out the possibility of *final* causality, which is what *religion* deals with.

If everything, as Dawkins supposes, can be explained by way of blind natural processes, on what basis can he rest his belief that evolution (contra the teleological argument) can provide a definitive answer that can be relied on? If evolution is 'unguided' as Dawkins claims, why should we believe that naturalistic explanations are in any way reliable? Since, according to Dawkins, we have no God-given soul (as theists believe), why should our neurological processes (resulting from unguided evolution) be expected to provide us with access to any truth about the world? As **Descartes** had already recognized, without the notion of a God who is not a deceiver, for all we know we may be living in a dream world controlled by an evil demon, where truth about reality is merely a chimera, or an illusion.

> ***Dawkins*** Everything evolved according to the needs of organisms, but evolution is ultimately the result of blind biological and physical forces. This is called *naturalism*.
>
> ***Plantinga*** The view of naturalism, that everything goes back to blind forces, rules out any reason why its product, human intelligence, can be relied on to arrive at objective truth.
>
> *How does ruling out an infinite regress add strength to Plantinga's argument?*

Theists, by contrast, as **Plantinga** points out, have reason to believe in the evidence of the senses because they believe what Descartes concluded, namely, that a good God could not be a deceiver. Only by grounding the evidence of the senses in some kind of metaphysical basis (such as the existence of God) can it be possible to trust that the evidence provided by experience can be relied on as an infallible basis of truth. For this reason, Plantinga puts it to Dawkins that the clash which he thinks is between science and religion is, really, between science and naturalism. This, he believes, leads to a galling choice for Dawkins. Either he accepts God as the ultimate guarantor of all truth-claims, or he trusts that all his truth-claims are valid, despite himself

THE EXISTENCE OF GOD

also being the outcome of the blind forces that produced what appears to be an orderly world.

> Dawkins, one of Britain's most outspoken critics of theism, is widely criticized for holding a confused and inconsistent position. If, as he claims, God is a delusion, then his existence is false. But he also claims that God is ***improbable*** (see p. 43). This still leaves open the ***possibility*** of God's existence. In which case God cannot be called a delusion.

How science challenges Paley's argument

The arguments suffered a big setback from the scientific discoveries in cosmology, geology and biology. These discoveries showed the workings of natural causes to explain many of the features of the world, including its origin. Natural causality had a particularly devastating effect on the teleological argument, which claimed that the appearance of 'order and design' present in the world and in nature pointed to God. The noted teleological argument of **William Paley**, in which he invokes God as the intelligence behind the intricate workings of the world by analogy with a watch, suffered particularly from the discoveries of **Charles Darwin**.

> The discovery of the extensive operation of natural laws and causes throughout the world made **Paley**'s argument look too presumptuous. To all outward appearances the world had no need of an intelligent 'watchmaker' because the evidence showed that it had evolved gradually over time.
>
> *But how far did this completely rule out any form of teleology?*

Many of the formerly awe-inspiring features of the physical universe, in particular the phenomenon of life, could now be explained without the 'God hypothesis' as **Laplace** called it. Instead they were shown to be explicable in terms of the physical laws of mechanics and natural selection (for more see Chapter 12, Religion and Science). However, theists would argue that Laplace failed to understand that religion was something other than an explanatory tool to rival science. For many believers, such a view of religion is misleading

41

and inadequate, because it supposes that religion can be introduced to short-circuit natural or scientific explanations. As we shall see, the 'God hypothesis' is not a rival to an evolutionary hypothesis: it merely claims that physical explanations fall short, because they remain at the level of the physical and the contingent, and fail to stop further questions being asked.

> ***God of the gaps*** An old idea by which religion was used to explain empirical problems that belonged to science.
>
> *But how, by retaining the word 'gap' to mean something **non-empirical**, might the idea still have relevance in showing that religion can fill some gaps that science cannot?*

The god of the gaps is not about efficient causality

To introduce religion as an interim explanation to rival science is then a serious mistake, because religion is about ultimate, or final, causality and not efficient causality (see also below, p. 188). No ultimate (religious) explanation can ever rival an efficient (scientific) one. For this reason a 'god of the gaps' introduced to explain causal gaps, in what science should in principle be able to explain, reveals a misunderstanding of how science and religion are related. Theists would point out that a correct understanding of the two allows science to go as far as it can in providing scientific explanations for empirical phenomena. But only when scientific explanations reach their limit in the realm of efficient causality, can religion be invoked to throw light on the 'dark background' which lies behind and beyond science. Hence the perceived need on the part of theists for some ultimate cause to explain the fact that things exist at all, regardless of the physical details of how they came to be.

> ***Efficient cause*** The cause of death was blood-loss from a gunshot wound (provable by science).
>
> ***Final (ultimate) cause*** The cause of death was revenge (not provable by science).

THE EXISTENCE OF GOD

More recently **Richard Dawkins** has failed to appreciate this distinction in using science in a head-to-head confrontation with religion over the question of which offers the best 'hypothesis' to explain the world. Failing to appreciate that both hypotheses are essentially different, he creates an unnecessary rivalry between science and faith. This enables him to mistakenly claim that science offers the 'most probable' explanation of the world, whereas he really means the most probable 'efficient' explanation. This he believes entitles him to challenge the 'religious hypothesis', and show that religion (or God) is highly 'improbable'. But far from closing the discussion with his own naturalistic/atheistic hypothesis, he merely begs the question of God's possibility, which he surprisingly does not rule out. The suggestion that God is improbable entails, after all, that God's existence is possible, something that Dawkins is obviously reluctant to consider.

> *Scientific hypothesis*   A scientific – for example, biological, geological, or physical – explanation for something.
>
> *Metaphysical hypothesis*   A trans-empirical explanation of origins, in terms, say, of blind chance.
>
> *Religious hypothesis*   An ultimate explanation in terms of an originating personal agency.

KANT'S MORAL ARGUMENT

Moral arguments proceed on the basis that certain moral facts such as 'it is a fact that raping a defenceless woman is wrong' have a peculiar, or 'transcendental', status. They cannot be established as true or false in the way that other facts can. Using this line of reasoning **C. S. Lewis** has argued that such moral facts give rise to the possibility of another realm where their full significance holds true. Therefore, he believes, it becomes more reasonable to suppose that in this realm there exists a being who is capable of seeing justice done to victims of evil, than to believe that moral facts are insignificant, and evildoers would never be brought to account for their actions (see also the moral vacuum argument, p. 47).

> **Aquinas** also had a moral argument in the fourth of his 'Five Ways'. He argued that the limited nature of all admirable human moral qualities, such as goodness, truth, beauty and the like, points to a maximum standard of excellence against which they can be seen to be limited. 'Therefore there must be something which to all beings is the cause of their being, goodness and every other perfection; and this we call God.'

God's existence suggested on the basis of moral duty

Having helped to undermine the traditional rational arguments of Anselm and Aquinas, Kant produced a new argument for God's existence 'by the back door' so to speak. The back door was the 'practical reason', which was not the same as 'pure reason'. The practical reason is what gives us an insight into what is required to make sense of our inner awareness of the moral law (see more on this below, p. 238). We are aware of being driven in a particular direction by the force of moral duty. To make sense of moral duty (or conscience) we need to have 'faith' that doing our duty leads somewhere. Having established the 'categorical imperative' or the 'absolute sense of duty' to abide by certain moral principles, Kant went on to argue that certain 'postulates' (requirements) were needed if the categorical imperative to act with moral seriousness was to make sense.

> Two things never fail to fill me with awe: the starry heavens above and the moral law within.
> *Words inscribed on Kant's tombstone*

> For **Kant**, the reality of moral duty pointed to the existence of three things.
> - The freedom of the will. If I *ought* to do something it implies that I *can* do it.
> - The immortality of the soul. Physical death would bring an unjust end to the moral life.
> - The existence of God. Only God can guarantee the *summum bonum* in the afterlife.

In other words if we are not to conclude that the moral life lacks any spiritual significance we need to assume three things: the freedom of the will, the immortality of the soul, and the existence of God. Kant stressed that there was no possibility of proving that these really existed. They were to be accepted on trust and held to be true, because not to do so would create an intolerable tension between what I ought to do and the ultimate rationality of doing it. For Kant, being morally 'programmed' to live by the categorical imperative, we are compelled to accept that God must be part of the picture.

The freedom of the will makes sense because it would be impossible to have a categorical imperative to do something unless we were free to carry it out. The immortality of

> Morality by itself constitutes a system, but happiness does not, unless it is distributed in exact proportion to morality. This, however, is possible in an intelligible world only under a wise author and ruler. Reason compels us to admit such a ruler, together with life in such a world, which we must consider as future life, or else all moral laws are to be considered as idle dreams.
>
> *Kant*

the soul seems almost certain since there is no possibility of the *summum bonum* (the equation of happiness with goodness) being enjoyed in this life. Unless the *summum bonum* existed as a real possibility, the moral life would have no just conclusion, and would lead to a dead end. In other words if man is compelled to live the moral life, then it makes sense to believe that one day the man of goodwill will be rewarded for his goodness. This requires us to assume a future realm of existence, and hence the immortality of the soul. Finally the existence of God is required to guarantee the *summum bonum* and ensure that the man of virtue will be crowned with happiness. Only God could provide such a guarantee.

Kant's moral argument is the outcome of what he saw as the dilemma facing us in the moral life. Either the categorical imperative will one day be rewarded, or it is merely an absurd contradiction. The question is, 'Does the road of the moral life lead somewhere or nowhere?' In producing this argument Kant said that he 'put aside knowledge to make room for faith'. In saying this, he accepted his argument was an invitation to believe that if the moral life was significant and worthwhile, God must exist to make it so.

The moral argument is not convincing to unbelievers and is faulted by believers

Critics of Kant have not been swayed by his reasoning. Surely, they say, Kant is merely begging the question of whether the moral life has ultimate mean-

GOD, FAITH AND PHILOSOPHY

> **Summary of Kant's moral argument**
> - Man's destiny is to enjoy the *summum bonum*.
> - The *summum bonum* is the equation of virtue and happiness.
> - Man has a categorical obligation to follow a virtuous life.
> - Virtue is not normally matched with happiness in this life.
> - If there is no afterlife man is doomed to be frustrated in his moral endeavours.
> - It is counter-intuitive to believe that virtue will never be rewarded.
> - Therefore it makes sense to believe in an afterlife.
> - The afterlife is where God can ensure the *summum bonum*.
> - Therefore it makes sense to believe in God.
>
> *How far is Kant's argument vulnerable to the charge, not only of illusory or wishful thinking, but lack of evidence? How can Kant's moral argument be compared with the 'Moral Vacuum Argument' below?*

ing or not. Yes, it would be nice to believe that a virtuous life is rewarded with happiness in some future realm, but sadly it is possible that this will never happen, and there is no real evidence to make us believe it. In the end Kant's proposal falls by the wayside for those who are not willing to accept his invitation to have faith that life, including the moral life, has any ultimate value. But can his reasoning be so easily dismissed on the basis of lack of evidence? Many would argue that an important feature of his argument is precisely an appeal to evidence, the evidence of the moral dimension of human existence. Kant would probably be happy to take on his opponents on the issue of evidence, but of course the evidence is ambivalent. It therefore remains a matter of choice how the evidence is interpreted, and on this many part company with Kant.

Criticism of Kant has also come from theists who reject his attempt to make God the 'product' of one (admittedly a significant) aspect of human experience. They say this reflects on the sovereignty of God and undermines his transcendence. Many however would consider this a weak objection, and one that overlooks Kant's attempt to suggest the existence of God from deficiencies that become apparent when our experience is analysed and thoughtfully considered. This after all is little

> *Kant held that the moral life was sufficient **evidence** to justify **belief** in God, but how far is his reasoning persuasive?*

THE EXISTENCE OF GOD

different from what **Anselm** or **Aquinas** were doing when using philosophic methods to established God's existence. In arguing that the moral life suggests the existence of God, many would say that Kant is following in the medieval tradition of showing how the findings of philosophy can converge with the beliefs of faith. It is for theology (not rational thinking) to go further and affirm the religious aspects of God's nature.

> **Kant** believed that virtue ***deserved*** to be crowned with happiness (the highest good) but only God could make this possible.
>
> *His argument has been rejected by many philosophers, but how far can his reasoning be seen as laying a foundation for the **possibility** of God's existence?*

THE MORAL VACUUM ARGUMENT

Before concluding this section on the relation between our moral awareness and the possible existence of God, it may be useful to look briefly at another argument for the possible existence of God, one that relies on our sense of moral outrage when we see great suffering caused to others. The argument relies on a thoughtful analysis of great evils such as the Holocaust, the Stalinist terror, and the well documented examples of pointless suffering of soldiers and civilians during times of war. The line of reasoning goes like this. If no scheme of natural retribution (or justice) is possible to make the perpetrators of great crimes responsible for the evils they inflict, then only 'heaven' can supply the answer. This comes from the ancient intuition that some things 'cry to heaven for vengeance'. At first sight this looks more applicable to moral evil than to physical evil. Yet because physical evil equally brings human suffering on innocent people, a similar question arises: are human beings ultimately at the mercy of the blind forces of life, as well as the evil that others perpetrate upon them?

> This argument depends on the most likely outcome of two possibilities. One is that evil goes ***unresolved***. The other, that evil is one day ***resolved***, especially in favour of innocent sufferers.
>
> *How far might this idea provide an argument for God's existence?*

GOD, FAITH AND PHILOSOPHY

> **The moral vacuum argument**
> - Great evil and suffering have happened and continue to happen.
> - Human justice is usually unable to deal with the effects of evil.
> - As a result many appear to 'get away' with the evil they cause.
> - Nature also would be seen as a blind force that causes evil.
> - This leaves a moral vacuum that cannot humanly be filled.
> - This causes outrage to our deepest moral sensibilities.
> - Therefore we should hope that the moral vacuum will one day be filled.
> - Only God could fill this moral vacuum.
> - Therefore it is reasonable to hope that God exists.
>
> *The argument is vulnerable to the charge of illusory or wishful thinking, because it reflects how we feel; but how far might the argument converge with other arguments to strengthen the rational case for God's existence?*

If it is supposed that no God exists, then undeserved human misfortune has the final say, and human criminality goes unpunished. This would leave a moral vacuum that human beings cannot fill. As a result our sense of natural justice makes us feel that it is somehow not right that this should happen. If I am simply an unlucky victim of an earthquake, or the random victim of a criminal, am I to accept that these are brute facts about the way the world is? Only a theist can think otherwise. Like other arguments for God's possible existence, this one appeals to facts about the world that call out for an explanation that is not forthcoming from within the world itself.

But like all the other arguments, it relies on faith to be added to the conclusions of rational thinking. As such it resembles the anthropic-principle argument, the 'human transcendence' argument and, probably even more, the moral argument of **Kant**. In each case questions arise that call for an answer. In each case one is confronted with the choice either to believe that no answer exists, or to believe that an answer does exist. (See also below, p. 143 for another form of this argument: the suggestion that religion can create the spiritual conditions needed to overcome, or prevent, the kind of evil shown to be characteristic of some modern atheistic regimes.)

> *Auschwitz is a historic symbol of moral evil at its worst, and a classic example of man's inhumanity to man, but how far can it be used to argue both for and against God's existence?*

THE EXISTENCE OF GOD

The strengths and weaknesses of the arguments

The answer to this question will obviously vary depending on whether the respondent is a believer or not. For theists the strength of the arguments may be seen in the way they provide a rational basis for what they believe about God through revelation, or on other grounds. Based as many of them are on a posteriori, inductive reasoning, they show that theism is a reasonable interpretation of the empirical world. While the ontological proof stands as an exception, inasmuch as it is based on a priori, deductive reasoning, it too has the strength of offering the power of logic to underline what God must be like.

> *Strengths* They demonstrate that religious beliefs can be supported by rational arguments.
>
> *Weaknesses* They depend too much on supposition and hypotheses rather than on empirical fact.

But theists would also recognize that the arguments have inherent weaknesses. If one is not a believer to begin with, it is unlikely any of them would be persuasive in themselves to demonstrate that God actually exists. With regard to the ontological argument, the main weakness would seem to be the move from arguing from the logical necessity of God's existence to the conclusion of his actual existence. With regard to the cosmological and teleological arguments, their main weakness would seem the way they move from facts about the empirical world (needing a cause, or designer, and so on) to conclusions that go beyond this world. With regard to the moral argument, the absence of empirical evidence to support its conclusions would seem to be a major weakness.

> Other arguments for God's existence appear later in connection with *religious experience* (p. 120), and the human need for **spirituality**. **Swinburne** has made the point that all the arguments can be combined to form what is called the *cumulative case* argument (see below).
>
> *Critics have suggested that if one argument fails the others might be seen to fall with it, but does this necessarily follow?*

The rational arguments in relation to faith

The rational arguments for God's existence continue to form the staple diet for students of the philosophy or religion both at A level and at university. While the arguments are generally seen to belong mainly to the academic sphere, it would be a mistake to see them as having no more than academic interest. The recognized popularity of debates on the subject of God and religion, as well as the recent success of books on these subjects at the time of writing, appears to confirm this. The twenty-first century public, widely assumed to be immersed in the attitudes of the materialistic age, appear to have a surprising appetite for engaging in a subject (religion) not normally associated with popular demand.

> While the arguments for God's existence may appear theoretical, and removed from popular interest, there is recent evidence that this is not quite the case.

Some might suggest, with a hint of faint cynicism, that modern interest in religion is really a search for reassurance that religion is indeed a fantasy, an illusion, or indeed a delusion. Such a search might not be unconnected with the fear that God, after all, might exist! This view had earlier been put forward by **John Calvin**, who took up **St Paul**'s idea that refusal to believe in God was the result of ignorance caused by humankind's selfish nature. Calvin here seems to mean that because religious faith typically involves a moral commitment, it would be naturally unpopular with those unwilling to accept its ethical implications. Those who contest the existence of God would, however, reject such allegations and would claim that their non-religious stance is justified on entirely different grounds. What is significant about this view, however, is how far removed it is from Freud's theory of religion. According to **Freud** wishful thinking leads to religion, while according to **Calvin** it leads away from it.

> *Calvin* Selfishness, or sin, lead *away* from religious faith.
> *Freud*   Selfishness, or wishful thinking, lead *towards* religious faith.

THE EXISTENCE OF GOD

But even for those who might see the arguments for God's existence in a positive light, it is generally accepted that they play little part in the actual support of faith. Which is to say that ordinary religious believers would tend to show little practical interest in the arguments. This is because, historically, faith is something inherited within a tradition, and is neither aided nor undermined by what philosophers (including religious ones) have to say.

> According to studies and researches most believers have little interest in, or knowledge of the **arguments** for God's existence. Religious faith is more likely to be something acquired through **upbringing**, and later sustained through a spiritual **relationship** with a personal God.

No doubt many may find encouragement from the rational underpinning of faith provided by philosophic thought, but others, perhaps the majority, are probably unaware of the arguments, and would be reassured by the words of **Aquinas** that, as far as faith is concerned, not everybody needs to be a philosopher. Instead, it seems, most theists are more likely to believe in God because of their initiation into faith through a religious upbringing, a belief later sustained through the experience of prayer and religious practice (see also Pascal and the God of the Philosophers in the next chapter).

> Indeed, the perversity of the impious, who though they struggle furiously are unable to extricate themselves from the fear of God, is abundant testimony that this conviction, namely, that there is some God, is naturally inborn in all, is fixed deep within . . . From this we conclude that it is not a doctrine that must first be learned at school, but is one of which each of us is master from his mother's womb, and which nature itself permits no man to forget.
>
> *John Calvin*

2 The Nature of God

- The Judaeo-Christian conception of God.
- Philosophy as only offering a rational idea of God.
- Classical theism and the qualities of God.
- The implications of God being a personal being.
- The problems of God's omnipotence and omniscience.
- Pros and cons of classical theism.
- The non-realist conception of God.

The Judaeo-Christian conception of God

When **Blaise Pascal** died in Paris, a piece of paper was found sewn into his cloak. On it was written a prayer he had composed after a moment of intense religious experience several years earlier. In it the devout Pascal thanked God for revealing himself to him. He added 'not the God of the Philosophers but you, the God of Abraham, Isaac and Jacob'. With this short prayer Pascal made famous an important distinction. For Pascal, the God of the *Philosophers*, especially the God of classical theism, was a product of academic, rational thinking which bore no resemblance to the living God he encountered in the Bible and the Church.

> *The God of the Philosophers*   The product of dry rational thinking.
>
> *The God of the Bible*   The living God of revelation found in the Bible.
>
> *But how far did Pascal exaggerate the difference between the two?*

THE NATURE OF GOD

Pascal's point is that the academic 'God' produced by the learned and the wise is only a pale shadow of the living God who is addressed by believers. The real, true God is the God who reaches out to give life and grace to mankind. He is not the product of intellectual argument but the Father of Jesus Christ who redeemed the world by his death on the cross. This is the God who raised Jesus from the dead and holds out the promise of immortality to all who accept him in their hearts by faith. This is the God who is addressed in prayer, and is the object of worship through his Son, Jesus. This is the God to whom people turn in time of need, for help, guidance and grace, or to express sorrow and repentance, confident that their prayers are heard. Whether, or how, they are answered is part of the trust that is part of faith, and is not revealed by way of temporal events on earth. All faith is eschatological, that is, directed to the future; is characterized by trust, inspired by hope and made visible by charity (agape, the selfless love of others). It is this God to whom Pascal expressed his gratitude (see also Pascal's wager below, p. 108).

Classical theism: the qualities that God must have

Yet many would insist that philosophers have made a very important contribution to bringing into a clearer light by means of rational thought the nature of God. The result of philosophical thinking about God has been an admittedly cold but important divine profile traditionally named the God of 'classical theism', a description in human philosophical language going back to **Plato** and **Aristotle**, and later developed by the Church, of the qualities God must have in order to be God, that is, the Supreme Being who alone is worthy of worship. Thus, arguing philosophically, there can only be one God, since a rival 'god' would have a separate and independent existence, which would limit the power of both, and this is impossible. Therefore God must be unique.

God must be omnipotent, omniscient and perfectly good

God must also have other necessary qualities. He must be *omnipotent*. This means he can have no limitations in respect of his power in regard to what is logically possible. Thus it would be absurd to say that God cannot make

> **The TETRAGRAMMATON** (four letter sacred word)
>
> Phoenician (1100 BC–135 AD. Found on stone): ヨYヨʎ
>
> Aramaic (1000 BC–300 AD. Found on stone): 𐤉𐤄𐤅𐤄
>
> Hebrew (1000 BC–AD) – **YHVH** (with vowels JeHoVaH)
>
> Greek – Κυριος (**LORD**)
>
> English – **YAHWEH** (Lord God)

a round square since such a concept is incoherent. God must also be *omniscient*, that is, he must be subject to no limitations in regard to his knowledge. There has been much controversy, however, even among Christian theologians about what this means. Taken to extreme it could imply that God has absolute foreknowledge of the future. If he did have, it would have obvious implications both for human freedom and for his own goodness (see more on God's foreknowledge below, p. 239).

Human freedom, it could be argued, would be compromised if God already knew how people would behave, and the key notions of reward and punishment would be thrown into disarray. Furthermore, if God had foreknowledge of people's choices, and knew that they would create evil, would this not reflect either on God's power or on his goodness? We return to this question below.

> *How far has God's omnipotence created problems for understanding aspects of life such as evil and suffering?*

A related necessary quality in God is that he must be maximally perfect, and absolutely *good*. If goodness is a positive attribute recognizable by everyone as such, and evil is a degenerative quality, then it would be absurd to deny that God must be absolutely good. Some see this as also related to God's omniscience. An all-knowing being will have the capacity to know what is best in every situation, as well as knowing what is worst. He will therefore always will what is best, because it would be an abuse of both his omniscience and omnipotence to will what is worst.

On the negative side God cannot be created, cannot either come into exist-

THE NATURE OF GOD

ence or go out of existence and can have no limitations. For these reasons God is acknowledged to be a spiritual mystery that cannot be fully comprehended by the human mind. Thus philosophy can help to enhance and highlight the mystery of God, by showing by purely rational methods, that God as the Supreme Being possesses all the positive qualities admired in human nature, but to a perfect degree.

> Philosophical theologians have argued that God must be absolutely good in order to be God. **Plato** called the 'Form of the Good' the *highest* reality. **Aquinas** held that goodness was part of God's *essence*.
>
> *What problems would be created by the idea of an evil God?*

Another aspect of God's nature highlighted by classical theism is (as we have seen in relation to the ontological and cosmological arguments) that God must be *self-existent*. Were he not self-existent he would require something else to explain his existence. This would reduce God to a contingent being (that is, dependent on something else). This would make no sense philosophically since God could never be dependent on some other being for his existence. Self-existence means that he cannot not exist, as Anselm, and later Descartes, also pointed out (see p. 11).

> In classical language God is said to have *aseity*, from the Latin '*a se*' meaning 'by himself', so that God is the self-sufficient cause of his existence, and can exist 'by himself'. This idea (also called God's necessary existence) is also contained in the ontological and cosmological arguments.
>
> *How far would these arguments work without this divine quality?*

This in turn implies that God is *eternal*, having no beginning and no end. This again is a function of being non-contingent. If God is not contingent there is no reason why he should have a beginning or an end. God is also infinite, meaning that there can be no limitations to his power, wisdom, knowledge and goodness. For God to be God he must be all-powerful (omnipotent), all-knowing (omniscient), all wise (omnisapient) and all-good (omnibenevolent). This implies that God is all-just in his judgements, and can therefore be trusted to be always in the right, or righteous.

Finally, according to classical theism God is immutable, meaning that God cannot change. This has been the subject of different interpretations. When the Bible says that God effectively 'changed his mind' on some occasions it appears that God can change. However, others have pointed out that God's immutability refers to his essence as possessing all the qualities already referred to. Thus God, for instance, can never change with respect to his goodness or justice, and is therefore always 'reliable', 'trustworthy' and 'faithful'.

God is a living personal being

Another aspect of God's nature highlighted by classical theism is his possession of *personal* qualities. God, it is pointed out, is not so much a 'person' as 'person-like'. This is because the analogy between God and humans has to be carefully interpreted. But because personhood is the highest category of existence we know, God must have this. A person is distinguished as the highest of the animals by having, either actually or potentially, intellect, will and self-consciousness. That God must possess these qualities, and to a perfect degree, also follows of course from his omnipotence, omniscience and perfect goodness.

> For Christians Jesus is the ultimate 'icon of God' revealing God's personal nature.

To possess these qualities means that God is not *impersonal* in any way. This has obvious implications for how God is to be conceived. It would be absurd, for instance, to identify God with impersonal forces, or even to call God a *'force'*. By extension this has implications for how the world began and how it continues to exist. If God is personal, the world did not come about by the activity of blind forces, and its destiny is not at the mercy of such forces. It also has important implications for the way humans understand the meaning of life. If God is personal then human destiny is in the hands of a supreme personal being.

> Atheists differ from theists in how they understand the universe. One sees it as the result of blind forces, the other as the product of a personal being.

THE NATURE OF GOD

Problems with classical theism: human freedom and the existence of evil

Classical theism gives rise to a number of problems concerning the nature of God and his relation to the world. One is the idea that God is immutable. This is difficult to reconcile with the Bible, where God is seen to change in relation to the chosen people, sometimes 'repenting' over what he had done, or 'deciding' either to punish or not to punish, and so on. Scholars have dealt with this by saying that this is how the biblical authors 'imagined' God, and did not necessarily mean exactly what it said. Others have added the idea that God is immutable in respect of his qualities of 'faithfulness', 'righteousness' and 'justice', which remain constant at all times.

> ***Classical theism*** implies that God is omniscient, omnipotent and perfectly good. As we shall see, these necessary qualities of God give rise to the practical problem of ***evil***, and the theoretical problem of human ***freewill***.

Another problem is the difficulty of reconciling certain aspects of experience with the nature of God. Thus, for example, how can an all-good and all-powerful God be reconciled with the existence of evil in the world? (see more in Chapter 11, 'God and Evil'). Second, to say that God is all-knowing implies that he knows in advance how people are going to behave. Does this not make it impossible to have freewill? Can I really be free if God already knows what I am going to do? (see more later on God's foreknowledge and freewill). Third, if God is all-knowing, why did he create a world knowing that it would contain so much evil and suffering? These are problems that crystallize into what is called the 'problem of evil' to which we shall return later (see p. 165).

Scholars, however, have debated what it means for God to know the future. If the future is 'not yet', some argue, then it is logically outside the range of possible knowledge, like criticizing God for not knowing what a round square might look like. Thus it is no limitation of God's knowledge for him not to know the future. The problem of God's foreknowledge interfering with human freedom is answered in much the same way. Aquinas held that there is no interference with human freedom since the important thing is that God always knows how human beings have used their freedom to act. In other

57

GOD, FAITH AND PHILOSOPHY

> **God in classical theism**
> - **Necessary** Not contingent. Either necessary or impossible.
> - **Eternal** Follows from necessary. God always was and always will be.
> - **Infinite** Has no limitations.
> - **Omnipotent** Is all-powerful with respect to what is logically possible.
> - **Omniscient** Is all-knowing because his knowledge is not limited by time.
> - **Omnibenevolent** Is all-loving and perfectly good. A 'bad' God would lack goodness.
> - **Unique** There can only be one God, since a rival 'god' would be impossible.
> - **Personal** Implies that God is not an objective, or blind, force.
> - **A spirit** God is not dependent on a material body.

words it is on the use of our freedom that we are judged, and theoretically God is only an observer of this, not someone whose foreknowledge interferes in its working.

Religious problems with classical theism

This takes us back in a way to **Pascal**'s original problem of why the true God cannot be captured by philosophical reasoning. For him philosophy had its place, but could not get beyond a cold, limited and fundamentally inadequate notion of God. Other thinkers, like **Martin Luther**, who was influenced by **Paul** and **Augustine**, also objected to using philosophy to bolster faith. They believed that faith, by its nature, is not meant to be rationally transparent. Faith can never be hostage to reason, since reason is merely a human capacity which is never able to access the mystery of God. Besides, reason is a depraved faculty, one that is corrupted by sin (see more on this below, p. 58). Others, however, like **Anselm** and **Aquinas**, took a more positive view of reason, seeing it as God-given gift to be used responsibly to show the rational credibility of religious faith. They believed that without a rational basis, or some point of intersection with reason, faith is open to the charge of being outside rational discussion.

> *Aquinas* Philosophy can show that God exists.
> *Luther* Philosophy should not be used to support faith.
> *Pascal* Philosophy only provides a limited, rational idea of God.

THE NATURE OF GOD

Besides, without subjecting faith to rational reflection, a human dialogue with doubters, sceptics and unbelievers would be impossible. After all, if faith and reason are not connected, how can believers make sense of their beliefs either to themselves or to others? For Aquinas, reason provided a rational infrastructure to religious belief which, if required, could demonstrate its rational foundation. However, Aquinas did not mean to imply that the ordinary believer must also be a philosopher. He knew that most people took faith on trust, being content to benefit from the guidance and authority provided by the Church, and leave it to scholars like himself to look after the philosophical side!

> God is not known, he is used.
> *William James*
>
> James was a pragmatist who believed that a thing's significance was in its usefulness for life. He believed the key question about God was not how far his existence was theoretically ***true***, but how far it was ***useful*** (significant) to human life.

God and non-realism: the suggestion that God is a symbol of what can make people human

We conclude this chapter on the nature of God by looking at a modern proposal for making the idea of God relevant in a godless age; what is called non-realism. This has come into vogue in recent times as part of the movement popularly called postmodernism. The idea became popular with the 'sea of faith' movement associated with **Don Cupitt** of Cambridge. It was another attempt to overcome what was seen as the unfashionable stumbling-block of the 'objectified' God of traditional faith, a problem that had been brought to light by the logical positivists. The challenge that religious language was meaningless (see more, p. 215) might be countered by shifting the understanding of God to make it relate more closely with human values and aspirations. Thus in contrast to classical theism, which proceeds from God to the human, non-realists go the other way – from the human to God. According to non-realists, since God is outside the realm of what we can experience, the idea of his real or objective existence should be left to one side. Instead

59

GOD, FAITH AND PHILOSOPHY

the focus should be on the fact that he 'exists' within the minds of believers, and is a 'potent symbol' that can affect the believer's understanding of the world.

> *Cupitt popularized the view that God was best seen as a 'focus' of human values. How far did this approach go to make religious language meaningful, and how far does it resemble the 'language games' theory of religious language (see below, p. 220)?*

The problems with non-realism: God as merely an imaginary function

Non-realism is clearly at variance with the traditional belief going back to **Anselm** and **Aquinas**, which emphasized the necessary existence of God as a Being who is non-contingent, and the source of all reality (see above, p. 11). Non-realism has interesting implications for atheism for the same reason, since atheism is the denial of the objective existence of a real God. Atheists could not seriously oppose a God who was merely within the 'minds of believers'. While many thinkers consider it a misguided attempt to evade the 'death of God' and logical positivist challenges, by (in a way) translating the meaning of God into human terms, its defenders would argue that the non-realist approach offers a better key to the understanding of God for modern believers.

God and non-realism
- Logical positivism showed up the problems of speaking of a 'real' God.
- A concept of God seen from within human experience might counter this.
- Focus on the meaning of God for human existence would be significant.
- The emphasis should shift from belief in 'God' to 'belief' in God.
- 'Belief' in God's existence has a legitimate place as a 'language game'.

3 The Knowledge of God

- Revelation as fundamental to western religions.
- Differences in belief about divine revelation.
- The meaning of idolatry in relation to revelation.
- Philosophical problems with revelation.
- Philosophical arguments for revelation.
- Faith as response to the truth of revelation.
- Propositional and non-propositional revelation.
- Problems with the scriptures as the record of revelation.
- The debate about scripture and tradition.
- The authority of scripture as a religious and moral guide.

Revelation as a fundamental concept in western religions

In addition to the use of reason as employed in the arguments for God's existence, as well as in the working out of classical theism, believers hold that the primary source of our knowledge about God comes from elsewhere. To access it one employs faith, not reason. This is the source called revelation, the record of which is believed to be in sacred texts such as the Hebrew Bible, the Christian Bible, or the Koran for Muslims. Revelation is the term used to describe what believers hold to be the principal means by which they come to understand the reality and nature of God. It is sometimes called God's self-disclosure. They believe that God has revealed his existence and, more importantly, his will for humankind in the course of history, and that this is recorded and documented in the sacred books or scriptures of each religion.

GOD, FAITH AND PHILOSOPHY

> ***Revelation***, also called revealed theology, is a faith-based source of knowledge about God, and is therefore not recognized as a valid area of knowledge by non-theists.

Although all three sacred books are separate and distinct, they are nevertheless historically interconnected. Each one is effectively a development from the other. For instance, all three faiths are collectively known as the 'Abrahamic religions' because the patriarch Abraham was the founding father of all three. Abraham's recorded encounter with God at the beginning of the biblical story (Genesis) makes him the father of divine revelation. On the basis of that fundamental revelation all three faiths have a common understanding of God. All three religions believe that God is the creator of heaven and earth; that he is supremely worthy of worship; that he demands ethical obedience to his laws; and that the perfect response to him is by way of faith, a response that involves trust rather than rational certainty (see faith, p. 78). Also common to all three faiths is the belief that one day there will be a Last Judgement, when God will judge all humankind, rewarding the good and punishing the wicked. This is why the three major western religions are called ethical theism, a reference to the necessary link between religious faith and ethical behaviour.

> **Revelation in Judaism, Christianity and Islam**
> - God created heaven and earth.
> - God revealed himself to humankind.
> - God revealed his will for humankind.
> - God demands ethical obedience to his will.
> - God's revelation is contained in sacred scripture.
> - God will one day judge all humankind.
> - The proper response to God is faith.

Difference in beliefs about God's revelation

Despite these areas of agreement about God, the three faiths differ significantly from one another on the details of God's revelation. In Judaism God's revelation is confined to the Hebrew Bible which effectively ends with the promise of a messiah. In Christianity God's revelation is completed in the New Testament with the arrival of Jesus Christ as the long-awaited messiah. In Islam God's revelation is contained in the Koran, which centres on the person of Muhammad as the recipient of that revelation. Only Christianity holds that Jesus was the Son of God, and that God is a mystery of three persons rather than one.

Revelation

Judaism God's revelation is contained in the Old Testament.

Christianity God's revelation has reached its final stage in Jesus Christ (New Testament).

Islam God's revelation has been given definitively to Muhammad (Koran).

Judaism is historically the earliest of the 'religions of the book', with its origins going back to around 2000 BC. Judaism is regarded as the parent faith of Christianity and Islam and gave the western world the concept of *ethical monotheism*, the existence of One God who has revealed his will in terms of ethical laws to be respected and obeyed. However, the human perception of God's revelation in Judaism is markedly different from that of Christianity or Islam. For Jews, God's promise of a messiah is still to be fulfilled, a belief which would have major historical implications for the separation of Judaism from Christianity.

Christianity can be seen as a development from Judaism in that the Old Testament provides the religious and historical background for Christian beliefs about Jesus as the *Christ* (the anointed one sent by God). Unlike Judaism (and Islam), the Christian faith is based on the belief that Jesus was the incarnation of God and the climax of God's revelation. By his death he redeemed the world from its alienation from God, and by his resurrection showed that he was one with God as master of life and death.

Islam is the 'youngest' of the three faiths, having its origins in the seventh century AD. The human response to God's revelation in Islam centres on the person of Muhammad, who is seen as God's definitive spokesman, the greatest of all the prophets, greater than Moses or Jesus. This put Islam in direct conflict with Judaism, which considers Moses to be the greatest prophet, and Christianity, which sees Jesus as the son of God, and God's definitive revelation.

> **Faith, reason and revelation (Aquinas)**
>
> ***Faith***
>
> - Is based on ***revelation*** (recorded in scripture).
> - Its content is called ***revealed theology*** (the study of revelation).
> - This is also called ***special revelation*** (more than reason could reveal).
>
> ***Reason***
>
> - Can demonstrate that God ***exists*** (the fundamental religious truth).
> - But it leads only to ***natural theology*** (knowledge of God's existence).
> - This is also called ***general revelation*** (because rational truth is universal).
>
> *Strict fideists reject the use of reason to support faith, which they claim is a matter of trust. How far is Aquinas justified in claiming that reason can support faith?*

The true God distinguished from the false gods of idolatry

The problem of idolatry appears in all three western religions. Allegiance and fidelity to the true biblical God would later be spelt out to mean living by the law of God. The law was enshrined in the 'ten words', or Decalogue, given to Moses on Mount Sinai. The sacredness of the Law was symbolically expressed by the Ark of the Covenant, a holy receptacle which was carried reverently at the head of ceremonial processions. The symbolism of the Ark had particular significance. It was the public face of the true God whose real face could not be looked at. Significantly it signalled that the presence of God was symbolically marked by the place where his Law was preserved. The true God is the God of the Decalogue. Any other 'god' is false, a fraud, bogus god, an impostor, an idol. This is because any other god would be religiously deficient because ethically deficient. Not surprisingly the worship of false gods became a big issue among the chosen people precisely because such gods pandered to decadent behaviour, and permitted lower moral standards than those required by the true God of the Decalogue.

> Idols, or false gods, detracted from the purity of faith in the true God. Worship of idols was seen as a deception, partly based on false hopes, and the placing of trust in that which was 'not God'.
>
> Idolatry was evil because it was seen to pander to human weakness, and lead to moral decadence.

Philosophical problems with the idea of revelation

The concept of revelation has been challenged by unbelievers. How, they ask, can a revelation from God be perceived, and how can the recipient know that it is from God? These are questions that will come up again in connection with religious experience (see below p. 123), and revolve around the claim that they are all merely subjective experiences originating in the mind of the alleged visionaries or prophets. The initial reply of believers is to show that history testifies to the conviction across three major religions that such a revelation from God did take place, despite disagreements about its nature and content. From an a priori, or logical, point of view there is nothing impossible about a God of infinite power finding ways of making his presence known to his creatures. The supposition behind all the biblical records is that this is what happened. The belief that Abraham, Moses, Jesus and other biblical figures were the subjects of a special encounter with God led to widespread acceptance that such events did take place.

> **Faith and philosophy**
>
> Sceptics question whether there could ever be *evidence* for a transcendent revelation, and question how a transcendent God could ever be identified as its source. Theists have argued that if God exists, revelation is *possible*, especially if it could be shown that humans stood in need of one. If revelation is *actual*, it will tell us more about God than could be known by reason. If *historical* events are grounds for reasonable beliefs, such events could be seen as evidence for what they meant to those who experienced them.

GOD, FAITH AND PHILOSOPHY

Philosophical grounds for the possibility of a revelation

Some have defended the notion of revelation on the grounds that humankind had a fundamental awareness of need for it, in the light of our existential deficiencies. Some religious thinkers have also argued that humankind, having experienced the Fall (the catastrophic effects of the disobedience of Adam and Eve), already had an implicit sense of 'something missing', a deep-down perception that a transcendent communication was needed from God to bring enlightenment about ultimate human fate and destiny. **Karl Rahner** has argued that the concept of revelation is possible because it answers questions that arise from how human beings see themselves. If life can be shown to have serious deficiencies, then the idea of salvation from that deficiency is not impossible to imagine.

> *Rahner believed that humans were 'tuned' to hear a revelation from God, something that would save them from the fate of death and meaninglessness, but how far might this be just wishful thinking?*

Rahner therefore argues that a historical revelation from God can be philosophically defended on the grounds that it was something humans needed in the light of the deficiencies of their existence, problems that have been universally recognized by all the existentialist writers. Ironically it is they, albeit from an atheistic perspective, who have been most active in highlighting those aspects of life which have also been at the heart of biblical revelation. These include the sense of meaningless, angst and guilt that characterize human life seen against the fact of death (see below). For Rahner such recognized problems besetting human life provide the ground for understanding the need for a revelation from God – especially one promising divine salvation from the fate of death and possible meaninglessness.

> **Martin Heidegger** was the leading existentialist, who held that human existence had three main aspects:
>
> *Facticity* Humans are born into circumstances over which they have no control.

THE KNOWLEDGE OF GOD

> ***Fallenness*** Humans are naturally prone to seek the easy way out and 'follow the crowd'.
>
> ***Potentiality*** We have the power within ourselves to find our own values, and truly 'exist', or exist 'authentically' until death.
>
> Thinkers like **Tillich** have accepted this analysis, but hold that without God human beings are unable to 'fully' exist, or find ultimate fulfilment.

Revelation as throwing light on the meaning of life

The outstanding Danish religious thinker **Søren Kierkegaard** believed that life was something that could be lived at a superficial level and not be taken seriously. It was possible to ask no questions and simply 'follow the crowd', and live by the standards set by others. For those who took it seriously, however, life was at best confused and frustrating, at worst meaningless. But to avoid the big questions and live for the moment is to live an illusory dream. The real solution to how life should be lived lay in understanding the truth of revelation found in the Bible. Unlike the atheistic existentialist writers who agreed with his analysis, Kierkegaard's own brand of existentialism was specifically Christian. He believed that the only hope for man was to receive help from outside, help that would save him from his predicament. He believed that this was offered in the Christian message of revelation, a message that centred on the death and resurrection of Jesus Christ.

> *Kierkegaard believed that revelation was the solution to human angst and despair, but many would argue that such pessimism about life is exaggerated. How far may his views be unlikely to appeal to those who find life in the materialistic age satisfying in itself?*

Kierkegaard saw that this was an event that came from out of the blue, a miracle of grace that no one could ever have predicted or expected. It was the finger of God reaching out to touch the finger of man. This was an event revealed in the contingencies of history, not something that could be predicted as inevitable, as **Hegel** had suggested, or some theory based on reason or mathematics. **Socrates** had said that all rational truth was already revealed and known to man: it only needed to be 'discovered'. But for Kierkegaard the crucial truth about human salvation was one that could never be discovered as a human truth by human means. It came from beyond, as a revelation, a free gift of God, a truth which, he warned, could appear to rational eyes as little short of 'paradoxical', 'irrational' or 'absurd'.

> ***Socrates*** The soul pre-existed the body, and knew all truth before birth, in the realm of ideas. Everything we know is a form of 'recollection', and 'there is nothing new under the sun' (*nec novum sub sole*)
>
> ***Kierkegaard*** Revelation is a source of ***new*** truth, a 'miracle' from God that could never otherwise be known.

Faith as the response to divine revelation

Kierkegaard believed that this gift had finally come in the person of **Jesus Christ**, who, as the God-man, could offer all men an escape from the angst and futility of life. There was only one condition. To benefit from God's revelation each individual had to suspend reason (that is, rational thinking) and summon the will to make a great 'leap of faith'. This was a daring, and apparently irrational, personal decision which no individual could make for anyone else. Each one had to accept the gift of salvation for themselves with a faith of 'intense passionate inwardness'. This must be done without any seeking for assurance, or prior supporting evidence, as might be provided by reason and common sense.

> **Kierkegaard** is famous for his view of faith as a 'leap' taken without assurance. He said it was like 'being suspended over 70,000 fathoms', but those who took the leap would discover its power.
>
> *How far might this view be called over-intense, or unrealistic for people today?*

The alternative is futility, angst and the possibility of profound despair about life. With his emphasis on faith Kierkegaard rejected the use of reason as a backup to faith. Therefore he was strongly opposed to the whole enterprise

THE KNOWLEDGE OF GOD

of proving God's existence, and looking for 'reasons' to believe before the leap of faith is taken. This he regarded as a form of irreverence, an insult to God. The issue, he said, is the same as in a court of law. It is not whether the prisoner exists, but whether he is guilty or innocent. For Kierkegaard the issue is not whether God exists, but what he means for mankind. The answer of revelation is that the meaning of life is intimately tied up with the grace of God. Those who respond positively by faith are on the road to salvation, both now and in the hereafter.

> *What did Kierkegaard mean by saying that proving God's existence was both futile and irreverent?*

Revelation as propositional

At this point it may be useful to deal with two views of how revelation can be understood. In one view revelation is seen as a process that ends with a message or truth. This is called the 'propositional' view of revelation. In this view the stress is put on revelation as essentially a communication of vital truths from God, truths concerning God's will for mankind. Such truths can be either in the form of agreed Christian beliefs, or in some cases dogmas; or in the form of a direct communication from God, such as Moses received on Mount Sinai. Traditionally the key truths of revelation included that God was Creator of the world; that humans sinned in the event called the Fall; that God willed the salvation of the world; that he sent his Son, Jesus, to redeem the world by his death, and confirmed it by his resurrection. In this view revelation has become identified with the message rather than the process, which many see as overlooking the part played by human factors in the process.

> ***Revelation*** can be seen both as an encounter with God (directly or indirectly), and as something that can later be reflected on as to its full significance, resulting in truths, dogmas or 'propositions'.

69

Revelation as non-propositional

The understanding of revelation as non-propositional can be taken in two ways. One is that revelation need not involve any message or communication from God. This is often applied to supposed mystical and other forms of religious experience in which the recipient merely claims to have encountered God. Such an event, for example, could have happened to **Moses** before the burning bush had God not spoken to him. Because God spoke, it may be called 'propositional revelation'. If God had not spoken, but merely revealed his presence, it would be called 'non-propositional revelation'.

The second way in which the term 'non-propositional revelation' can be taken arises from the view that revelation comes primarily through events that are claimed to have happened involving God, and only later resulted in truths, or dogmas of belief. Supporters of this view point to the fact that God rarely 'spoke' in the Old Testament. Instead, it is claimed, revelation happened indirectly through normal events of history. Holders of this view claim that the traditional emphasis on the 'truths of revelation' creates the impression that God spoke directly to human beings, rather than indirectly through certain historical happenings. They claim that the propositional view overlooks and conceals the historical method by which God communicates with man.

> Many point out that revelation came ***indirectly*** through events in history, including the life of **Jesus**. Only later was the ***significance*** of such events codified in the 'truths' of revelation.
>
> *This suggests that both aspects of revelation go together, but why have some thinkers expressed reservations about starting with the 'end product' and ignoring the historical process?*

This, they claim, is even more apparent in the New Testament, where Jesus is not concerned with revealing truths from God, but rather with calling for repentance and belief in his moral and religious teaching. In this sense Jesus appears as a religious prophet with a human message for his hearers, not as a speaker of divine oracles. This, they claim, is further highlighted in the fact that it was mainly others, not Jesus himself, who worked out the full significance of his identity as the bearer of God's revelation. They point out that Jesus himself only lightly touched on the meaning of his death and resurrection. Only later, after his death, did the full import of his life and significance become apparent, and become fully worked out in 'propositional' terms such as we find in the writings of **St Paul**, and later in the teachings, or dogmas, of the Church.

> **Revelation**
>
> *Propositional* Revelation boiled down to certain key truths about God and his relation to man, for example that God made the world, and redeemed mankind from sin (Christian revelation).
>
> *Non-propositional* Revelation seen as an inward sense of awareness of God's working in the world. In this view revelation is the result of how certain events are interpreted, and only later became revelatory about God in his relations to humankind.
>
> *While the two aspects can be separated, how far are they also interconnected?*

Revelation and the scriptures

Agreement about the Bible as the record of revelation

We end this chapter by looking at some of the problems arising from the belief that the scriptures are the record of God's revelation. First, there is wide agreement on some fundamental beliefs about the meaning of the Christian revelation. Christians of all denominations believe that the scriptures (Old and New Testaments) are a record of God's revealing of himself to mankind. Unless God chose to reveal himself to us, Christians believe that we would be left in the dark about his ultimate destiny but, as the scriptures testify, with the arrival of Jesus Christ came the 'good news' that humankind was destined to be reconciled to God. According to **Augustine**, from the scriptures we learn that God initially intended his creation to be good, but his will was thwarted by his creatures. By selfishly challenging God, humans (in the myth of Adam and Eve) upset the whole order of nature, and brought disorder and chaos on themselves and the whole of creation. But this was not the end of the story. God, in his mercy, arranged to make up for mankind's failure in the person of Adam by sending a saviour, Jesus Christ (see more on this in connection with theodicy, p. 166).

> ***Revelation*** God's communication to mankind.
>
> ***Scripture*** The official record of that communication.
>
> ***Faith*** The believer's response to revelation.

The debate about religious authority in regard to Scripture and the Church

While all Christian traditions are in basic agreement about the religious authority of Scripture, this did not prevent a major conflict at the Reformation precisely about the position of Scripture in relation to the Church. The Catholic tradition holds that Scripture should always be interpreted by the Church since, after all, the original identification of texts as being worthy of being called 'Sacred Scripture' was originally the work of church authorities. This collection is called the 'canon' of Scripture.

> **The canon of Scripture**
>
> The official list of books considered to be inspired by God, and deemed worthy to make up the Old and New Testaments. The canon was finalized by the early Church after rejecting a number of books because they were considered not to be inspired.

At the Reformation **Luther** rejected the Catholic claim, saying the Scripture holds prior authority as a guide to faith and practice. As a result the Protestant tradition adopted the *sola scriptura* principle and allowed Scripture to be interpreted freely by the individual believer. The result has been a serious divide between the two traditions about the nature, purpose and role of Scripture. Historically the Catholic Church has been perceived as holding an ultra-conservative view of the moral guidance contained in Scripture, while the Protestant view has allowed for a more liberal interpretation of its moral guidance. This has resulted in the strict Catholic teachings on divorce, sex outside marriage, contraception, abortion and euthanasia. At the same time, it may be noted, in practice neither Catholic nor Protestant believers are necessarily at one in these matters.

THE KNOWLEDGE OF GOD

> **Scripture and Tradition**
>
> *Catholic*
>
> - Scripture needs official interpretation by the Church.
> - The Church is bound by the teachings of Scripture.
> - Scripture lays down clear rules for moral guidance.
>
> *Protestant*
>
> - Scripture is the word of God and has absolute authority.
> - Scripture can be interpreted freely by the individual.
> - The moral rules of Scripture are subject to modern interpretation.
>
> *What are the strengths and weaknesses of both traditions, and how far are they really different?*

> *Luther opposed the Catholic position by giving absolute authority to Scripture, but what problems did this create?*

The role of Scripture and issues about its interpretation

While, as we have seen, Christians can agree about the overall significance of the scriptures as the record of divine revelation, especially in regard to fundamental matters of faith, there is considerable disagreement about the nature, purpose and role of Scripture both as a source of reliable empirical knowledge, and as a guide to life. Fundamentalists and some ultra-conservatives see Scripture as the literal word of God, and interpret it at its face value. However, as we shall see below in connection with science (p. 181), mainstream religious leaders had to accept that the scriptures cannot be treated as a rival to science in empirical matters. The classic example is the understanding of how the world came about. If Genesis is taken literally as a factually reliable account of how the world was 'created by God in six days', then it comes into conflict with scientific knowledge. However, if Genesis is interpreted symbolically as, say, a poetic account of beginnings (genesis), one that focuses on the personal power of God in bringing creation into being, then room can be made for both accounts (see below, p. 180).

> **Literal interpretation** Favoured by fundamentalists, and some conservatives. The Bible should be interpreted literally because it is the word of God.
>
> **Non-literal interpretation** Favoured by biblical scholars and liberal theists. They accept the findings of science, and believe that passages such as the creation story are meant to teach religious truths within a framework of myth and symbol.

How modern knowledge affects biblical morality

Another area of greatest controversy today concerns how far moral principles contained in Scripture are to be understood, principles affecting areas of human behaviour such as abortion, euthanasia, homosexuality, divorce, sex outside marriage and so on. Are biblical rules laid down as absolutely binding or is there room for interpretation? The 'conservative' view is that moral principles are fixed by Scripture and cannot be altered, while the more 'liberal' view is that such principles need to be reinterpreted in the light of a modern understanding of human nature and human needs. The liberal view is based on the claim that more is known today about human needs, emotions, and desires and drives. Today, they claim, we have a better understanding of the human condition in the light of the known impact of social, genetic and psychological influences. This raises questions about the authority of Scripture as a specific guide in matters of ethical behaviour and religious understanding.

> **Views on Scripture as a moral guide**
>
> **Conservatives** Scripture lays down specific rules of behaviour that cannot be altered.
>
> **Liberals** Scripture lays down moral guidelines rather than strict rules. Its message is more about living a virtuous life in the light of God's will, seen against the background of a modern understanding of the human nature and the human condition.
>
> *How far do these disagreements create problems for understanding biblical teachings on questions like divorce, contraception and abortion?*

THE KNOWLEDGE OF GOD

Many liberal thinkers believe that the Bible did not intend to lay down specific 'rules' for living beyond the more general rules set out in the Decalogue. For this reason the Bible should be seen as less a 'handbook of ethics' than a religious and moral guide that calls for virtuous behaviour either in the light of God's overall will or, for Christians, in the light of the story of redemption (see the virtuous life below, p. 273). In this view the Bible's essential authority lies not in what 'rules' it is perceived to lay down, but in the religious reasons it gives for living a virtuous life. Some see this confirmed by the way that the Bible prefers the method of parable to direct instruction (classically exemplified in the case of **Jesus**), a method of teaching, it is claimed, that leaves the listener (or reader) some latitude in how it should be understood, or lived up to.

The authority of Scripture

Agreement

- Scripture (Old and New Testaments) is the record of revelation.
- Scripture is the revelation of God's will for humankind.
- Scripture is a fundamental guide to moral and religious values.

Disagreement

- Scripture is the inspired word of God (conservative/fundamentalist view).
- Scripture is inspired by God, but written by *humans* (liberal, scholarly view).
- Scripture should be interpreted by the *Church* (Catholic view).
- Scripture should be interpreted *privately* by the individual (Protestant view).
- Scripture should be interpreted *literally* (conservative/fundamentalist view).
- Scripture should be interpreted *reasonably* in the light of science (liberal, scholarly view).
- Scripture lays down specific moral *rules* about living (conservative view).
- Scripture is a moral guide only in respect to basic moral *values* (liberal view).

> From this it can be seen that the **authority** of Scripture is dependent on whichever view is taken on its nature, purpose and role in the life of faith. The most controversial area is its significance as a **moral** guide to Christians. If it is taken **literally**, moral principles are clearly laid down; if not then there is room for **interpretation**. A key area of disagreement is how far Scripture can be said to be the '**word of God**'. In one view Scripture is '**inspired**' in the sense that God '**dictated**' its contents. In the other view Scripture is inspired in a way that allows for the 'human' character of the writer working within his own culture.
>
> *What are the implications of these two views for understanding the moral principles laid down in Scripture?*

4 Religious Faith

- Faith as involving inward trust and will.
- Faith as an I–Thou relationship.
- Faith as not about believing in facts.
- Faith and trust.
- Faith and values.
- Faith and evidence.
- Faith and religious authority.
- The idea of implicit faith through a virtuous life.

The nature of religious faith as involving intellect and will

If God is believed to exist, faith may be broadly defined as the positive response to that belief. *Faith* may also be distinguished from *belief* in the sense that faith is the *subjective* pole of the religious response, while belief is the *objective* pole, involving the acceptance of certain truths about God and his revelation. In medieval terms the subjective aspect of faith was called *fides qua* (faith *by which*) while the objective aspect was known as *fides quae* (faith *of which*) and refers to the beliefs of faith. The former implied the active personal response characteristic of faith as a commitment to God, while the latter referred to the *content* of faith. It could also be said that *fides qua* has more to do with the will and the inward attitude of trust, while *fides quae* has more to do with the specifics of religious belief.

GOD, FAITH AND PHILOSOPHY

> ***Fides quae*** The ***objective*** content of faith (truths of revelation). Usually means 'beliefs'.
>
> ***Fides qua*** The ***subjective*** commitment by which faith is lived. Usually means 'faith'.

Religious faith as something different from belief in facts

Many religious thinkers have pointed out that faith cannot be properly understood unless it is seen in terms of a *personal relationship* with God. In this relationship a human being stands before God as a subject addressing a subject. If this is not understood, faith becomes stuck at the level of belief in facts, and thus suffers the fate of belonging to just another form of belief, such as that God might exist, or that death might be the end, or that science will eventually have all the answers, or that the economy will recover. By contrast, they point out, religious faith is a quite different form of belief inasmuch as it involves a personal commitment of *trust* in God and what he stands for. **Kierkegaard** made this point by using the example of someone before a court of law. In such a situation there is no issue about the existence of the accused, only about whether he is innocent or guilty. In other words he is saying that it is theoretically possible to believe in God's existence but miss the more important point of what his existence 'means for me' in the light of revelation.

> ### Three aspects of faith
>
> - ***Belief*** in revelation as something that has happened, as recorded in the Bible.
> - ***Trust*** in a personal God who offers salvation.
> - ***Love*** in response to God who has offered salvation, and directed to love of neighbour.
>
> *Aquinas called these the theological virtues, faith, hope and charity. How far do these three aspects show faith is incomplete unless it leads to moral action, at least in desire?*

RELIGIOUS FAITH

The nature of faith as involving an I–Thou relationship between the human person and God

The idea of faith as a personal relationship with God was especially brought to the fore by the Jewish thinker **Martin Buber**. He believed that religious faith is something profoundly spiritual because it involves a sense of being in relation with a divine *person* (God), a relationship of cosmic importance that embraces one's whole being. In his view, if God is a person, faith is not just about whether such a person exists. It may involve this, but is primarily about having an active relationship with that person in a way analogous with how we relate to human beings as persons. The highest form of personal relationship known to human beings is what Buber calls an **'I–Thou'** relationship.

> ***Martin Buber*** *emphasized that religious faith is about forming an I–Thou relationship with God. How far is this idea helpful in understanding the nature of religious faith?*

The alternative is a reduced 'I–It' relationship, one which is easy to fall into, and one that is totally inappropriate in the relationship to God that is called faith. An I–It relationship is a relationship between a person and an object (me and my car). But to reduce God to an object would be to ignore the reality that he is a living subject. To apply the concept of 'person' to God is to use an analogy with human beings, whose 'personhood' is the highest quality they have as living beings. For Buber an important significance of God being a person is the imperative to treat him as a *subject*, not an object. God cannot be put on a par with a scientific fact, and therefore cannot be known as another 'fact of life'. For Buber, God is always a 'You' (not even a 'He'), something made clear by the biblical writers. Once God is merely a 'He' he becomes detached, objectified, distant, and thus becomes removed from the orbit of faith.

> *I–It* relationship   An ***objectified*** relationship with a thing or idea.
>
> *I–He/She* relationship   An ***objectified*** 'third person' relationship with another person.
>
> *I–Thou* relationship   A ***personal*** 'second person' relationship with another person.

GOD, FAITH AND PHILOSOPHY

> *Buber claims that the only proper **religious** relationship with God is an I–Thou relationship, but how far might this be seen as either incomplete, or too idealistic?*

The I–Thou relationship with God is sustained through an active faith in which God is directly 'addressed' through prayer, worship and the acceptance of a life of ethical obligation expressed in the love of others. One implication of this analysis is that when non-believers attack or criticize faith for being naive, childish, irrational, and so forth, they usually do so simply by not understanding what it means to believers. In holding up faith for inspection and treating it as an object of academic analysis, they do something foreign to what believers do, and therefore cannot do justice to its spiritual and inspirational nature. In terms borrowed from **Wittgenstein**, they may be said not to understand the 'form of life' to which faith belongs, and are thus incapable of understanding its nature as understood by believers (see language games, p. 220).

Treating God as an object

> By its very nature the eternal You cannot become an It . . . because by its very nature it cannot be grasped as a sum of qualities, not even as an infinite sum of qualities that have been raised to transcendence . . . And yet we reduce the eternal You ever again to an It, to something, turning God into a thing, in accordance with our nature . . . through religion and its marginal forms.
>
> *Martin Buber*

Here Buber warns against the common tendency to treat God as an object. This can happen during philosophical analysis of issues of faith, and even in the practice of religion, but the cost is to lose sight of the true nature of faith as a relationship to God.

The implications of religious faith for life and values

However, granted Buber's analysis of the internal *subjective* nature of faith, there is also the *objective* side of faith. This refers to the *content* of faith, those things that are held as *beliefs*. Traditionally religious faith was seen to involve three things. First, faith meant a particular world view or perspective on life. From the viewpoint of faith life was to be seen *sub specie aeternitatis*, that is, from the perspective of God and the afterlife. This meant seeing earthly life as temporary, the afterlife as eternal, and spiritual values as superior to earthly ones. In the perspective of faith, *material* values such as money, fame or happiness must always give way to, or be consistent with, *spiritual* values, such as honesty, truth, justice and love of neighbour (see also religion and ethics, and virtue ethics, below, p. 264).

> **Faith and values**
> - Life has a transcendent dimension, with the promise of an afterlife.
> - Life should be seen from the perspective of the afterlife.
> - Life involves a competition between different sets of values.
> - Spiritual and moral values are superior to earthly values.
> - Moral values are summed up in the Decalogue.
> - The love of God cannot be separated from the love of neighbour.

The claim that faith is not supported by empirical evidence

An important aspect of faith is the way it may be subjected to analysis and criticism by unbelievers, and challenged for its credibility as a true perspective on life. One of the big challenges to religious faith is the apparent absence of empirical evidence to support it. People who believe anything without evidence, it is claimed, are simply foolish, and naive. What is usually meant by evidence is of course irrefutable empirical grounds for factual belief of the kind that can be tested and verified by scientific methods. Believers, however, would claim that this is an oversimplified view of both faith and evidence. **Basil Mitchell** pointed out (see p. 230) that beside those things that can be seen to support faith, nothing in the world *decisively* undermines it.

> Certainly it is salutary to recognize that *even* our belief in so-called hard facts rests in the end on a faith, a commitment, which is not in or to facts, but in that without which there would be not be any facts.
>
> R. M. *Hare*

Believers would also say that the nature of faith is to show trust in God despite whatever may tend to shake that trust. In this sense it is part of faith to live with the temptation to have doubts about it, for otherwise it would not be the free commitment that it is.

> Some religious thinkers argue that faith is a *commitment* to trust, both God and the *evidence* of the historic trust of others within the religious community to which one belongs.
>
> *How far might this counter the charge that faith is blind?*

Believers would also point out that there are many areas of life involving convictions where undisputed empirical evidence (rather than 'indicators') is impossible to find. Declarations of *love* between two people, judgements about the *beauty* of a Picasso or a Beethoven concerto, or judgements, say, about human motivation (such as revenge, jealousy or prejudice) are not the kinds of things that are amenable to empirical evidence in the way that everyday factual claims are. Judgements about beauty, goodness or morality, they would say, are usually more related to feelings and *intuitions* than to clear factual evidence, and involve an important element of *trust* about the accuracy of belief. Yet many would argue that such judgements are perfectly valid, and involve important claims to truth, but come from the mystical, spiritual, numinous or intuitive side of human nature.

> It would be difficult to offer empirical evidence that a painting by Rembrandt is a work of art, although many are convinced that it is. But the question might also be: is it a genuine Rembrandt? Recently in London a picture went on sale amid doubts about its provenance. The buyer made a wager on it being a genuine Rembrandt. Like Pascal's wager the outlay was small but the rewards could be great.
>
> *How far does this counter the principle that 'nobody should believe anything without sufficient evidence' as propounded by Richard Dawkins?*

Believers would also point out that unbelievers often gloss over the counter claim that alternative world views to faith, such as scientism (the belief that all that are worthy to be called facts are scientifically explainable) and naturalism (the belief that everything happened naturally, and by chance), involve

RELIGIOUS FAITH

holding beliefs that also go beyond the world of empirical facts, and ultimately rest on some kind of 'belief' as opposed to 'knowledge'. Theists would point out that the belief that nothing exists outside the world observable by science (scientism) is a metaphysical belief that can be neither confirmed nor denied, exactly the sort of characteristics alleged to make faith irrational.

> *Scientism*   All facts within the world are explainable by *science*. Any fact about the world not explainable by science is not a true fact.
>
> *Naturalism*   All events in the world, and those that led to the world coming about, happened naturally, and by *chance*.
>
> *Evidentialism*   The theory that all beliefs must be supported by *empirical* evidence.
>
> *Theism*   Facts *within* the world can be explained by science, but facts *about* the world are different. The world is not the result of chance, but was created by a personal being, God.

The urgency of believing (wagering) that something is true without conclusive evidence

William James seems to echo **Pascal** with his view that because of our 'passional nature' we need to make decisions about life *now*, decisions that are based on trust and judgement rather than certainty. Without such trust normal human relations would be impossible. Pascal saw the need for a wager on life because of the high stakes involved, and the impossibility of being able to examine all the relevant issues now. Pascal, a realist as well as a mystic, was keenly aware that people in real life give little time to working out the credibility or otherwise of religious faith. He disagreed with **Descartes** that people were mainly interested in life's certainties. People were far more interested in horse-racing and gambling and other everyday pursuits, than about philosophy or religion (much less philosophy of religion!). For Pascal there were no rational certainties in life. People are human beings, and typically tend to rely on trust, hope, and guesswork in everyday life, knowing that they have to live with uncertainty. When it comes to the big questions of life they have to work out the odds on who is right and who is wrong. They have to wager on the truth (see Pascal's Wager below, p. 108).

> **Pascal** and **James** held that faith was an *urgent* decision that could not be made to wait for 'sufficient evidence'. **Plantinga** holds that faith is a *basic belief* (beliefs are 'properly basic', i.e. they do not depend on any other beliefs, if they are consistent with a reasonable world view). He agrees with **Descartes** that belief in experience cannot be properly basic since it can be wrong. Basic beliefs include belief in our *senses*, belief in our *memories*, belief in our *reasoning*, and belief in God.

Religious faith as a possible source of personal fulfilment

> **C. G. Jung** differed from **Freud** by seeing religion, not as the result of emotional drives, but as arising naturally, and as capable of being seen as psychologically beneficial to the inner psyche.

An important question for the credibility of religious faith might be its value in relation to the personal search for inner peace and contentment, a universally recognized good desired by all people. The critical question would be how far faith contributes to such a value, or whether it can be shown not to. The view that religion does matter for the welfare of the psyche was one of the convictions of the psychologist **Carl Gustav Jung**, who reached very different conclusions about religious faith from his colleague **Freud**. Where Freud saw religious faith as illusory and damaging, Jung saw it as a therapeutic and positive value for the health of the inner psyche. He agreed with Freud that religion was something that people wanted to be true, but unlike Freud he held that without it people were in fact psychologically deprived. Religion brought 'wholeness and integration' to the personality, something, he believed, that all people desire to bring about, but try to do so in other, less successful ways (see box).

> The desire for alcohol symbolized at a low level our spiritual thirst for wholeness; expressed in medieval language as union with God . . . man lives wholly when, and only when, he is related to God.
>
> *Jung*

RELIGIOUS FAITH

> This echoes **Tillich**'s view that God, and all that he means, is the only object worthy to be our 'ultimate concern' because all else is transient, but **Jung** was only making observations about what religion actually meant for his patients at the experiential level. How might the two views be brought together?

Unlike Freud, who rationalized religion as a temporary, but false, human solution to personal fears and anxieties, Jung saw religious faith as an emotionally fulfilling experience in its own right coming from outside the individual, not something 'produced from traumas within' as Freud had claimed. He therefore widened the basis of religious faith as something arising from a universal experience, and an important factor in the search for inner peace. The modern, internationally respected psychologist of religion **Antoine Vergote** of Louvain has argued against Freud that religious faith, although sometimes a factor in mental neurosis, is, in the normal case, important for human fulfilment and the search for emotional happiness.

> *Freud* Religion is a rationalized, but false, solution to human fears and anxieties.
>
> *Jung* Religion is an inner experience that is beneficial to the human psyche.
>
> *Vergote* Religion can be an important factor in the search for good emotional adjustment.
>
> *In the light of these different assessments of religion, how far do all agree that many find a solution to human problems, rightly or wrongly, in religious faith?*

Religious authority in regard to faith and religious values

The history of Christianity shows that there have been many disputes about faith, disputes that have usually centred on the question of who is the correct 'authority' in deciding about its content and meaning. Originally it was agreed that the early Church was the recognized authority in matters of faith and morals. This authority was exercised first by the apostles, who were held to have a privileged right to be the spokespersons for God's revelation. After the apostles their successors as leaders of the Church took on the mantle of God's authority on earth. While God is strictly the ultimate authority in everything to do with faith, it is his human representatives on earth who mediate this authority. This is where the problems have arisen. Eventually disputes would arise about where God's authority was 'most truly' mediated. History would show that this was a problem difficult for human beings to resolve.

> ***Religious authority*** ultimately resided in God, but both the ***scriptures*** and ***religious leaders*** are theoretically the official ***mediators*** of that authority.
>
> *How far is it humanly understandable that disputes should arise about who is best qualified to speak for God, and how might such disputes be best settled?*

There was, for instance, a major disagreement at the Reformation as to whether Scripture was the sole authority, or whether the Church with its established traditions was a more reliable authority in the interpretation of Scripture (see also above, p. 75). Thus arose a major clash over religious authority, resulting in claims between rival groups about who was best qualified to speak for God. For the Reformers real religious authority lay in 'Scripture alone', which meant the rejection of the authority of Catholic church leaders, and their claim to be the 'guardians' of Scripture, and the ultimate earthly authority in faith and morals. However, all agree that whatever form it takes, whether through Scripture or religious leaders, the purpose of religious authority is to represent the truth in matters of faith and values.

> *Catholics believe the Pope is the supreme leader of the Church and the guardian of revelation. His authority was rejected by the Reformers, but how far is the authority of religious leaders important in religion today?*

RELIGIOUS FAITH

How authority is exercised today

In the Catholic tradition the Pope is the supreme authority on earth. This is exercised normally through the agency of bishops and priests. This authority is expressed through papal pronouncements (usually called encyclicals); sometimes through council decisions (meetings of all the bishops with the Pope); individual bishops' letters to the faithful; and priest-centred teachings in the various parishes that make up the Church. All in all the Church keeps control of the interpretation of Scripture, and issues teachings from time to time on matters of faith, morality and worship. In the Protestant tradition authority is less centralized, and more emphasis is placed on the private interpretation of Scripture by the faithful.

The Church and religious authority

Catholic The Pope is the supreme authority acting on behalf of God in matters of 'faith and morals'. He rules over the Church, but is bound by the teachings of Scripture and tradition. He is normally advised by other church leaders, such as a Council of Bishops.

Protestant The supreme authority is Scripture alone. Church leaders help to interpret it, but the faithful are free to interpret it for themselves with the guidance of the Holy Spirit.

How far can it be argued that some churches place more importance on the authority of religious leaders in matters of faith and morals than others?

A final source of authority in religious matters is the exercise of conscience, which is universally accepted as the most immediate authority in moral matters for each individual. (For more on conscience see below, p. 276.) Aquinas, however, held that conscience could be a misleading authority unless it is fully informed and educated, by which he meant in conformity with official church teachings. The question of church authority, understood as something vested in the hands of human beings, is seen as controversial by many people. In a secular age where personal independence is highly valued, church leaders inevitably find that the authority they once enjoyed in the age of faith is no longer as compelling as it was.

> **Religious authorities**
>
> ***God*** Theoretically the ultimate authority, but God's authority must be *mediated* by humans.
>
> ***Sacred texts (Scripture)*** Regarded my most Christians as highly authoritative, but all sacred texts have to be initially *selected* by humans, and later interpreted by them.
>
> ***Church traditions*** Catholics have traditionally stressed the authority of its traditions, claiming that the interpretation of Scripture must be controlled *officially* by the Church, not done individually by believers.
>
> ***Conscience*** Recognized as a *sovereign* authority in matters of faith and morals, but is held to need *guidance* and direction (Aquinas) to avoid being over-subjective, and therefore potentially deceptive.
>
> *What might be the problems or merits in having* **church leaders** *as sources of religious* **moral** *authority, compared with the authority of individual conscience?*

The idea that faith can be implicit as well as explicit

> **Karl Rahner** *believed human beings whose lives were admirable could be called 'anonymous Christians', but why might some people, while agreeing with his point, find the label offensive?*

We end this chapter by briefly considering a view that appears to throw open the traditional distinction between believers and non-believers. This is the view that people without religion might qualify as having the 'essence' of faith, by reason of the *virtuous* character of their lives. In the view of some religious thinkers faith can be present, even if only implicitly, in those who may have no outward connection with an official religion, and who may even reject religious belief. This idea has been put forward by the noted Austrian theologian **Karl Rahner**. He has argued that 'official' faith, that is, faith merely on the outside, which is carried as a sort of label or badge of identity, has little spiritual value unless matched with the reality which the badge represents, that is, a life of integrity and virtue (see more in Religion and Virtue below, p. 269).

> ***Believers*** Could be officially 'baptized' members of their church, but only nominally Christian, showing no commitment to religious faith or values.
>
> ***Non-believers*** May have no connection, or even sympathy, with religion, but may be conscientious and good living.
>
> *Jesus had already been aware of the difference between those who 'say' and those who 'do', but how far is Rahner's view appropriate in an age of declining religious practice?*

Rahner argued that unbelievers and even those hostile to religion were capable of being able to show 'implicit faith' by the quality of their lives. According to Rahner, people who lived lives of integrity and moral goodness were displaying the true essence of faith, and were higher up the spiritual scale than so-called badge-carrying Christians. By this method Rahner is taking an essential element of faith (ethical integrity) and arguing that where such ethical commitment is present it qualifies the subject to be implicitly included among the ranks of the 'faithful'. It honours being religious in deed, or character, without necessarily being religious in the traditional sense.

> ***Explicit faith*** Possessed by those who are baptized, and are official members of the Church.
>
> ***Implicit faith*** Possessed by those who may be unbelievers, but whose lives are morally virtuous.

In this way Rahner highlighted the theoretical gap that can exist between God and religion. Serving God may be aided by official religion, but in the end true religious faith is something that transcends all earthly religious forms, and is a task that can be carried out in a secular form through life in the world. The validity of such an approach is exemplified in two contrasting situations. In one, a person may be hostile to religion but may show good character and live a virtuous life. In the other, a person may claim to be a 'Christian' but show by their lives that such a label is purely a sham. The Russian prisoner and writer **Solzhenitsyn** gave a small illustration of this when he remembered how interrogators wearing crosses turned out to be as brutal as any of the others.

> Why believe that there is a God at all? My answer is that to suppose that there is a God explains why there is a world at all; why there are the scientific laws there are: why animals and then humans have evolved... why we have the well authenticated accounts of Christ's life, death and resurrection; why throughout the centuries men have had the apparent experience of being in touch with and guided by God; and so much else. In fact, the hypothesis of the existence of God makes sense of the whole of our experience, and it does so better than any other explanation which can be put forward, and that is the grounds for believing it to be true.
> *Richard Swinburne*

5 The Language of Faith

- The problems of religious language.
- The use of analogy.
- The use of myth.
- The use of symbol.
- The use of religious symbols to express beliefs.
- The problems with analogy, myth and symbol.
- The idea of art as a medium of the transcendent.

Religious language is ordinary language but used to refer to transcendent realities

One of the immediate difficulties raised by religious language is that it refers to a spiritual, transcendent reality called God. The question then arises to what extent it is possible to use language about things *within* the world to refer to things *beyond* the world. The linguistic philosophy called logical positivism (see below) held that the function of language is to 'mirror the world' and its main business is dealing with 'facts' about the world. An implication of this is that all assertions must be able to be 'verified' or 'falsified' by the methods of science. This was a serious challenge to religious language because its assertions (about God, creation, sin, redemption and so on) could not be verified by experience or confirmed by proof (see more on this in the challenge to religious language, p. 215).

Aquinas may not have imagined that one day religious language would be classed as meaningless, but he was fully aware that it was not quite the same

> ***Ordinary language*** Refers to things in the world which can be directly experienced.
>
> ***Religious language*** Refers to transcendent realities that cannot be directly experienced.

as 'ordinary language', that is, language about things in the empirical world, also known as 'empirical language'. Aquinas knew that God was not a person who could be spoken of on the same level as human persons. One is infinite and belongs to the realm of the spirit, and is transcendent; the other is finite and belongs to the everyday world of sight, hearing, touch, taste and smell. Thus to say 'God is in heaven' is grammatically similar to, but logically different from, saying 'Moses is on the mountain'. To ignore this is known as 'anthropomorphism', that is, treating God as a human being. It is also a form of 'literalism', the mistake of taking things literally instead of metaphorically, as when we say we were 'over the moon' with delight.

> ***Religious assertion*** God is in heaven.
>
> ***Empirical assertion*** The book is in the library.
>
> *The two statements may be said to be grammatically similar but logically different.*

Religious language and the use of analogy

Recognizing the 'infinite qualitative difference' between God and humanity, Aquinas proposed the use of analogy, a literary device by which one thing is compared to another. He held that this was possible because we are in some way related to God since we are 'made in God's image and likeness'. Yet we must be aware that language about God is bound to be as limited and inadequate as our limited human understanding of God's nature.

> **Analogy (comparison)**
> - 'God is good' (analogy of ***attribution***).
> - 'God is infinitely powerful' (analogy of ***proportion***).

THE LANGUAGE OF FAITH

Aquinas explained how analogy can be used to speak of God, as when we say 'God is wise' or that God is 'all-powerful', or 'merciful' and so on. In these examples we are using the analogy of 'attribution', attributing to God qualities that are highly esteemed by human beings, such as that God is good. Likewise, we use analogy of 'proportion' when we recognize that God is proportionately greater than humans. So God is 'infinitely' wise, good, loving, just, and so on.

> *Model*   Goodness, wisdom, power.
>
> *Qualifier*   ***Perfectly*** good, ***all***-wise, ***infinitely*** powerful.
>
> **Ramsey** claimed that the purpose of religious language was to be not *descriptive*, but *evocative*.

Ian Ramsey preferred to talk in terms of 'models' and 'qualifiers'. To say God is wise is to employ a model 'wisdom' from everyday experience. To say that God is 'infinitely' wise is to use the qualifier 'infinitely' to describe the uniqueness of God. This, according to Ramsey, 'lights up' the meaning of God, and leads to a religious 'disclosure' which in turn leads to a religious 'commitment'. Ramsey's concern was to show that religious language was above all not descriptive but evocative, meaning that its purpose is not to arrive at an accurate description of God, but to move the believer to make a religious response to a Being who is ultimately beyond words, but whose significance for human beings can be grasped by human language.

> **Language about God**
>
> *Equivocal* (wrong)   This is to speak of God in a ***different*** sense from how we speak of earthly things.
>
> *Univocal* (wrong)   This is to speak of God in the ***same*** sense as we speak of earthly things.
>
> *Analogical* (correct)   This is to speak of God cautiously by *comparison* with earthly things.
>
> Aquinas also spoke of the via *affirmativa*, the via *negativa*, as well as the via *analogia*, as methods of speaking about God.

Religious language and the use of myth

The word myth is commonly understood to mean a story that is false, and is popularly linked to legend and folklore. However, in a religious context a myth expresses fundamental beliefs of a community where the myth is regarded as a sacred narrative. The earliest mythological stories concerned how the world came about by the power of the gods or supernatural agents. The classic example of myth in the Old Testament is the creation narrative from Genesis, some of the elements of which were borrowed from earlier existing myths. Only comparatively recently did such mythical accounts come under examination. The big issue was whether they should be taken literally or metaphorically. Biblical scholars today are generally agreed that myths like the creation narrative are important vehicles of religious truth, but should not be taken literally. Under the impact of science, especially, it became necessary to see this (see Religion and Science below, p. 177).

> A renowned New Testament scholar, **Rudolf Bultmann**, believed that biblical myths were stories that were factually untrue but contained truths of vital religious and moral significance. The creation myth, for instance, was about the sovereignty of God and the creaturely status of sinful man. Its mythical 'frame' was understandable but unimportant.

> *Myths* present God in anthropomorphic terms, making him act like a human being.

The early Christian thinker **Origen** had already raised the rhetorical questions: Did anyone think that the fruit eaten by Adam and Eve was a real fruit, or that God really 'walked in the garden in the cool of the evening' as the Bible colourfully puts it? This reflected an early understanding of the difference between the 'literal' meaning of Scripture, and its deeper 'spiritual' or metaphorical meaning. More recent studies of ancient texts have highlighted the use of particular literary forms which appear throughout the Bible. Thus God is described as 'working', 'resting', 'regretting', 'admonishing', 'promising', 'praising', 'threatening', 'punishing'. These are typical mythic terms and are used by way of analogy (comparison) with the actions and thought processes of human beings. Another common myth is the picturing of God as 'an old man in the sky'.

THE LANGUAGE OF FAITH

> *The idea that God is an old man in the sky is literally untrue, but how far can this myth be a vehicle of religious truth?*

This is a good illustration of how a religious myth if taken literally can appear as 'naive', or 'unbelievable'. Yet for theists the elements of this homely image preserve some deep theological truths. Theists would say that even in the space age, the sky still appears to us as a place, or space, that looks limitless, infinite. Hence it becomes an 'appropriate' location for a God who is infinite and limitless. The sky also suggests height and majesty, and indeed is something truly awesome, hence its suitability as the 'home' of a God who is transcendent, mysterious, awesome, who rules from 'on high' and whose presence is invisible but ubiquitous. The idea of God as an 'old man' is of course an image of age and wisdom. Even **Wittgenstein** recognized that when someone 'raises their eyes to heaven' they are showing a mythical awareness of the divine, without necessarily believing that God is literally 'up there'.

Religious language and the use of symbols

The use of symbols to express profound ideas related to the understanding of human life was commonplace before even the biblical era. Two examples will suffice. The serpent as a symbol of evil and deception was already well recognized before the story of Adam and Eve. Eve fell for the deception by listening to the serpent, and convinced Adam that the fruit of what appeared to be the tree of the knowledge of good and evil was safe to eat even though God warned against it. The idea that the serpent's head would be crushed in a reversal of his triumph in the garden became a powerful image of how humanity through Christ would eventually bring about his nemesis, and the victory of good over evil in the redemption. Likewise the dragon was a symbol familiar in Greek mythology which stood for the beast who has to be overcome if the realm of the sacred could be reached. In turn the dragon also becomes a symbol of the 'beast within', the animal instincts which prevent the attainment of spiritual freedom. Therefore images of the archangel Michael and St George defeating the dragon came to have a strong spiritual significance.

> **Biblical symbols**
>
> ***Angels*** Messengers of God, and symbols of purity and goodness.
>
> ***Satan*** The 'fallen' angel, symbol of temptation and evil.
>
> ***Serpent*** Classical symbol of evil and deception.
>
> ***Tree*** Symbol of knowledge of good and evil.
>
> ***Fruit*** Symbol of earthly desires.
>
> ***Garden*** Symbol of order and beauty.
>
> ***Sword*** Symbol of power and justice.
>
> ***Fire*** Symbol of purification.
>
> ***Light*** Symbol of goodness and truth.
>
> ***Darkness*** Symbol of ignorance and evil.
>
> ***Water*** Symbol of life and spiritual regeneration.
>
> ***Bread*** Symbol of sustenance and spiritual nourishment.

The religious philosopher **Paul Tillich** held that religion (or God) can only be expressed through symbols, which are always finite things, but their function is to point to the infinite. Symbols can be 'things, persons or events'. Unlike signs which are human conventions (such as traffic lights), and can change, religious symbols can never change in respect to how they function as finite things pointing to the infinite or, as he prefers, the 'ultimate'. In Tillich's complex thought some religious symbols can 'die' and cease to function, such as a church building, or even a religious picture. At the same time non-religious things can be effective symbols of the infinite (he cites cubist art as an example). He holds that although God can be symbolized, he is not himself a symbol, but the focal point of all earthly symbols, being the infinite that always 'lies behind' the finite.

> For **Tillich** the key function of *finite* things is to be symbolic of the *infinite*. Hence his liking for secular art as an example of how this can work.
>
> *But how far might this be criticized as an over-intellectual approach, one that is unlikely to have much appeal to ordinary people?*

Tillich's concern seems to have been to break the conventional dependence on traditional religious symbols, such as 'holy' images and pictures. He prefers the idea that anything finite can be used to point to the infinite, and that there are a wide variety of resources from the natural finite world that can to do this. While this is theoretically a provocative, interesting, and certainly challenging idea, it is unlikely to cut much ice with ordinary believers, who normally rely on the established or traditional symbols commonly found in churches, shrines, art galleries, books and so on.

> Man's ultimate concern (God) must be expressed symbolically, because symbolic language alone is able to express the ultimate.
> *Paul Tillich*

Tillich believed that all symbols functioned to show how the finite, and finite concerns, could reveal what is ultimate and infinite. A Cezanne landscape with its 'displaced' details can be a reminder of the contingent nature of earthly things, a vision that can convey an understanding of the permanent, the infinite, the ultimate, and the eternal.

Symbolic images expressing key aspects of faith

One of the earliest symbolic images of Christ was 'the good shepherd' with a lamb on his shoulders. The lamb was a well-known image of sacrifice, and echoed John the Baptist's description of Christ as the 'lamb of God'. When it appeared on Christian gravestones it also became an image of the Christian soul, an allusion to the words of Christ to Peter, 'feed my lambs', meaning his followers. Another symbol of the soul was the peacock, originally a pagan symbol of immortality. The fish symbol was widely used as a focus of devotion, and appeared early on the walls of the Roman catacombs where the early Christians worshipped, as well as on graves and tombs across the Roman Empire from North Africa to Europe and the Middle East. This image represented the Saviour, probably because the initials 'Jesus Christ Son of God Saviour' made *'ichthus'*, meaning a fish in Greek. The image of the dove became an image of the Holy Spirit, from his appearance 'in the form of a dove' at the Baptism of Christ, and on the occasion of his descent on the apostles on the Day of Pentecost.

> **Christian symbols**
> - ***Cross***   Instrument of salvation.
> - ***Fish***   Symbol of Jesus Christ.
> - ***Shepherd***   Symbol of pastoral care (Jesus).
> - ***Lamb***   Symbol of sacrifice (Jesus).
> - ***Dove***   Symbol of the Holy Spirit.
> - ***Fire***   Symbol of inspiration.
> - ***Bread and wine***   Symbols of eucharistic worship.

The Eastern Church: icons express and embody the holiness of the human person as follower of Christ

In the Eastern Church icons became an important feature of church interiors (in some cases exteriors), and were meant to enhance worship by acting as an inspiration for prayer and reflection. However, the figure of God is rarely seen except in symbolic form as a hand appearing through clouds. Icons reflect and call attention to the incarnational aspect of Christianity and show human images usually of Christ, the saints and martyrs. The icon is traditionally a manifestation of the divine in human form, echoing the truth of the incarnation. To avoid any danger of an icon becoming a focus of worship in itself, it is pointed out that the image is merely a window into the spiritual world. To dwell on an icon is to see into the world 'beyond', the world to which the figure now belongs. Icons remind the worshipper that their destiny in not limited to this life, but is one day to be with the saints in heaven.

> An icon of the Trinity, created by the Russian icon painter **Andrei Rublev** in the thirteenth century, is on view in the Tretyakov Gallery in Moscow.
>
>> Andrew Rublev painted this icon not only to share the fruits of his own meditation on the mystery of the Holy Trinity but also to offer his fellow monks a way to keep their hearts centred on God in the midst of political unrest. The more we look at this holy image with the eyes of

THE LANGUAGE OF FAITH

> faith, the more we realize that it is painted not as a holy decoration... but as a holy place to enter and stay within... The movement of the Father towards the Son, and the Son and Spirit towards the Father becomes a movement in which the one who prays is lifted up and held secure.
>
> *Henri Nouwen*
>
> *Here Nouwen expresses the idea of the Trinity as something human and consoling. But to create this feeling, how far is the icon dependent on Christian faith?*

Religious symbols that express beliefs about life after death

An important area of symbolism in Christianity is their use in expressing beliefs about life after death. Christian belief about the afterlife inevitably showed a strong connection to their beliefs about Jesus' death and resurrection. Such symbols can be found in churches and cathedrals, but they also appear significantly on tombstones and places where Christians were buried. One of the most popular symbols was the cross, the instrument of salvation and the source of hope. The *chi–rho* (the Greek letters *KR* standing for the first two letters of *KRistos*) became widespread as a badge of identity on Christian graves, pointing to faith in Christ as the victor over death. This monogram is somewhat misleading today because the letters KR appear as XP. Although it is not obvious that it stands for the initials KR, it became popular because the K could also conveniently be made into a cross *(X)*.

> ☧
>
> The *chi-rho* symbol of Christ appears almost universally in early Christian grave steles across north Africa, Rome and the Middle East.

GOD, FAITH AND PHILOSOPHY

> **Popular Christian symbols on gravestones**
> - ***Anchor***   Salvation referring to Christ.
> - ***Olive wreath***   Victory over death.
> - ***Palm leaf***   Victory over death.
> - ***Evergreen tree or leaves***   Everlasting life.
> - ***Birds in the air***   The soul and resurrection.
> - ***Alpha and Omega*** (A–Z)   Christ as divine, the beginning and the end.
> - ***The Chi-Ro (KR) monogram***   Christ the author of salvation.
> - ***The Cross***   Redemption leading to resurrection.
>
> *Religious symbols on gravestones or tombs typically convey reassuring truths about life after death. The focus of each symbol is the person of Christ. Explain why this is so, and why all these are symbols of hope and reassurance.*

The problem of expressing spiritual truths by means of analogies and symbols

> ***Scientific symbols***   Depend on their ability to express scientific facts meaningfully.
>
> ***Religious symbols***   Depend for their meaning on religious beliefs.
>
> *How far does this distinction affect the intelligibility of religious symbols?*

Metaphors and symbols are an accepted literary device to explain something in terms of something else (a camel is a ship of the desert). Not surprisingly analogies, metaphors and symbols are frequently used in science to explain phenomena that need to be explained using more familiar terms. Therefore science uses terms such as 'waves', 'particles', 'pulses', 'fields', 'holes', 'probes' and the like to illustrate certain scientific facts that would otherwise be unintelligible. Science also depends on symbols to express the presence of invisible

THE LANGUAGE OF FAITH

things like gas, electricity or radiation. In the same way believers claim it is justifiable to use religious metaphors (God is my rock, the Lord is my shepherd, and so on) as a legitimate way to express certain beliefs about God. For believers, however, the problem of using analogy through myth, symbol and metaphor is in justifying the claim that they are making comparisons with an invisible God.

> Science employs symbols to warn of hidden dangers.
>
> *Religious symbols also refer to hidden realities, but what limitations or problems do theists face in claiming the validity of such symbols?*

Unbelievers will claim that the uses of religious analogies and symbols are meaningless because they refer to supposed realities that cannot be experienced, and are beyond verification and falsification. They would argue that comparisons with scientific metaphors or symbols are misleading since science can always verify the validity of their use in scientific contexts, for example defining an abstract reality such as light in terms of waves or particles. Believers, however, will claim that their use of religious language is valid simply because the religious world view is itself valid. If religion is true, then symbols and metaphors referring to God are both meaningful, and capable of expressing religious truths. Believers would also point out that the use of religious language bears comparison with aesthetic language or poetic language, or moral language, all of which may employ metaphors, analogies or symbols, but which are not amenable to strict verification or falsification.

Different metaphors and symbols

- **Religious metaphor**   Jesus is the **light** of the world.
- **Poetic metaphor**   You are my **sunshine**.
- **Artistic metaphor**   The painting was a unique **experience**.
- **Aesthetic metaphor**   That music was the **tonic** I needed.
- **Moral metaphor**   Evil is the **poison** of society.
- **Scientific metaphor**   Light travels in **waves** or in **particles**.

Why would many say that the scientific metaphor is the odd one out?

The use of art in communicating Christian beliefs

From the earliest days of the Church, visual art was used to illustrate and express fundamental beliefs. The earliest examples can be found in places like the Roman catacombs, where the early Christians met secretly for worship. Other examples have survived on gravestones found all around the Mediterranean, from North Africa in the south, to the Holy Land and Asia Minor in the east, and to Britain and Ireland in the west. The earliest images were naturally of Christ, the Virgin Mary and the Apostles, the founding figures of the faith. Later with the growth of Christian churches, cathedrals and basilicas there came a growing need for visual images of the faith. Their earliest forms were frescos and mosaics, remarkable examples of which can be found throughout Christian Europe, but especially in Constantinople, Rome and Ravenna. Later artists like Giotto, Michelangelo, Raphael, Leonardo, El Greco and Rembrandt (to name a few) added a new dimension to the visual depiction of the faith.

> Art ennobles the human spirit, and presents us with a justifying vision of ourselves, as something higher than nature and apart from it ... knowledge of God is not a knowledge *that*, nor a knowledge *how*, but a knowledge *what*: a knowledge what to feel in the face of nature ... (we find in Kant) this elevation of the aesthetic to the highest spiritual position.
>
> Roger Scruton
>
> *What might be required for this vision to work?*

The notion that art is a universal language with intimations of the transcendent

We end this chapter with a consideration of views that hold that art, even where it is not meant to be the language of faith, can in principle contain, if not a vision, an intuitive insight into the world of the transcendent. In support of this view some thinkers have gone so far as to say that all art can best be seen in a theological context. **George Steiner** has argued that all great art provides an 'entrance into our lives of the mystery of otherness ... of a metaphysical–religious kind'.

THE LANGUAGE OF FAITH

> Art is not meaningful without a wager on transcendence . . . a wager that there is in the art experience a meaningful form, a presence . . . the entrance into our lives of the mystery of otherness in art and music is of a metaphysical-religious kind.
>
> George Steiner
>
> *Steiner here seems to imply that art reaches out to the 'beyond', to that which lies outside or beyond the visual image, and transcends it. How far is this open to challenge from a scientific point of view?*

Trevor Pateman says, 'it is an arguable claim that all serious art is in some sense an attempt to articulate something ineffable, something that transcends everyday reality and is in consequence religious art, whatever the conscious beliefs of the artist or audience. On this basis one can think of artistic creation as (in some sense) a religious act.' **Roger Scruton** sees art as an avenue into an understanding of the world that explicitly relates to a religious understanding, but that in a secular age would not be called that. For this reason he sees art as secular language through which we learn how to feel about the world. Pateman suggests that there is something significant in the way we react to the destruction or vandalism of a work of art. Our reaction is often expressed in religious terms. 'Anyone who feels shock and outrage at the destruction of an artistic work . . . is probably not far from seeing such acts as literally sacrilegious.'

> Even in a world mostly secular, the arts can make space for our intuition of mystery, which is not the same as saying that the arts are a substitute for religion. It's enough that the arts make space for those intuitions and feelings that are crowded out in our works and days. With the arts people can make a space for themselves and fill it with intimations of freedom and presence.
>
> Denis Donoghue
>
> *If this view be seen as a non-religious attempt to widen our understanding of life, how far does it suggest the limitations of a purely scientific view?*

6 Faith and Reason

- Faith and reason.
- Faith and the question of reality.
- Plato's cave.
- Fideism and reason.
- The views of Augustine, Luther and Kierkegaard.
- The view of Aquinas.
- Pascal's wager.

The dispute about how faith is related to reason

The relationship between faith and reason has been an important topic in the history of philosophy of religion. One view is that faith (as a system of belief) should in some sense depend on reason, and be subordinate to it, while a counter view is that reason should be subordinate to faith because of the superior knowledge that faith is claimed to provide. In this view faith is superior to reason and is independent of it. In the other view faith can be shown to be consistent with reason, and offer a 'reasonable' interpretation of life. As we saw above, there are two conflicting traditions regarding the relationship between the two. One tradition, called fideism, mainly represented by **Luther** and his followers, holds that faith is its own justification, and has no need for rationally justifying reasons to uphold its credibility. A variant of this view was also held by **Augustine** and **Anselm**, both of whom believed that faith was superior to reason because of the knowledge provided by revelation. The other view is the one represented by **Aquinas**, who believed that reason can legitimately be used to support faith (as in the arguments for God's existence). (See also Plantinga on faith as a 'basic belief' above, p. 84.)

FAITH AND REASON

> ***Paul, Augustine, Luther, Kierkegaard*** All were said to be ***fideists***. In its extreme form fideism means that faith needs no support from reason, and can stand by itself. All believed that faith was 'rationally absurd', a 'paradox', and was a 'scandal' from a 'reasonable' point of view.
>
> *Why did they believe this, and how far does fideism really dispense with reason?*

The idea that the world of the spirit is the real world

According to **Augustine** the insights of faith could never be supplied by human reason. Already **Paul** had made a similar point when he said that the wisdom of faith was 'foolishness' in the eyes of the world. Augustine was influenced by **Plato**, who favoured a mystical or ideal view of reality, not one which depended on reason and experience. He thereby reversed the normal understanding of what is counted as 'real'. According to Plato the full truth of reality is only gained through an understanding of the spiritual realm, where true 'reality' is to be found. Here is the realm where the 'important' things in life take place: love, justice, truth, evil. This makes for an easy link with religious faith since its object, God, belongs more to the ideal, spiritual world than to the so-called 'real' world of science, where experience is limited to the empirical and the scientifically verifiable.

> In a famous phrase **Tertullian** said that 'Jerusalem owed nothing to Athens'. Athens was the centre of reason and philosophy, Jerusalem the location of the events which were the source of the Christian faith.

The allegory of the cave: earthly reality is only an illusion of the real thing

> ***Spiritual world*** The real world. The world of good and evil, right and wrong (Plato).
>
> ***Material world*** The world of illusion, which needs to be seen for what it is (Plato).

Paradoxically, for **Plato** reality in the fullest sense exists as 'ideal forms' only perceived by the mind. The real world is an 'ideal' or 'spiritual' world, of which earthly things are only pale and transient shadows. The world of everyday experience, Plato held, is similar to people living in a cave who, seeing the shadows of things projected on a wall by the background light, take them for the real thing. Only when they leave the cave and come into the sunlight of reality do they enter the real world. Plato for instance saw ideal beauty as the original idea or model from which all manifestations of beauty are derived. He also highlighted the distinction between things that are true, and 'ideal truth', between things that are good and 'ideal goodness'. In each case the 'shadow' of truth is contrasted with the 'light' of truth, the discovery of which everyone, with effort, can make.

> *Plato used the cave to show that earthly knowledge was a mere shadow of true reality. How effectively does this image introduce the idea of spiritual truths and values, and how convincing is Plato's vision of reality?*

The ideas of Plato were revived in the third century by **Plotinus**, who claimed that we are all tuned to go beyond everyday realities and search after the ideal. He saw love as something normally directed to earthly realities but held that its real target was in the spiritual realm. 'Love', he said, was 'the activity of the soul desiring the Good'. Augustine saw this as evidence that earthly love really pointed to the Highest Good, which is God. God is the ideal Reality who is dimly reflected in earthly forms of love, beauty, truth and goodness. In this way experience of the world gives rise to intuitions which provided access to a reality beyond that which can be obtained from rational thinking. Augustine's understanding of faith, therefore, was something that was derived more from intuition and inner perception than from rational thinking. He felt that faith belonged to the heart rather than the head, because the heart was more in touch with the deeper reality to which faith provides access. Significantly, the heart is also the seat of trust and commitment, which are both central to faith.

> **Plato**'s influence lay behind **Augustine**'s view that faith provided access to the 'real' world, in contrast to the earthly world which was full of shadow and illusion. He believed that faith was an ***intuition*** that made sense of experience. It came from the heart rather than the head.

Whether faith needs the support of reason

Luther was critical of **Aquinas**, whom he accused of using reason to uphold faith. Supporters of Aquinas, however, would say that he was only trying to show that faith could rest on reason, not that faith *needed* to rest on reason. Aquinas felt that faith could be shown to be at least consistent with reason, and that the existence of God in particular could be worked out from observed facts about the world. However, when it came to religious faith in the life of a believer, Aquinas saw it as a matter of accepting 'the authority of God who has revealed himself'. This means that faith in practice means making a direct response to God, not a response via the assurances gained by rational thinking. Luther's thinking, of course, was bound up with his concern to clarify the theological nature of faith, in contrast to Aquinas, who was concerned to address unbelievers, and argue for the credibility of faith against the rationalist challenges of his time.

> ***Luther*** Reason is corrupt because of the fallen nature of man, and cannot be relied on to provide full access to truth, much less religious truth. Faith supplements reason and goes beyond it.
>
> ***Aquinas*** Reason contains some measure of enlightenment being a gift of God, and can show that God exists. Faith can, but need not, build on reason. Faith supplements reason and goes beyond it.
>
> *Luther was pessimistic about reason, Aquinas more optimistic, but how far can both views be reconciled?*

Faith as a free response to God for his own sake

Kierkegaard made the point that faith was not the result of human reasoning or calculation but a free response to God, who offers the gift of salvation. He believed that if God had wanted to he could have revealed himself in such a way that human beings would have no choice but to accept him. As it is, God is hidden (at an epistemic distance) from humankind, and therefore we have the choice to accept God for himself on the basis of a revelation that looks 'irrational', 'paradoxical' and 'absurd': the story of God becoming incarnate in a humble man from Palestine. Yet good things come to those who trust what they experience with goodwill. Kierkegaard illustrated this with the story of the prince and the maiden. The prince knows that if he fully reveals his identity the maiden will be overwhelmed enough to marry him. Because this would be a poor reason for gaining the hand of the maiden, the prince conceals his identity and relies on the maiden to marry him for his own sake.

> **Kierkegaard** believed that there were reasons for having faith, but the act of faith must not be supported by any further reasons: it must be accepted on its own terms, like the maiden and the prince.

Pascal's wager: a reason to bet on faith in the interests of eternal salvation

A somewhat novel attempt to employ reason in conjunction with faith was put forward by **Pascal**. Like Aquinas he too was concerned to address unbelievers and make a case for the wisdom of accepting religious faith. Pascal was brought up a devout Christian but later joined a circle of freethinkers and unbelievers in the Paris of the 1700s. As a result of a mystical experience he underwent a revival of faith, and began to see its true significance. It was his renewed faith in God that produced his famous declaration that the God he came to know was not the cold God of the Philosophers, but the 'living' God of Abraham, Isaac and Jacob. Later, he made the famous statement that 'the heart has reasons that the mind never thought of', a reference back to **Augustine**, and to his awareness of God not as a 'fact' that could be shown to be true, but as a living truth of existential relevance felt by the heart.

> **Blaise Pascal** had a religious experience that changed his life, but he felt that the wager approach might appeal to those less religiously enlightened, or inclined, than himself.

Pascal went on to produce an argument for choosing religious faith called the *Wager*. After his religious conversion he became acutely aware of the importance of faith for a *virtuous life*, and ultimately for securing salvation.

FAITH AND REASON

In Pascal's day religious faith was inextricably linked to the moral life: both were seen as two sides of the same coin. He felt that the bohemian life lead by his freethinking friends might be fun for a while, but was ultimately unable to provide the satisfaction that all humans craved. It was then he hit upon the famous wager. As he saw it, life was a gamble. You could bet on there being no eternal life, or bet that there was.

> **Pascal's wager**
>
> Let us weigh the gain and loss in wagering that God is. Let us consider the two possibilities. If you win you gain all; if you lose you lose nothing. Hesitate not, then, to wager that He is.
>
> *Pascal*
>
> *How valid is the criticism that the wager is a cold and calculating way to gain salvation, and unworthy of religious faith?*

How the wager is proposed as a moral gamble on the good life

If you bet on there being no afterlife you could feel free to ignore moral restraints, have a good time and enjoy this life while it lasted. If you bet on there being an afterlife you had to change your lifestyle, but the reward was beyond calculation. Betting on the claims of faith was a safe bet, argued Pascal, because it merely involved living an upright life and enjoying the satisfaction that came from that. But by not betting on the truth of faith you take a great risk. If you lose you lose eternity.

> ***Pascal's wager*** was a proposal to bet on God by living a virtuous life, not just an opportunist bet that God might exist.

Some have accused Pascal of degrading faith and making it disreputable by presenting it in these terms. Surely God would have little time for anyone with so calculating an approach! Pascal would no doubt agree if the wager was understood as a shallow act of cold calculation driven by self-interest. But this is to caricature the wager. In Pascal's terms the wager was a commitment to the spiritual and moral life. The essence of the bet was taking on the kind of life that, with grace, would merit the eternal reward. Such a life, based on religious and moral values, would not be easy. It would require faith and devotion, and a commitment to the virtues of honesty, justice, chastity, truth and so on. It would leave no room for selfishness, hypocrisy, falsehood or wickedness. Seen in this light the wisdom of Pascal's wager is not the cold calculating act of a gambler: it is a gamble on reasons for changing one's life for the better.

> The debate about **faith** and **reason** has sometimes revolved around the difference between the **correspondence** and **coherence** theories of truth. The former is the standard theory of science, that 'knowledge should correspond with its object'; for example, certain chemicals will explode when heated. In the coherence theory, truth is that which 'coheres', or agrees, with certain possible truths, for example, the possible truth that God exists coheres with a certain understanding of the world, and vice versa.

Part 2 Religion and Human Experience

> Unlike the finite part of our life, the religious or infinite part of our life is impartial. Its impartiality leads to truth in thought, justice in action, and universal love in feeling.
> *Wittgenstein*

7 The Meaning of Religion

- Religion as the human perception of the divine.
- From religion to religions.
- Common features of organized religion.
- Christianity and cultural values.
- The modern impact of the Christian churches.
- The contribution of the churches to peace and reconciliation.

Religion as the human perception of the divine

Believers would accept that it is at least partly true, even if open to misinterpretation, that religion is a human phenomenon. Non-believers hold that it is merely a human phenomenon, something that can be explained completely in human terms, whether through the early experience of social grouping (**Durkheim**), living in an unequal society (**Marx**), or the experience of psychological conditioning in the family (**Freud**). To disagree with these theories is not to deny that religion as it exists in the world can have a significant and often unattractive human element. This is especially the case when its adherents show characteristics of immaturity, egoism, selfishness, arrogance, intolerance or other negative elements. But we may begin by accepting

> Religion is the art of the remaking of man. Man is not a finished product.
>
> *Edmund Burke*

RELIGION AND HUMAN EXPERIENCE

> Religion is the feelings, acts and experiences of people apprehending themselves to stand in solemn relation to what they consider to be the divine.
>
> *William James*

Features of western religion
- A communal system of belief.
- Directed to a divine being.
- Involving belief in revelation.
- Involving the use of sacred scriptures.
- Involving the practice of worship.
- Involving a moral code for living.
- Involving the authority of religious leaders.

Features of Christianity
- Belief in revelation as recorded in Scripture.
- Use of sacred scriptures for worship and reflection.
- Use of sacred buildings for communal worship.
- Use of sacred rituals such as baptism and the eucharist.
- Influence of religious leaders such as bishops, and the Pope.
- Recognized moral code such as the Decalogue.

William James's broad definition of religion as a relationship between human beings and the divine.

We can add to that by saying that religion is a communal system of belief which involves faith in a divine being, usually expressed through ritual practices of worship, and accompanied by a moral code.

Common features of organized religions within society

What is called 'organized' religion is religion in a noticeably structured form. It is religion as it has historically emerged from less structured or more 'primitive' forms. Organized religions have their own distinctive features. They are typically guided by sacred books, controlled by an official authority, and identified by specific beliefs, ethical codes and religious practices. Another common feature of organized religions is the social (and often, for better or worse, political) impact they make on the societies in which they take root. All three major religions have a definite social impact through their various offices, agencies, officials, customs, beliefs: and through the influence they have as an established organization within society at large. It may be useful therefore to dwell briefly on how religion impacts on society, and therefore how it relates to modern culture.

Religion and the cultural values of society

It may be said that all the main religions have a presence in society which makes them an important influence in what we may call modern culture. Allowing for claims about the decline of religion, we might say at the 'cultural level', each religion continues to have a significant social impact through its presence in society. This can be seen when, say, the Church is looked at as a human organization similar in many respects to a large business corporation. It will have 'offices' for 'administration', often the administration of large 'budgets' to cover its many social, educational and religious programmes.

> The Church is a ***human*** and ***social***, as well as a ***divinely*** established ***spiritual*** organization.

It will have its 'manpower needs' like any other social organization. It will have its 'mission statement' outlining its essential nature and purpose. It will want to attract 'customers' to its 'brand' or 'product'; it will 'advertise' its 'services' and it will have 'running costs' sometimes even to 'stay in business'. Many churches for instances have 'plant' that needs upkeep and repair, and sometimes renewal and expansion, plant that not only includes its religious buildings, but also schools, study centres, youth clubs, and of course places for the training and preparation of future leaders.

The Church as a social organization
- Manpower to be recruited and trained (vocations, seminaries, priests).
- Leaders to exercise authority (religious and pastoral leadership).
- Religious duties for leaders to fulfil (baptisms, marriages, deaths).
- Pastoral duties for leaders to fulfil (visiting the sick and bereaved).
- Buildings for education and worship (schools, colleges, churches).
- Plant for administration (international, diocesan and parish offices).
- Offices for local, national, and international charity works.
- Running costs to be paid for (salaries, buildings, and other costs).
- Budgets to be balanced (financial income to cover costs).

The internal commitments of churches

Most churches have *internal* commitments to the study, reform and renewal of their basic beliefs and raison d'être (reason for existing). These will usually be done through meetings of leaders in such assemblies as a General Council (Catholic), the General Synod (C of E) or the Methodist Conference. Issues of faith and practice may include modern areas of controversy such as the question of women priests, homosexuals, euthanasia, abortion, marriage and divorce and the problems of the family. Churches also have internal commitments to recruit and train suitable ministers and leaders. Some of the internal structures for these purposes include training colleges, seminaries and other centres of preparation directed to those who will do the work of the Church. Some leaders will be in 'holy orders' or 'ordained', which means they will play a central part in worship, and other sacramental activities such as baptisms, marriages and funerals. Others will be 'lay' people, called to help with and support the work of the ordained ministers. Other leaders may be involved in the more 'secular' work of the Church which may be called its *external* commitments.

> The Church's mission is spiritual, but much of its work is carried out through its social involvement in local communities: through service to the family, the sick, the poor and the bereaved; and through its pastoral work in hospitals, schools and colleges.

The external commitments of churches

These include not only international charity work, but also local charity initiatives directed to the neighbourhood poor irrespective of whether they are church members, and people with problems. The church is often looked to for help at a local level. Other commitments at the local level may involve work in education. Most churches have responsibility for schools, which are seen as serving the needs of the future religious community, as well as the more immediate needs of their pupils, who may come from a variety of backgrounds, beliefs, cultures and religions. Traditionally the task of education was taken over by religious orders such as Dominicans and Jesuits, while the Franciscans were associated with promoting the gospel ideal of service to the poor. Many present-day initiatives see the Church involved with the Samaritans, the Emmaus Community, the L'Arche foundation, Oxfam, Save the Children, Christian Aid, and the Catholic Fund for Overseas Development (Cafod).

> The ***Corrymeela Community*** is a pan-Christian organization situated in Northern Ireland, dedicated to bringing people together from diverse backgrounds, and initiating people into the principles of non-discrimination, equality and justice, leading to community harmony and peace.
>
> The ***Iona Community***, founded in 1938 on the island of Iona, is a Christian ecumenical community dedicated to living by gospel principles (agape) in today's world, with special reference to peacemaking and love of neighbour without discrimination.
>
> Both communities aim to attract, and involve, people from all over the world.

In these ways the Christian Church can claim to make its contribution to modern culture through its evangelical mission to 'spread the word' and promote the Christian way of life. It can do this with its emphasis on spiritual and moral values, and through its special vision about the meaning of life expressed through its moral and spiritual message based on revelation. It can therefore claim to be a potentially important resource in challenging such negative 'cultural' phenomena as binge-drinking, drug-trafficking, sexual exploitation, racial discrimination, street violence, family disintegration, and the modern tendency towards the cult of transient values, such as wealth, celebrity, social status, pleasure and the widespread appeal of popular 'entertainment'.

> **Christianity and culture**
>
> Christianity like other religions has the potential to have an important impact on modern society and its so-called 'cultural' values such as the pursuit of wealth, the drive towards self- indulgence through alcohol,

drugs, sexual exploitation and avoidable debt, and the rising tendency towards social violence and family disharmony.

Given the nature of the Church's mission, what difficulties is it likely to face in meeting these challenges, and what aspects of its work are most important today?

8 Religious Experience

- Religious experience as encounter with the divine.
- Direct and indirect religious experiences.
- Religion based on feeling and experience rather than rational thought.
- Strengths and weaknesses of this claim.
- Religion and the numinous.
- Religious experience as foundation of major religions.
- Types of religious experience: conversions, visions and mysticism.
- Contribution of mysticism in major religions.
- Authority of religious experience in sacred texts.
- The question of the verification of religious experience.
- Naturalistic explanations of mysticism.
- Mysticism and the need for spiritual preparation.
- The place of religious experience in the Church.

Different kinds of religious experience

The term 'religious experience' does not have a single meaning, but it may be divided into two kinds. One is the kind of experience that its recipient is convinced comes from a direct encounter with the divine, the supernatural, or God. All the major religions accept the reality of such a phenomenon. All look back in their history to chosen individuals who were believed to have experienced the mysterious reality of God. These have been described as 'primordial' experiences such as those associated principally with people like **Abraham, Moses, Jesus** and **Muhammad**. In addition, religions such as Christianity are replete with cases of individuals who have claimed to have

RELIGION AND HUMAN EXPERIENCE

religious experiences, some of which have led individuals to new levels of religious commitment.

> **Religious experience**
>
> ***Direct*** The experience of God claimed by religious founders, and later by mystics.
>
> ***Indirect*** The experience of seeing a religious aspect to experiences in life.
>
> *Some claimed experiences of a spiritual or unusual kind may, or may not, be given a religious significance. The claim to 'feel a presence' in a certain place is of this kind, but how far can ordinary experiences be called religious experiences?*

The other kind of experience is that often spoken of in secular language, but which refers to the kind of experience that goes beyond the mere experience of empirical objects or people in the world. Such an experience is usually spoken of as a depth or limit experience, and is often linked to the experience of nature, beauty or even (in the case of **Kant**) to the experience of morality. In this type of experience there is no claim for any encounter with the divine, although believers may want to term it an indirect type of religious experience. Many would claim that at a basic level there is a perception given in ordinary experience that something more is involved. A starry sky may arouse a sense of that something more, or the beauty of a landscape, or in some cases even the experience of evil may give rise to feelings that point beyond it to something else. For many people these kinds of experiences are ambivalent inasmuch as their object is difficult to identify: to the eyes of religious faith they may be called religious experiences, but to non-believers they may or may not be regarded as in some way spiritual, but in the end are seen as merely natural.

> *Some experiences may arouse feelings of religious awareness, while to non-believers they are merely human feelings of unusual depth. What makes such experiences open to different interpretations?*

RELIGIOUS EXPERIENCE

Religion to be found in feeling rather than rational thought

> What I see in Nature is a magnificent structure that we can only comprehend very imperfectly, and that must fill a thinking person with a feeling of humility. This is a genuinely religious feeling and has nothing to do with mysticism.
>
> *Albert Einstein*
>
> *How far might this be described as a direct or indirect religious experience?*

Kant argued that our experience of moral obligation indirectly pointed to God. He is less well known for holding that our experience of beauty pointed to transcendent features of our being, those features that cannot be grasped in rational thought. Many writers on art claim that while we know that our knowledge of the world is limited to the empirical, that is not how we feel (see above, p. 103). The experience of beauty is related to our *feelings* rather than to our reason, and in the profound feelings it generates we get a sense of something that lies beyond the mundane world, something overwhelming and inexpressible. The modern philosopher **Roger Scruton** defends the notion that some experiences, including especially those we get from art, can provide insights that match up with what religion speaks about (see above, p. 103).

> **Kant** held that art and beauty were transcendent features of our being, ones which pointed to beyond the empirical world.

Nobody developed the idea that religion was rooted in feeling more clearly than the renowned German philosopher-theologian **Friedrich Schleiermacher**. Addressing the 'cultured despisers of religion' from his church in Berlin, he asked them to forget about the rational arguments that were used to support religious belief, and look instead at the realm of feeling where he believed the reality of religion and God was to be found.

RELIGION AND HUMAN EXPERIENCE

Religion to be found in the feeling of absolute dependence

> Schleiermacher broke new ground with his view that religion was based on experience, not on intellectual reasoning.

One of the most influential thinkers of the nineteenth century, Schleiermacher argued that our creaturely sense of inadequacy and incompleteness was the root of all religious feeling. What he called the 'feeling of absolute dependence', was a feeling that is inescapable and holds the key to the reality of God. This was really an appeal to the sense of contingency that makes the creature aware of his creatureliness. As such it was a new, an emotional, not a rational appeal to the truth of religion that was to have a profound effect on subsequent religious thinking. It owed much to Schleiermacher's Pietist upbringing, from which he learned that religious faith was not about reason or rational thinking, but all about feeling, emotion, sentiment, experience. Yes, he conceded, it was possible to dismiss the rational arguments made famous by **Anselm** and **Aquinas**, and agree with **Kant** and **Hume** that they had no power to convince the sceptic. But it was not possible to disregard the plain fact of our helplessness in the face of the immensity of the universe, the uncertainties of life, and the certainty of death.

> **Schleiermacher** *claimed that the 'feeling of absolute dependence' lay at the root of religion, but how well would this be likely to go down in the modern scientific age, the age of 'independence'?*

In distinction to Kant's idea that God can be perceived in the experience of moral duty, Schleiermacher argued for religion from an even deeper sentiment, the sentiment that gives us the feeling of 'absolute dependence' in a universe that is at once immense and overpowering, but also finite, contingent, uncertain. An interesting connection here can be found in the thought of **Wittgenstein**, who spoke of the experience of feeling 'absolutely safe', a feeling that

> I mean the state of mind in which one is inclined to say 'I am safe, nothing can injure me no matter what happens'.
> *Wittgenstein*

goes beyond those feelings that have a clear object, such as a fear of flying. Schleiermacher later argued that a deeper and more specific level of religious experience was possible, one that led to what he called a 'God consciousness'. It was this, he believed, which **Jesus** and other religious leaders possessed to an eminent degree.

The God discovered in emotional experience might only be imaginary

By his appeal to the deeper intuitions and emotions as the real roots of faith, Schleiermacher became a pivotal figure in modern Christian philosophical theology. God was to be sought no longer in the 'starry heavens above' but in 'the emotional (not moral) life within', to paraphrase **Kant**. By insisting that this is exactly the way the world is, and the way the world makes us feel, he points out why religion reveals itself as that which arises from those feelings, and offers an insight into how we might cope with them. But many would claim that the weakness of his approach would be exposed in the end by the 'cultured despisers' that he hoped to convince. These were later led by **Freud**, who would provide a devastating exposure of the risks of assuming that because the world appeared aimless and inhospitable, an imaginary 'God' was the answer. It can be argued, however, that Schleiermacher's theory of religion is not the same as Freud's. One speaks of an overpowering sense of something that transcends rational thinking, a level of awareness that takes in the *whole*, and produces religious awareness. The other theorizes about inner drives and wishes which force the individual to seek a 'solution' in terms of religious belief. One is talking about direct experience, the other about psychological reasoning.

> Many would argue that **Schleiermacher** was appealing to inner feelings that came directly from the ***experience*** of the world. **Freud** later went on to theorize about more complex feelings of fear and guilt that arose from psychological ***conflicts***. If this is true, then there is a big difference between the respective views of Schleiermacher and Freud on the roots of religion.
>
> *But how far does Schleiermacher's theory of religion escape the charge of being an illusion?*

At the same time his proposal was not without its strengths, and its ultimate appeal. Renowned as a philosopher and religious thinker of the highest stature, Schleiermacher called attention to those aspects of human life that would occupy the existentialists a century later. These were the aspects brought to light by inner feeling, the emotional sense of meaninglessness, the dreaded feeling of angst, and the overwhelming sense of finitude produced by the looming certainty of death (see more, p. 66). Here was an appeal to pure experience. The choice was simple and challenging. Are we to perceive ourselves as cast 'on the sea of life' without any reason for hope that the sense of being lost and overwhelmed is only an illusion? For Schleiermacher, this encounter with the bleaker side of life gave rise to the inner feeling that something else was there, something that was a source of hope and salvation: for him this encounter with life in all its starkness, was able to produce a genuine religious experience.

> ***Schleiermacher*** Religion is produced by adult feelings that arise in the face of life.
>
> ***Freud*** Religion is produced by emotional traumas in childhood, carried into adult life.
>
> *Obviously both arrived at different conclusions about religion, but how far is it true that for both human experience was a major theme?*

The idea that religion comes from a sense of the numinous

> Without this faculty (of religious awareness), no religion, not even the lowest worship of idols and fetishes, would be possible; and if we will but listen attentively, we can hear in all religions the groaning of the spirit, a struggle to conceive the inconceivable, to utter the unutterable, a longing for the infinite, a love of God.
>
> Max Müller
>
> *This is often called an intuitive awareness of the transcendent. How far could this, and Schleiermacher's view, be called a **pre-religious**, rather than a strictly religious experience?*

RELIGIOUS EXPERIENCE

As a result of extensive studies of religion in tribal cultures, the German **Max Müller** put forward the view that all religion is rooted in a fundamental capacity of people for 'religious awareness'. This he believed was a particularly human capacity which found its earliest expression in tribal religions (see box above). But it was his contemporary **Rudolf Otto**, a Lutheran theologian, who became famous for his penetrating analysis of human experience in its full depth, identifying what he believed lies at the root of all religion. He rejected ideas current at the time that religion was an illusion thrown up for historical, economic, sociological or psychological reasons. He argued instead that the root of religion was an awareness of the 'numinous', a term borrowed from **Kant** to denote something that lies behind and beyond pure 'phenomena'. The numinous is associated with an indescribable feeling of awe and wonder, the object of which, though profound and even 'dreadful', can only be described as a mystery, what he called a *mysterium tremendum et fascinans*.

> The ***numinous*** is a term used by Otto to mean a deep sense of mystery in life which evokes an overwhelming feeling of awe and fear, yet has a mysterious attraction, leading to a sense of the holy.
>
> *But how far is such a feeling only open to those who either seek for it or are able to perceive it?*

Otto gives as an illustration of the numinous the feeling that came over people in a German town during the building of a massive bridge over the Rhine. After a storm suddenly caused the bridge to collapse an eerie silence fell over the river, leaving people awe-struck at the mysterious power of nature. For Otto, this was analogous to the sense of the numinous that underlies all the great religions, making experience the real root of religion. The experience of the numinous is the experience of being in the presence of what he called '*the holy*'. The presence of the holy brings a sense of 'fascination' and attraction; but at the same time it brings a feeling of something that is 'fearsome' and 'overwhelming'. The term 'numinous experience', however, is often used today in a weaker sense to denote the religious feelings of people during worship, or during a visit to a holy site or place of pilgrimage.

> *Otto held that the experience of the numinous was the basis of all religion. How far do his ideas both resemble and differ from Schleiermacher's?*

RELIGION AND HUMAN EXPERIENCE

Religious experience as the origin of the great religions

Otto applied his analysis to some of the great religious leaders whose mystical experiences have been decisive, such as **Abraham, Moses, Jesus, Muhammad** and many of the other prophets. He believed that it was their personal experiences of the holy through which they became intensely aware of God, and which inspired them to become the religious leaders they were. These were recognized by their followers as special experiences, and historically became so significant that major religions arose from them. Some writers have called them 'primordial' experiences or 'revelatory' experiences and have distinguished them from later claims of religious experience by saints and mystics (see below, p. 129) which historically have not been accorded the same significance or authority.

> **Kinds of religious experience**
>
> ***Primordial or revelatory*** The ***direct*** experience of the divine associated with great religious founders such as Abraham, Moses, Jesus and Muhammad.
>
> ***Dependency*** Indirect experience of the divine through the feeling of ***contingency*** leading eventually to a sense of 'God consciousness' (Schleiermacher).
>
> ***Numinous*** Indirect experience of the divine through a sense of awe and wonder (Otto). Such an experience is often said to accompany prayer and worship.
>
> ***Mystical experience*** A perceived direct experience of the divine as testified by saints and mystics (St Paul and others), often leading to religious ***conversion***.

The question of the authority of religious experience

When it comes to questions about the authority of religious experience, therefore, it is important to distinguish those experiences just mentioned, which were seen as the medium through which *revelation* was received, from other later forms of religious experience that appear in the history of religion. All three major religions of the West recognize the religious experiences of **Abra-**

RELIGIOUS EXPERIENCE

ham and **Moses** as experiences that have acquired a special authority because they have been seen as carrying an authentic insight into the being and will of God. For Christians the experiences of **Jesus**, and to a lesser degree the apostles, have had a special authority for a similar reason. For Muslims the experiences of **Muhammad** are regarded as having supreme authority. For these reasons the sacred books of the Bible and Koran are seen as products of the religious encounters of uniquely chosen individuals with God.

Mysticism as a phenomenon in religious traditions

Turning to those kinds of experiences frequently claimed within religious traditions we begin with the experience known as mysticism. For convenience and limitations of space we can bring under this heading other forms of religious experience such as conversion experiences, apparitions and visions. We can define a mystic as someone who claims to have had a personal encounter

> The mystical experience leaves the subject absolutely convinced of its reality.
>
> *St Teresa of Avila*

with God. In keeping with the transcendent nature of God, the experience of mysticism is typically characterized by elements of mystery and surprise: the experience usually leaves the mystic at a loss for words to describe it. This leaves the mystic open to the typical charge of the sceptic, represented by **A. J. Ayer,** when he said that if the supposed mystic is unable to describe his experience he/she is bound to talk nonsense in attempting to do so (see

> If a mystic admits that the object of his vision is something that cannot be described, then he must also admit that he is bound to talk nonsense when he attempts to describe it . . . in describing his vision the mystic does not give us any knowledge about the external world; he merely gives us indirect information about the condition of his own mind.
>
> A. J. Ayer
>
> *Here Ayer applies a detached interpretation to mystical claims, reducing them to phenomena imagined by the supposed mystic, but how far can evidence be used to counter this view?*

box). Historically, mysticism has occupied an important place in religious traditions because their claims have often been seen to bear the hallmarks of authenticity.

The contribution of mysticism within Judaism and Christianity

Although usually classed as a prophet, **Moses** of the Old Testament must count as one of history's great mystics. His experiences of God were so influential as to be one of the formative factors in the history and development of Judaism. These experiences are recorded in the Bible and include his famous vision of God in the burning bush. Later, he encounters God on Mount Sinai and receives from him the Decalogue, or the Ten Commandments. The second great recipient of mystical experience was **Jesus**. Several times he communes with God and speaks to him as his Father. On occasions, such as at his baptism, he is the centre of strange and mysterious happenings. For the Gospel writers this is no surprise, since he is the incarnate Son of God.

> *Paul's experience on the road to Damascus was both a mystical and a conversion experience. How far can this experience be verified, and how open is it to a psychological explanation? How far would such an explanation invalidate it as a religious experience?*

Next to Jesus comes the apostle **Paul**, whose remarkable experience on the road to Damascus was decisive for shaping his own future and the future of the Christian faith. The incident is described in his own writings, but is easier to read about than fully understand. He is thrown from his horse and blinded by a strange light. He encounters Jesus, who rebukes him for being his persecutor. Paul is transformed by the encounter, and goes from being an enemy of the new faith to becoming one of its main leaders. His subsequent life is spent on hard missionary work, spreading the gospel message until he is martyred in Rome around 64 AD. His series of inspired epistles provide a unique insight into the meaning of the cross and the resurrection, a contribution which made him one of the early founders of the Christian Church.

> **St Paul** is generally regarded as one of the greatest Christian visionaries, but others have been part of the Church's visionary or mystical tradition.

Other examples of mysticism include **Augustine**, a highly educated scholar who held university posts in both North African and European centres of learning. A mystical experience changed his life from that of a non-believer, and he became one of the giants of the early Christian Church. The renowned mystics of the medieval period include the Spanish saints **Teresa of Avila, John of the Cross** and **Ignatius Loyola,** all notable for their religious insights into the nature of God. In Germany **Meister Eckhart**, a Dominican prior and teacher, was famous for the mystical experiences which became the basis for his inspired social teachings. He stressed above all the role of the mystic in spreading the message of God's love for the world by word and example. In England **Julian of Norwich** and **Richard Rolle** made similar contributions to understanding God's relation to the world. What is notable is that in all cases there are no new messages, or no new revelations, merely a confirmation of what believers already know from the official channels of the Bible and the Church.

> The history of the Church testifies to a well documented mystical tradition, but believers are not necessarily obliged to give credence to any of the famous mystics.

Mysticism and the problem of its verification

Mystical claims are usually dismissed by sceptics on the grounds of lack of evidence, but theists would hold that they cannot so easily be dismissed. The American philosopher and psychologist **William James** made a special study of mystics and mysticism. Having studied the history of mystics and saints like Augustine, John of the Cross and Ignatius Loyola, he became convinced that intense religious awareness was a real phenomenon, one that made a deep impact on those who experienced it. He was not, however, prepared to say whether the experience pointed to God. But he insisted that those who had such experiences often became outstanding individuals who were seen as a positive asset to the societies around them. Their lives were, said James, evidence of 'the best fruits history has to show'.

RELIGION AND HUMAN EXPERIENCE

> **James** is famous for his study of religious experience. Its qualities were ineffable (impossible to describe), noetic (providing some form of insight), transient, but overwhelming for the recipient.
>
> *How far can James's observations be used to support the validity of religious experience?*

He saw that religious faith was a source of strength and power, able to change individuals from being confused, anxious and depressed to people with new drive and enthusiasm. Such an experience usually left them with a heightened sense that life was good and worthwhile. James's studies of religious experience were not meant to be an open proof that God existed, or that their experiences were necessarily a valid contact with a supernatural world. As an empiricist he merely highlighted what he saw as positive evidence of the good that religious experience brought to certain people. His work was a counterpoise to the ideas put forward by the likes of **Nietzsche** and **Freud**, who had argued that religion was synonymous with weakness, illness or neurosis.

> **James** was a pragmatist who saw the 'truth' of religious experience confirmed by its beneficial effects, both on the individual and the society around them.
>
> *This may be seen as **necessary** evidence for the involvement of God, but how far can it be seen as **sufficient**?*

On the contrary it could be shown that belief in God was not confined to the weak, the ignorant or the ill. Neither was religion, as James put it, a sign 'of a degenerative brain', as alleged by many of its detractors. For this reason it is generally held that one of the tests of the credibility of such experiences is how far it advances the character of its recipient, and how far its effect on others is for the good or for the bad. Taking this approach therefore can be a possible way of verifying the validity of such experiences, and assessing the degree to which they deserve to be taken seriously. Clearly if a mystic had the effect of glorifying evil it would be a prima facie sign that their alleged mysticism was not from a good God and would therefore be falsified.

RELIGIOUS EXPERIENCE

> Theists generally hold that the **character**, and subsequent **effects** of mystical claims are an important 'verification test' of whether the mystic is reporting a genuine experience. Unless the effects are **good**, they cannot be traced to a good God.

Can mysticism have a natural rather than a religious explanation?

In dealing with the validity of mystical experience **James** felt that it could only be said to be valid for the individual who has had the experience. Others are free to accept or reject the claims of the mystic which, as we have seen, is also the official position of the Christian Church. For unbelievers, however, mysticism is impossible and has to be dismissed as the sign, or result, of the working of (probably) psychological forces. **Russell** made the witty remark that there is little difference between the man who has drunk too much and sees snakes, and the person who eats too little and sees heaven. **Ayer** with equal scepticism insisted that mystical claims are no more than claims about the content of the mind. Thus mystics are often dismissed as either mentally disturbed or in any case people who, though sane and well-meaning, simply cannot be taken seriously.

> **Mysticism**
>
> **Theists** Mystical encounters with God are possible because God exists.
>
> **Non-theists** Mystical claims are false because God does not exist.

Theists, however, would argue that there is no necessary contradiction between a natural explanation for mystical experience, and a supernatural explanation of the same event (see different causalities, p. 188). Indeed it is perfectly legitimate to find natural explanations for some mystical phenomena, some of which may help to explain the more precise forms that mysticism takes. Sceptics could argue, for example, that **Jesus** often went without much sleep, causing him to have perceived 'mystical' encounters with God. **Paul** the Jew could be psychologically analysed as a crypto-Christian sympathizer

> Feeling the world as a limited whole ... seeing the world as a miracle ... (not) the scientific way of looking at a fact. .. (this) shows a tendency of the human mind which I personally cannot help respecting deeply ... there are indeed things that cannot be put into words, they make themselves manifest, they are what is mystical.
>
> Wittgenstein

who strove hard to deny his sympathies. His violent persecution of Christians meant he was 'kicking against the goad' of his inner conscience, resulting in a level of emotional stress that could produce his tortured experience on the road to Damascus, as **C. G. Jung** suggested. All this may help to explain the inner mechanisms of his experience, but his own testimony and understanding of the event stands as a serious challenge to naturalistic explanations which, of course, can be neither verified nor falsified.

Naturalist explanations and reductionist conclusions

Theists point out that explaining mystical experiences naturalistically is called reductionism. This is where an event is 'explained away' as a natural phenomenon that has no religious significance, and thus is 'reduced' completely to purely natural elements. It is also an example of what is called the *genetic fallacy*. This is the supposed mistake of attempting to explain a phenomenon on the basis of how it originated. Jung did not mean to do this, but his explanation of Paul's experience is inevitably open to a naturalistic interpretation. Theists would argue that if God exists, then it would not be surprising if he made contact with people through channels appropriate to their particular nature, whether these were rational, psychic, emotional or physical.

> The ***genetic fallacy*** is the supposed error of explaining a phenomenon in terms of how it ***originated***. If Jack said he believed in God because of his parents, the origin of his belief may be said to be his parents, which would clearly be a fallacy. In the same way Paul's experience may appear to have originated as a ***psychological*** phenomenon, but according to the genetic fallacy it is possible that there may have been another, deeper explanation.

Thus the *apparent* origin of Paul's encounter with Jesus may have been *psychological*, but in reality it may have been more than this. It may also have been what Paul thought it was, a mystical encounter with the supernatural figure of Jesus, the target of his persecuting zeal. Paul's stresses and inner conflict may have been very real, something he may have been painfully aware of, yet theists would claim that his experience may have ultimately been the pathway to a new level or religious awareness. This is how Paul saw it, and even if the principle of testimony and credulity is not foolproof, many would argue that even the most impartial observer has at least to suspend judgement in the light both of Paul's claims, and of the historic effects of his experience.

Assessment of mystical experience

Theistic Mystical experience is possible given the existence of God. Some mystical experiences are historically documented and have resulted in major religions (Moses, Jesus, Muhammad). Such experiences have absolute authority for believers. Other mystical experiences do not have binding authority.

Non-Theistic Mystical experience is impossible given the non-existence of God. Claims for such experiences can be explained as having natural causes, probably emotional or psychological.

Rational/Religious Mystical experience may well originate from the impact of psychological forces on the recipient, but this does not mean it can be explained in purely natural terms. A mystical claim has credibility if the mystic is of a character likely to be pleasing to God, that is, showing holiness and virtue. If the character of the mystic is otherwise it would be unlikely that their experience came from God.

But in the end whether mystical claims are what they purport to be, that is to say manifestations of the divine, or something arising from within the personalities of the supposed mystics themselves, will always remain unconfirmed for the sceptic. It is certainly the case that mystical claims have not, historically, been persuasive enough to convince the unbeliever. This is because naturalistic explanations of such alleged phenomena are always considered sufficiently convincing. This is only to say that recognizing even the

> The case for the existence of God is a cumulative one. I claim that the existence and continued operation of God (normally through the laws of nature, but sometimes setting them aside), can explain the whole pattern of science and history, and also men's most intimate religious experiences.
>
> *Richard Swinburne*

possibility of mysticism will always be dependent on the prior possession of religious faith.

The problem of mysticism being a special privilege

Another objection is that mysticism, if true, raises the question of whether the mystic is in some way given privileged access to God. If the mystic is so favoured by God, it is said, why does God not make his presence more accessible to more people? Theists would point out that this objection overlooks an important aspect of mysticism, namely the contribution of the mystics themselves to receiving the experience. History shows that mysticism is partly the fruit of the intense religious devotion of the mystics themselves. One of the common themes running through the history of mysticism is the important role played by faith, piety and asceticism. All the great mystics were people who were in some way searching or reaching out for communion with God. As a result they can be seen to have put themselves in a receptive position to be able to 'divine' the signals they believed came from God. This is not unlike the special training in art or music required to develop the ability to appreciate (or create) artistic beauty.

> The argument that mysticism is a special privilege granted by God is countered by the claim that mystical experience is a special 'illumination' gained only after arduous training in contemplation and asceticism, as pointed out by **St Bonaventure**.

The place of religious experience in Christianity

We end this chapter by taking a look at the significance given to those experiences that occur in the later history of the Christian faith in the form of mystical and conversion experiences, apparitions and visions. Historically

RELIGIOUS EXPERIENCE

the Christian Church, while usually respecting such claims, has not accorded all of them a high level of significance, allowing for the possibility of such experiences being rooted in emotional or psychological factors within the personalities of their recipients. The Church appears to have little problem with claims of what may be called numinous experiences, those gained, say, during prayer or worship, or in the surroundings of a great cathedral, or during a visit to a holy site, or even in the presence of great art. The Church's attitude has been largely determined by the words of St Paul that 'faith is the acceptance of things we cannot see' and the words of Jesus to Thomas, 'Blessed are those who have believed and have not seen'. Therefore the authority of religious experience is primarily confined to the recipients themselves, and has no necessary binding force on the faithful in general. The possibility that such experiences might make a case for the existence of God could easily be accepted by believers, but is seen by many to be undermined by the possibility of naturalistic explanations for such experiences.

The authority of religious experience

Revelatory experience The experience of God described in sacred texts. Such experiences are regarded as having unique authority for believers within their tradition.

Mystical experience The experience of communion with God claimed by mystics. These experiences are respected if the mystic is of holy character, but have no binding authority on believers.

Conversion experience A mystical experience that leads to a religious conversion. Such an experience has a special authority if its effects are positive.

Visionary experience Includes visions and apparitions. Taken seriously if the visionary is of holy character, but has no official authority over believers.

Numinous experience A kind of experience commonly claimed by believers during worship, or in religious surroundings. This is usually called 'indirect' religious experience. Some forms of numinous experience may be more intense, giving the recipient a 'sense of the holy', but claims for such experiences have no official authority.

RELIGION AND HUMAN EXPERIENCE

Communal experience A form of religious experience claimed to occur among groups, usually during worship. Especially associated with worship of emotional or fervent character as found in Pentecostal or Charismatic communities. Such experiences have little authority outside the experiencing group.

9 Religion and Spirituality

- Spirituality as an essential aspect of being human.
- Spirituality and man's moral and religious sense.
- The distinction between material and spiritual values.
- The value of a religious spirituality.
- Spirituality from a philosophical viewpoint.

Spirituality as related to man's intellectual, moral and religious development

The meaning of the word spirituality may be said to have to do with the development of the 'spiritual side' of human life in contrast to its 'material side', or in terms drawn from **Mill** (see more, p. 245), the development of 'higher' powers (intellect, emotions, will) in contrast to 'lower' powers (physical prowess, sensual satisfactions). Spirituality may be said to show itself in the search for meaning in life; in the search for truth in relation to reality; in the pursuit of aesthetic appreciation in relation to art and music; and in the pursuit of love and justice in relation to the needs and rights of others. In the context of religious belief, it means recognizing that human existence is subject to the overall dominion of God.

> **Spirituality** is usually associated with the pursuit of spiritual or religious values, or the 'noble' as opposed to the 'base' side of human nature.

If all these are the mark of human spirituality, a spiritual person may be contrasted with one whose values are seen to be passing pleasures, frivolous entertainment, sensual enjoyments, and the exclusive pursuit of earthly happiness. For many, a religious spirituality has a strong emotional or experiential aspect, which is both expressed and found through prayer, worship, pilgrimage and other forms of piety and religious dedication. It also has a distinct ethical aspect since the recognition of God's existence means the acceptance of ethical obligations. A specific Christian spirituality is about ordering one's life in the light of the truths of revelation. A 'non-religious' spirituality must equally be concerned with the ordering of human life in ways that ensure the highest possible satisfaction in living life. If **Aristotle** is correct, this would mean following the good, since the good life is that which brings happiness and fulfilment (see more in virtue ethics, p. 265). For this reason, while spirituality is usually associated with religion, it is by no means exclusively connected with it.

> **Human spirituality**
>
> *Intellectual*   The search for truth.
>
> *Aesthetic*   The appreciation of beauty.
>
> *Moral*   The pursuit of the good.
>
> *Religious*   The pursuit of God's will.
>
> *Social*   The pursuit of justice for others.
>
> *Clearly there are overlaps between the different kinds of spirituality, but what have they all in common?*

Spirituality as a function of human intellectual, emotional and volitional powers

It can easily be observed that human beings have spiritual powers which contrast sharply with the more limited instinctual powers of the lower animals. **Kant** pointed out that while angels are pure spirits with purely intellectual powers, and animals are creatures driven only by instinct, human nature has the complexity of being a mixture of the two. As a result man has traditionally been seen as obliged to exercise dominion over his instincts or 'warring passions', and follow the higher moral path mapped out by his intellect. For Kant, humans, who are supposedly a 'product' of their environment (now confirmed by evolution) are capable of rising above the environment, and are not, like the lower animals, imprisoned within it. According to Kant we are endowed with freewill, for without it we would not be capable of morality, the true hallmark of human beings (see more in 'freewill and determinism', p. 289).

> **Man and spirituality**
>
> *Angels* Angels are pure spirits, so they are naturally endowed with spirituality.
>
> *Humans* Humans have a capacity for spirituality in virtue of their intellect and will. But they also have instincts and passions which can be a barrier to the pursuit of spirituality.
>
> *Animals* Driven purely by instinct, appear to have little capacity for spirituality.

Hence the rejection by many of the idea that the human can be reduced to a material substance, a mere product of material evolution but with 'non-spiritual' powers that can be explained in terms of brain and nerve processes. The power of reason; the faculty of understanding (intelligence) and self-consciousness (including imagination and memory); and the ability to make autonomous decisions (freewill), especially in the form of courage or love, are all widely recognized as outstanding aspects of the spiritual nature of humankind. These human powers might suggest, as **Kant** claimed, a transcendent destiny beyond death, but from a rational and neutral perspective they may be seen merely as the sum of what makes us human in the best sense.

Human moral sense as an aspect of spirituality

In assessing the extent of human spiritual powers, many would include the intellectual capacity to pursue truth, and to understand how the world works (including scientific discoveries). They would also include the aesthetic capacity to create art and appreciate it (including art, literature and music).

But for our purposes another major sign of human spirituality is the human moral capacity to understand right from wrong, our moral or ethical sense. A human being may be an animal in the Darwinian sense but is unique in being able to make moral judgements. There is a universal awareness that because something can be done does not mean that it ought to be done. From the earliest Greek thinkers there is a perception of what is called the 'good', that which ought to be pursued, either for its own sake or for the benefits it brings to the individual and society.

> ***Aristotle*** Morality is a personal quest, and is crucial for man's eudemonia, or fulfilment.
>
> ***Kant*** The capacity for morality is the distinctive mark of being human, and is the proof of our spiritual powers and spiritual destiny.
>
> ***Hume*** Morality is purely a practical need for the running of human society, and has no transcendent or spiritual significance.

According to **Aristotle**, the question of what the good life means is the most fundamental question that we can ask. 'What is the good life for man?' and 'How should it be lived?' are the two key questions underlying all human and moral endeavour. Man's moral awareness finds historical expression in law, which is formed for the common good, and is the guardian of justice. Some see law as the secular expression of the human inner awareness that there is right and wrong, two concepts which, however understood, relate to an inner moral sense about how we should relate to others. Others, however, like **Hume**, see law in empirical and utilitarian terms. In his view law is something created to make possible the social goods of order, security, the peaceful possession of property, the protection of life, and all the things that make for a harmonious society (see more in Religion and Ethics below, p. 243).

> For **Aristotle**, living the ***good life*** was the highest form of human spirituality.

RELIGION AND SPIRITUALITY

Man's religious sense as an aspect of his spirituality

While religion and spirituality are conceptually distinct, there is no religion that does not stress the need for the development of all aspects of human spirituality, physical, intellectual and moral, as well as religious. Believers would see spirituality in terms of 'making the best use of the gifts God has given us' in whatever field one's particular talents lie: intellectual, physical, moral, educational, artistic, literary and so on. The basic will to work through physical striving is itself often seen as a function of the human spirit, and from a religious perspective the honest endeavour it involves is seen as an important spiritual value.

Religion, as belief in the supernatural, is of its nature concerned with the contemplation of spiritual things. This includes the awareness of God's presence, and the implications that follow from having a relationship with God. For Christians it means an understanding of the religious and moral aspects of revelation; the development of attitudes appropriate to being created by God. These include: an overall sense of the need for grace to overcome temptation to evil; a sense of being sinful or 'fallen' to counteract hubris and false pride; a sense of love of neighbour to counter selfishness, and the seeking of glory in material success alone; and a sense of the need for hope to counter angst and despair.

Such attitudes are part of a spiritual vision of life which is at odds with one which puts the highest values on all things worldly (fame, celebrity, admiration, wealth, pleasure and self-indulgence). But how far believers today live up to their declared spiritual and moral ideals is another question, partly answered by the observations of **Solzhenitsyn**.

> **Christian spirituality**
> - Awareness of God's presence.
> - Desire to imitate Christ.
> - Pursuit of Christian values.
> - Recognition of need for God's grace.
> - Participation in Christian prayer, contemplation and worship.

> European democracy was ordinarily imbued with a sense of Christian responsibility and self-discipline, but these spiritual principles have been found to have lost their force. Spiritual independence is being pressured on all sides by the dictatorship of self-satisfied vulgarity, of the latest fads, and of group interests.
> *Alexander Solzhenitsyn*

RELIGION AND HUMAN EXPERIENCE

Material values	**Spiritual values**
Wealth	Goodness
Fame	Truth
Power	Honesty
Self-indulgence	Self-sacrifice
Financial security	Forgiveness
Pleasure	Tolerance
Entertainment	Courage
	Compassion

Today is often described as a materialistic age, but how far is it possible to reconcile material values with spiritual ones, and what are the moral advantages, as well as the moral difficulties of doing so?

The perceived need for a spiritual understanding of life

Many would argue that one of the lessons of recent history is that where a purely material vision of life became dominant there was little regard for the **Kantian** vision of a kingdom of ends, a moral (or spiritual) utopia where everyone is treated as an end rather than a means, and where a sense of moral obligation defines the nature of the kingdom. In a move that became an inspiration for many, and a paradox to some, **Solzhenitsyn** emerged from his brutalization in the labour camps with a deep spiritual faith. Undaunted by the apparent 'absence of God' he came to have a deep spiritual sense that although 'he had once abandoned God, God had not abandoned him'. This led him to re-embrace the Christian faith he had earlier renounced under the heady impression that the future of mankind lay with atheistic communism. He was appalled by what he experienced first-hand; by what happens when the world falls into the misguided hands of men: dehumanization,

> The most terrible thing about materialism, even more than its proneness to violence, is its boredom, from which sex, alcohol, drugs, all devices for putting out the light of reason and suppressing the unrealizable aspirations of love, offer a prospect of deliverance.
> *Malcolm Muggeridge*

brutalization, flagrant injustice, unspeakable tyranny, mindless death. Only through the vision provided by spiritual faith, he believed, could humanity ever have a hope of overcoming the ruthless, evil side of its base human nature (a danger which, ironically, both **Nietzsche** and **Freud** were keenly aware of).

> Widely respected for his outspoken views of human nature, **Alexander Solzhenitsyn**'s vision is openly spiritual. His survival of the labour camps, and his critical views of the contemporary age, have caused many to see him as a modern prophet. But while he never claimed to have had a religious experience, he had a spiritual conversion that sprang from his awareness of human moral limitations, revealed in his experience of mindless torture and brutality.

Spirituality from a philosophical perspective

We conclude this chapter with a look at the issue of spirituality from a philosophical point of view. If spirituality is the cultivation of thoughts and attitudes that help us cope with life, and form the best kinds of relationships with others which lead to personal fulfilment, then it becomes a legitimate subject for practical philosophy. **John Haldane** takes this view when he considers philosophy, as it was originally conceived, to be as much about how we live as about how we think (see box below). He sees this confirmed by the sixth-century **Boethius**, who famously saw philosophy as a source of consolation, because through it we are given the power to counter the downward pull of material attractions, and engage intellectually with transcendent realities that elevate the human spirit (questions of truth, reality, beauty, goodness). He is also impressed by the secular wisdom of the seventeenth-century French Jesuit **Caussade**, who, although writing from a Christian perspective, suggested a spirituality based on a 'passive loyalty' to God (or in secular terms, fate) by accepting everything we cannot change. This was also an ancient Greek idea seen as part of the answer to the problem of 'hubris', the arrogance of feeling self-sufficient in the face of opposing, and sometimes overwhelming, forces.

> If it should seem that the necessary condition for the possibility of spirituality is some religious truth, and if the need and possibility of spirituality should seem compelling, then might we have the beginnings of an argument for religion?
>
> J. Haldane
>
> *Haldane sees spirituality as a human pursuit, but suggests that religion is an important medium for its attainment. Many would disagree, but how far can religion be seen as essentially about the development of human spiritual powers?*

10 Religion and the Afterlife

- The afterlife as an integral part of religious faith.
- Plato and Descartes on an independent soul.
- Kant and the afterlife: the link with moral integrity.
- The afterlife seen as necessary for ultimate human fulfilment.
- Arguments about the coherence of an afterlife.
- Religion not necessarily linked to belief in an afterlife.
- The afterlife as an illusory belief.
- The afterlife in eastern religions.
- The afterlife not dependent on Plato's idea of the soul.
- Evidence of an afterlife from human history (the resurrection).
- Near-death experiences.

The afterlife as a problem if separated from God's existence

For most religions belief in an afterlife is central to their world view. Theists would claim that it is not a problem for faith for three reasons. First, that it follows from belief in an eternal God: an eternal God would create the possibility that human beings might not be limited to a temporary existence on earth. Second, if God is omnipotent, the problems of understanding the nature of the afterlife are not the concern of believers: such problems can be 'left in the hands of God'. Third, for theists there is sufficient reason to believe that an afterlife is the will of God, because revelation shows it to be our final destiny.

> If God does not exist an afterlife is impossible, since humans die naturally.

Against this background, therefore, theists would see it as a problem not for faith, but for philosophy. Philosophy can clearly challenge the claims about an afterlife because the evidence for it is not empirically compelling. If the philosopher rejects the idea of God to start with, the door is already closed to accepting a possibility that clearly depends on God's existence. Therefore if God does not exist, the notion of an afterlife collapses. By way of riposte, however, an atheist could claim that the absence of evidence for an afterlife is part of his case for the non-existence of God.

Religion and the afterlife
- If God exists, an afterlife is *possible*.
- An omnipotent God *could* give humans an afterlife.
- A good God might have *reasons* to give humans an afterlife.
- An omnipotent God would be able to *identify* those who might deserve an afterlife.
- For Christians *revelation* has confirmed the existence of an afterlife.

The human soul as the seat of human spiritual powers

A great impetus to the notion of an afterlife was given by **Plato** with his metaphysical theory of the existence of an immortal soul. Plato held a dualistic view of man with his theory that the soul is something independent and separate from the body. He believed that this could be seen from the fact that certain activities are peculiar to the soul, such as the power of reason, our understanding of things like justice and truth, and the free movement of the will. This means the soul is seen not only as the principle of life, but also as the spiritual principle that underlies those activities that are characteristically and specifically human, the ability to be self-conscious, to show the powers of imagination and rational thought, and the ability to make free decisions.

RELIGION AND THE AFTERLIFE

> **Plato** held that the soul was the seat of human spiritual powers, those powers that are the origin of the 'important' things we know, and do.
>
> *How far is Plato right, and how might this idea support belief in the immortality of the soul?*

Plato said that the soul was the origin of all the 'important' things that we do: such as show love, pursue the truth, act from duty, and show loyalty, courage and self-sacrifice. He also said the soul is the origin of the important things that we know: the difference between good and evil, truth and falsehood, beauty and ugliness, love and hate, courage and cowardice. All these powers and activities convey a sense that they transcend the body, because they appear to be independent of it. This view was also held by **Descartes**, who saw the soul as being a different 'substance' from the body.

> **Aristotle and the soul**
>
> The soul does not exist without a body, and is not itself a kind of body. For it is not a body, but something which belongs to a body, and for this reason exists in a body, and in a body of such and such a kind.
>
> *Aristotle.*
>
> *Here **Aristotle** shows how his view of the soul differs from that of **Plato**. Unlike Plato, he denies that the soul can have independent existence. For Aristotle the soul is part of the body, and cannot exist without it. But if there is a sense in which the soul, that by which a person has **life** and can choose **how to live**, leaves behind some kind of lasting moral impression, then how far could this be the basis for the possibility of an afterlife?*

Plato's idea that the soul is the 'driver' of the body

Plato argued that the activities and powers specifically connected with the body were those dependent on the senses. The powers of the sense organs, unlike the powers of the soul, were notoriously unreliable. Without the intellectual activity of the soul presiding over the senses, the knowledge that comes from the latter could never be trusted. Besides, said Plato, what we

RELIGION AND HUMAN EXPERIENCE

take for goodness, truth or beauty are only 'shadows' of what these things are in reality, because the way we perceive them belongs to the world of the senses. Hence we have to look beyond the sense world, to the realm of the soul, where the 'ideal forms' of truth, goodness and beauty are to be found. For Plato the soul consists of three parts (see box on p. 149). He saw the rational side of the soul as a charioteer in charge of two horses, representing the passions and the physical desires. Only when the soul is fully in charge of the passions, and the desires of the body, can harmony be achieved.

> *Plato believed that the soul was like a charioteer guiding two horses. No debate about a life after death can ignore Plato's metaphysical beliefs about the soul, but how is the Christian view of the afterlife different from Plato's?*

The possibility of an extra-terrestrial realm where the ideal forms exist brings with it the possibility that the soul really belongs there rather than on earth, and the possibility that the soul will go there after death. If this were true there would be a case in defence of an afterlife. Not surprisingly, Platonic ideas gave great impetus to the Christian view which emphasized the transience of earthly realities when compared to the more permanent, and superior, spiritual ones. In particular, Platonic ideas opened the way for an understanding of the notion of eschatological happiness in contrast to earthly happiness, an idea that would have special implications for ethical behaviour in relation to both Christian belief and the moral philosophy of **Kant** (see more on this, p. 252).

> *Socrates, like Plato, highlighted the importance of our spiritual powers, which seem not to depend on the body. This appeared to provide grounds for thinking of the soul (as the seat of those powers) as incapable of death, but what could be shown to be the weaknesses of his position?*

The idea of the soul existing independently of the body was later taken up by **Descartes**, who famously declared a substantive 'duality' between the body and the soul. The soul, or mind, was the seat of reliable and unchanging rational truths, accessible through philosophy and mathematics. By contrast, the body often provided misleading experiences whose truth always needed

RELIGION AND THE AFTERLIFE

to be judged and confirmed by the reasoning mind. This so-called 'Cartesian dualism', and the notion of an independent soul, later became central to the ethical system of **Kant**, who argued that humans' destiny lay in the enduring spiritual record of their ethical behaviour, rather than being confined to the transient physical reality of the body.

> **Plato: The soul has three powers**
>
> 1 The power of reason (*nous*).
> 2 The power of emotion (*thymos*).
> 3 The power of bodily desire (*eros*).
>
> Plato believed that the soul was superior to the body, and could exist independently of it. Platonist ideas gave credibility to the Christian belief in the ***immortality*** of the soul, and by extension, belief in an afterlife. However, the notion of immortality may not necessarily entail an independent or identifiable 'spiritual substance'. This could be argued, if God's ***memory*** of the soul is taken to be sufficient to judge the lives of those who embodied it. In this sense immortality would be a spiritual reality in the mind of God, and would not entail dualism.

Kant and the philosophical reasons for an afterlife

Kant adopted the dualism of Plato and held that humans possessed an immortal soul that would be the real centre of their human identity. This identity would survive the death of the body, and in doing so would confirm the existence of an afterlife. Kant saw the afterlife as the arena where only the most deserving would achieve happiness, thus undermining the idea that the afterlife is merely the product of naive dreams and wishes. Kant argued philosophically that the aim of the moral life was happiness, but happiness understood as the *reward* for virtue.

> According to **Kant** the key issue in ethics is not the importance of happiness, but the importance of ***deserving*** to be happy.
>
> *How far does this influence Kant's view of morality and the afterlife?*

This has been frequently overlooked because Kantian ethics are usually contrasted with the ethics of utility, which is assumed to have the franchise on the pursuit of happiness. But in contrast to Kant, the ethics of utility are based on a rather limited and vague concept of earthly happiness, one not shared philosophically by Kant, and not accepted on religious grounds by Christianity.

> **Kant** believed that our sense of justice demanded the existence of an afterlife, otherwise the just would go unrewarded for ever, while the wicked could both prosper in this life, and never be held accountable for their actions.
>
> *But how far is this a compelling philosophical reason for thinking there will be an afterlife?*

The idea that happiness might be best understood in terms of an afterlife

Kant agreed with **Aristotle** that the only real form of earthly happiness is that which is obtained through living the good, or virtuous life. For Kant it was the satisfaction of doing the categorical imperative, that is, seeing the moral law as a call to duty, that brought the highest human fulfilment, even though it might lead to more pain than happiness in the short term. Since the essence of duty (and indeed virtue) is acting in an unselfish way, it is obvious that Kantian ethics has great potential for contributing to the happiness of others. That of course was not the primary aim of Kant's ethics, and the happiness he is concerned with is not of this world. In this view, happiness is seen as something which in due time is divinely bestowed, not something that can either be legitimately sought after in this life for its own sake, or realistically found in it.

> **Kant** held that the afterlife was the gateway to the ***summum bonum***, when virtue is crowned with happiness by a good God.
>
> *But how far would Kant's notion of an afterlife survive without the existence of God?*

Kant's view can be seen to bear a remarkable resemblance to the Christian philosophy of happiness. But although it is similar to Kant's view in that it sees happiness as an ultimate state of bliss, and locates it in a transcendent realm (an afterlife), believers would point out that it differs from Kant in being dependent not on the insights of philosophical reasoning, but on the received wisdom of revelation. However, as we shall see below, the Christian view is also different from Kant's in that it does not necessarily entail the notion of the soul as an independent entity separate from the body. It is the integrated resurrection of the body, not the detached immortality of the soul, that lies at the heart of Christian eschatology.

> **Dualism** is not necessarily implied in the Christian concept of death if it can be argued that it is the ***living body***, not ***the body*** that dies. In this case ***life*** could be restored to a person by God if he so willed.

The coherence of the notion of an afterlife

In more recent times the notion of an independent soul has been challenged by the empirical view that the human being is a psycho-somatic unity. This is to say that what appear to be powers of the soul are in reality the powers of a living body. To put it negatively, it would make no sense to talk of things like love, or duty, or courage in a disembodied 'soul'. If this is correct, the so-called 'powers of the soul' are more properly called the 'powers of a human person', and the notion of an independent soul collapses. In turn, it is generally held that if there is no reality corresponding to what Plato and others called the soul, then the notion of an afterlife loses its force. But does it? First we look at how the notion of an afterlife has been challenged by philosophers. They do so either on the logical grounds of its incoherence, or on the empirical grounds of the absence of sufficient evidence for its existence.

> Empirical philosophers reject the ***dualist*** argument of both **Plato** and **Descartes** that the soul, as the seat of human spiritual powers, can exist independently of the body – because they claim the human being is a psycho-somatic (soul–body) unity, and subject to certain disintegration at death.

If human life is a reality that within the limits of empirical evidence is terminated at death, then by definition the concept of an afterlife has no coherence. Besides, since the body is an essential component of human existence, once it disintegrates at death it is difficult to make logical sense of talking about an afterlife. For this reason any talk of a 'soul' makes no sense because, although the word soul can be used to speak of the 'life-principle' (*animus*) of the person, once the person dies it appears to be nonsense to talk of a 'disembodied' soul. Supporters of this school of thought argue that the human principle of life, the soul, cannot be viewed independently of the body any more than the *esprit de corps* can be separated from an army unit, or the concept of a hospital from its wards and clinics. To make such a separation, it is claimed, is a logical, or category, mistake, and shows a misunderstanding of what a soul is. But if the concept of a soul as some entity 'independent' of the body is *not* crucial to the religious understanding of an afterlife, then such problems disappear.

> If the soul is seen as the life-principle of humans, it is reasonable to speak of the soul as 'leaving' the body at death. From a ***rational/empirical*** perspective neither soul nor body have any further existence, since both 'need' each other for human life. But for **Kant**, the soul was not just the life-principle, but the ***moral*-life-principle**.
>
> *How far does this make a difference?*

The notion of the soul as a metaphor for a person's spiritual identity

Although belief in an afterlife was strongly boosted by the metaphysics of **Plato**, who postulated the idea of a separate immortal soul, it also lost credibility with the modern empirical challenge to the notion of an independent soul. But if the understanding of the soul is that which carries the identity of the deceased beyond death (something that seems implicit in Kant), then it is possible to argue that belief in an afterlife does not depend on the concept of a soul as Plato understood it, as something independent in itself. If the soul is understood as the spiritual essence of the deceased person, the so-called dualist objections to an afterlife collapse.

> If the soul is seen as the centre of a person's moral *identity*, and spiritual *dignity*, its *immortality* would simply depend on the existence of God, and would have no meaning apart from God.
>
> *What would be the implications of this view for body–soul dualism?*

If the concept of the soul is taken to be a way of speaking about a person's spiritual or moral identity, then it is quite conceivable that an all-powerful God could recognize a deceased person on the basis of their past deeds, without the need to suppose the existence of an independent 'soul' in the Platonic sense.

Hence in the Christian belief about the afterlife, God could reward the good and punish the wicked, because he is able to know which is which, regardless of any claim about an 'independent soul'. Leaving out the notion of a soul as some alleged 'entity' independent of the body, it then becomes possible (and reasonable) to talk instead about the reality of a person's past deeds (or 'track record'), something that many believe 'lives after them' in a way that could be described as 'immortal' in the eyes of God. Therefore if the notion of a 'soul' is merely a metaphor for speaking of a person's human and moral identity before God, it need not be thought of as in any sense 'independent' of the person who once lived.

> **Gilbert Ryle** famously argued against the existence of a soul, deriding it as a supposed 'ghost in a machine', but he seems to have missed the point if the soul is seen as a metaphor for a person's moral or spiritual identity. This is normally recognized as making sense, as when we speak of a deceased person deserving reward or punishment for their good or bad deeds. Kant accepted this, but retained the language of the 'soul' to mean the enduring moral identity of a person. Kant implicitly assumed that rewarding the *soul* was equivalent to rewarding the ***person***.

> ### Christian eschatology
> Concerning beliefs about the end of the world and the afterlife. The 'four last things' are death, judgement, heaven and hell. The just will be separated from the wicked and given the beatific vision (communion with

RELIGION AND HUMAN EXPERIENCE

> God) in **heaven**. The wicked will lose communion with God (often described as **hell**). Those needing to be 'purged' of their sins go to an interim place of punishment called **purgatory**. Christians believe that the world will end with a Day of Judgement, but by then all individuals will have been privately judged by God. Some believe in an apocalyptic ending of the world as an earth-shattering event, based on passages in the Gospels. How these future prophetic events should be interpreted is a matter of dispute among scholars.

Reasons for the claim that an afterlife is illusory

In addition to the challenge to an afterlife posed by philosophy, there has also been the challenge from psychology. **Freud** claimed that belief in an afterlife was an illusion created by wishful thinking, an illusion which lay at the heart of religion from the beginning. Who does not wish to escape from the hardships of life? Who would not wish for a life of endless bliss? For **Marx**, heaven was 'invented' to give hope to the hopeless, a kind of mental opium to bring emotional comfort, only to distract people from dealing with the temporal problems of poverty and misery in the here and now. Both theories were based on partially true observations of current trends in religious belief at that time. Marx felt his analysis of religion was true for his time; Freud that it was true from his clinical experience. But the idea that religion itself is rooted in, or explicable by, comforting notions of an afterlife is now shown to be historically erroneous and factually wide of the mark (see below). This means that both Marx and Freud were greatly mistaken in theorizing about religion in general on the basis of selective observations.

> If religion can be shown to have existed independently of, or prior to, belief in an afterlife, **Freud**'s theory of religion collapses.
>
> *But in what sense might part of his theory be valid?*

Religion as existing without beliefs about an afterlife

In a strong rebuttal of both thinkers, **John Bowker** has shown that the earliest religions held no comforting views about death being the gateway to a blissful afterlife. On the contrary they believed that life was the most desirable state, and death something to be postponed as long as possible. It is well known that not until near the end of the biblical story, for instance, is there any reference to an afterlife of bliss. Before that, death was seen as an unfortunate interruption both to the experience of life and to a relationship with God. An existence after death was regarded as difficult to comprehend, with the souls of the deceased going to a shadowy 'underground'. This undercuts theories that religion is an invention to provide illusory comfort from the miseries of life. Studies have shown that religions grew and prospered for centuries without any concept of an afterlife. Only later, with the benefits of revelation, did an afterlife come to occupy such a large part in religious belief, but when it did it was not in isolation from other factors, such as the need for a virtuous life, or a life of moral integrity, by the grace of God.

> **Bowker** shows that the belief in the existence of God does not necessarily entail belief in an afterlife.

The claim that Christian belief in the afterlife is supported by history

Christians believe that the afterlife is part of revelation, and involves an existence in which body and soul are united, as they are in earthly life. This belief is founded on the resurrection of Christ, but Christians are divided on the nature of this event. Some see it as a foundational belief that does not depend on factual evidence from the past. But others believe it was an historical event open to empirical investigation. If it can be shown that Jesus did rise from the dead, then the possibility of other humans living in an afterlife is established. This is the argument put forward by one eminent philosopher and theologian.

The German philosopher **Wolfhart Pannenberg** believes that the resurrection of Jesus was a clear and transparent revelation from God that the dead are divinely destined to rise again. He rejected the anti-historical position of

RELIGION AND HUMAN EXPERIENCE

> ***Wolfhart Pannenberg*** *believes the resurrection was a truly historical event, but other believers do not agree that it need have been. If Pannenberg is correct, the resurrection confirms the existence of an afterlife, but how persuasive is his case?*

Bultmann, who argued that claims for such miraculous events are unacceptable in the age of science, and that what is important is to look for the existential significance of the belief that Jesus had risen. He also rejected the position taken by **Barth** that the resurrection of Jesus was an event of faith that belonged to 'sacred history'. This meant that the event was only transparent to faith, and could not be established as an historical event. For Pannenberg the resurrection of Jesus could not be adequately understood from either of those positions. Bultmann's was an evasion of the historical facts. Barth's was an attempt to shield the resurrection behind the walls of faith, and render it invisible to unbelieving eyes.

Views of the resurrection

Barth It was an event of 'sacred history', and can only be known to faith.

Bultmann It was a mythical event that showed the power of God over death.

Pannenberg It was an historical event of 'universal history' and happened as reported.

Hume It was a physical impossibility because the dead do not rise.

The resurrection as an event of universal history

Pannenberg instead has taken the daring position that the resurrection was an event of universal history, that is, an event that it was possible to prove had actually happened using the tools of ordinary historical research. This meant that both believers and non-believers could be shown that Jesus rose from the dead. The role of faith was in the religious trust that the resurrection evoked, namely, that God would extend the same destiny to those who

RELIGION AND THE AFTERLIFE

believed in Jesus and became his followers. Pannenberg used two approaches in establishing his position. One was the philosophical approach based on anthropology. Here he argues that humans are by nature geared for transcendence, that is, for a destiny beyond the present world. He believes that this is a reasonable assumption since human beings are never satisfied with a purely material vision of things. We are always tending towards 'going beyond' every achievement, every discovery, every arrival point. There are clear similarities between this position and that of **Rahner** (see p. 310).

His second approach is purely historical, based on a threefold analysis of the event which is recorded as having happened, and seen in the context of its time. According to Pannenberg there was a strong biblical conviction at the time of Jesus that a resurrection from the dead would be shown to be not just a hope, but a reality. The resurrection of Jesus was therefore seen at the time as the fulfilment of this hope. Second, there was the evidence of the empty tomb. Despite efforts to suppress this evidence, as mentioned in the Gospels, the empty tomb became a linchpin in the evidence that Jesus had risen. Following this there is the clear evidence of the testimony of the apostles, the people closest to the event. The conviction of the apostles was not about something marginal or insignificant. It was a conviction that something of cosmic significance had taken place. For this conviction they would give their lives, another fact of universal history.

> I claim to be an historian. My approach to Classics is historical, and I tell you that the evidence for the life, death and resurrection of Christ is better authenticated than most of the facts of ancient history.
>
> E. M. Blaiklock

Arguments for the resurrection
- An event expected to happen.
- Recorded in the Gospels.
- Consistent with human aspirations.
- Confirmed by the empty tomb.
- Further confirmed by the apostles.
- The apostles died for their beliefs.
- Belief spread widely and quickly.
- Foundational belief of Christianity since.

RELIGION AND HUMAN EXPERIENCE

The credibility of the resurrection as an historical event

Pannenberg's compelling case for the historicity of the resurrection is closely linked to his view that, first, history is the arena where God becomes manifest in the world. And, second, that the meaning of history will not be fully understood until the end of time, in much the same way that the meaning of a novel lies hidden until its final page is reached. In this regard the resurrection of Jesus is a revelation by way of 'provisional insight' into the meaning of human destiny. The insight that the dead are destined to rise again will, for Pannenberg, be confirmed in the future when the end of the world comes. He believes that the idea of an 'end time' (*eschaton*), when human life and history will be concluded, is not only an article of faith, but is something confirmed by science. According to modern science, time began with the Big Bang, and will end with the Big Crunch. In religious terms this means for Pannenberg that it began with divine creation, and it will end with an apocalypse, when the power of God as Lord of life and history will be finally revealed.

> **Objections to Pannenberg**
> - His appeal to history is not convincing.
> - The events he refers to are too far back to be fully known about.
> - The evidence he appeals to is vague and unreliable.
> - The accounts of the resurrection are not consistent with each other.
> - There were no actual witnesses to the resurrection.
> - If God wanted the resurrection to be believed why was the evidence not clearer?
> - Unless God is shown to exist, claims for a resurrection are necessarily false.

The credibility of Pannenberg's view of history is of course enhanced by religious faith, but is claimed not to be dependent on it. Whether it is sufficiently compelling to convince historians is another question, but then all historical events are subject to doubt and revision. Atheists will inevitably dispute the claim that universal history contains the history of God's dealings with the world. Even if they believed that Jesus rose from the dead, their prior world view would prevent them from according it any *religious* significance. But, as Pannenberg has argued, if someone has risen from the dead it automatically poses religious questions. In this sense history may at best provide the evidence, but it is for faith to determine its significance.

RELIGION AND THE AFTERLIFE

> That Jesus rose from the dead is central to the Christian faith, but there is dispute among religious thinkers as to whether Jesus' resurrection needs to be seen as an empirically verifiable event, in order to be the foundation of faith in life after death.

The afterlife in eastern religions

Before concluding this chapter we will consider briefly beliefs about the afterlife such as found in **Hinduism** and **Buddhism**, neither of which has a concept of a soul similar to that found in the western tradition. Hindus do allow for a transfer of identity in the doctrine of reincarnation, so that the 'same' person continues to suffer or benefit from the moral quality of their previous existence. However, despite the complexities of Hindu beliefs, it must be remembered that they are framed within belief in a supernatural order where all human problems connected with faith can be expected to be ironed out by a supernatural power. Not so with Buddhism, which has no concept of the supernatural. Like Hindus, Buddhists have a cyclical understanding of life and death, but believe that life is about overcoming ignorance and gaining enlightenment. In the process called rebirth only a person's consciousness continues, making it difficult to understand how the 'same' person continues on the much sought after path to enlightenment (see box).

> **The afterlife in Hinduism and Buddhism**
>
> **Reincarnation** Central to **Hinduism**. Called **samsara** (the continuing cycle of birth, death and rebirth) and linked to **dharma** (ethical duties), **karma** (one's personal deeds) and **moksha** (final release from samsara). Hindus believe that one's karma determines one's future state after reincarnation. Good karma ensures a happy reincarnation, bad karma an unhappy one. But the human's destiny remains in the hands of Brahman, the ultimate deity.
>
> **Rebirth** Associated with **Buddhism**. Retains the cyclical view of life contained in Hinduism, but denies continuity of identity. There is no 'fixed self' reborn. Rather there is a rebirth of a similar **consciousness**, so that the faults of **ignorance** which always lead to rebirth are re-experienced. Once ignorance is overcome there is **enlightenment**,

RELIGION AND HUMAN EXPERIENCE

> the cycle is broken, rebirth ends and the individual enjoys a state of bliss called **nirvana**. Nirvana is seen as a state of being 'extinguished' (like a light) and the miseries of rebirth are avoided.
>
> *Both views give rise to philosophical problems of considerable complexity, especially in regard to how a person's karma (actions) can be ultimately rewarded if, as in Hinduism, reincarnation is not of the 'same' person in any normal sense. If, as in Buddhism, only the consciousness of the previous person survives, in what sense is that consciousness reborn if not in the 'same' person again? But Buddhists deny that any 'fixed self' is reborn. Who then goes on to enjoy nirvana?*

Near-death experiences

Finally, we conclude this chapter with a brief look at the alleged phenomena known as 'near-death experiences'. The experiences are variously described as of a 'mystical' kind, involving visions of bright lights, travelling through tunnels, out-of-the-body sensations, beautiful vistas, encountering dead relatives and so on. Another common feature of such experiences is a deep feeling of calm, and some would say love. The experiences are valued by those who have had them, but how they originate, and what their significance is, is widely disputed. Since they are not necessarily related to virtue or holiness church leaders tend to disregard them, and there is little religious support for the idea that they provide insights into an afterlife, or can be claimed as evidence of it.

> Near-death experiences are philosophically open to various interpretations. For some they have a religious significance, for others they do not. Christian leaders have little to say about such claims.

Various explanations range from hallucinations, the effect of drugs, the physiological and psychological effects of a 'dying brain', and the like. Since there are usually no specific claims about their significance (as there are in the case of religious or mystical experience; see p. 128), and since they are not normally claimed to have any theistic or religious significance, they are open to various naturalistic explanations. Whether they are *subject-related* experiences or have some *objective* basis, is an issue seen by many to be of only medical or psychological interest.

> The best argument I know for an immortal life is the existence of a man who deserves one.
> *William James*

Part 3 Religion and the Challenge of Atheism

11 God and Evil

- The problem of evil and suffering.
- Theodicy and the justification of God.
- The freewill defence.
- The Augustine and Irenaeus theodicies.
- New Testament theodicy.
- Process theodicy.
- Philosophical theodicy.
- Assessment of theodicy.

Differing responses to the problem of evil and suffering

The existence of evil and suffering has long been considered one of the major arguments for the non-existence of God. Great natural disasters such as tornados, earthquakes, floods and tsunamis, which cause widespread suffering to the innocent, seem to take place without any regard for their victims, proving for many that no loving God exists as claimed by religion. Equally the sufferings caused by man-made evils such as war and other crimes, raise questions about the existence of an all-powerful and loving God. While the response from some is to claim that these phenomena simply prove that no God exists, for others it has often become a reason for 'giving up' faith in a God who permits such things.

The latter response has historically been made by some, and represents an instinctive or emotional reaction to evils that are particularly repugnant, such as the suffering of innocent children. Whether such a response is temporary or lasting, or whether it should be categorized as agnostic or theistic, is

> **Responses to evil and suffering**
> 1 Evil and suffering show that no God exists (atheist).
> 2 Evil and suffering raise doubts about God's love (agnostic).
> 3 Evil and suffering are allowed by God for a reason (theist).

difficult to ascertain. The problem of evil, therefore, takes two forms. One is that God, since he exists, should intervene and stop such evils happening. The other is that the existence of such evils provides compelling evidence that no God exists.

Theodicy: arguing in defence of God

Theodicy is the name given to traditional attempts to justify God in face of evil and suffering (*theo* = God; *dice* = justify). Classical theism raises the problem of how an omnipotent and loving God could allow evil to exist because of the human suffering it causes. **Hume**, paraphrasing **Epicurus** from the ancient world, and later **Augustine**, stated the problem in terms of two apparent contradictions. The first is between a God allowing evil, yet being able to prevent it. The second is between a God allowing evil and yet being called all-loving. Either God can or cannot do something about evil. If he cannot, he is not God, because God is supposed to be omnipotent. Since evil exists, the only other conclusion is that God is unwilling to prevent it. If he is unwilling then he is not all-good, an essential quality of the true God. However, it is these conclusions which believers question. They argue that the existence of evil and suffering is neither proof that God lacks love for humanity, nor proof that he lacks the power to remove its sufferings.

> **The inconsistent triad**
>
> If God is not *able* to prevent evil he is not God.
> If God is not *willing* to prevent evil he is not Good.
> Therefore evil and God are contradictory.
> But evil exists, therefore God does not.

The term '*theodicy*' was first coined by **Leibniz**, who argued that evil was a necessary part of God's creation. His starting point was the goodness of God, a quality of God which he worked out philosophically: God had to be good. If evil exists then God must have a good reason for allowing it. Because creation is the work of God, this world is 'the best of all possible worlds'. Leibniz agreed with **Irenaeus, Augustine** and **Aquinas** that evil is allowed by God for the sake of a greater good, which he is able to see but we are not. In philosophical terms, argues Leibniz, the evil or imperfection of the part does not prejudice the good of the whole. We as creatures can only see the imperfections of the part, while God sees the wider perfection, and ultimate value of the whole. It is as if a viewer of Michelangelo's Last Judgement is only allowed to see the section on the suffering of the damned. This would give a false impression of the fate of mankind which, as the full picture shows, is about the overall goodness of God, and the happiness he has destined for humanity.

> Michelangelo's painting of *The Last Judgement* shows the blessed going to heaven, and the damned going to hell. Leibniz effectively said that seeing only part of the picture of life is bound to be misleading. In this case, if only the damned are shown a false impression is created, concealing the message that our real destiny is heaven.

The freewill defence (1): God allows evil for a greater purpose

Christian thinkers from the earliest times have used what is called the freewill defence to argue that God is not responsible for the evil in the world, but instead allows it for moral and other reasons. **Irenaeus** in the second century argued that it was important to God that his creatures should possess moral freedom. This moral freedom, or freewill, would have two aspects. First, it would make humans responsible for how they used their moral freedom, and compel them to accept the consequences of its good use and its misuse. Second, moral freedom would be the means to enable them to cope with the challenge of evil as they encounter it in the world. This would include coping with the mental sufferings of frustration, anxiety, despair, as well as the physical sufferings of pain and discomfort. Any alternative to this moral freedom would be a spiritual loss to human beings.

> *Irenaeus* God allows evil for the attainment of a greater good through the moral *use* of freewill.

RELIGION AND THE CHALLENGE OF ATHEISM

> Man needs difficulties. They are necessary for health.
>
> C. G. Jung

Thus a good God, as **Richard Swinburne** argued, could allow natural and moral evil to be part of the world so that it would be a true 'vale of soul-making', a place where human beings, after being tested in the crucible of suffering, would grow in goodness, love, trust and moral character.

In this perspective evil is an opportunity for the development of moral goodness, a quality of moral character excellence that cannot be achieved in any other way. This view has found compelling support in recent years from **Alexander Solzhenitsyn**, who, after years of unjust imprisonment and misery in the Russian labour camps, renounced his atheism for his original faith, Christianity.

Solzhenitsyn believed that the experience of suffering brought a spiritual transformation to its victims, and helped them preserve their humanity in contrast to the degradation and decadence manifested by their more animal-like oppressors. He found that this insight led him to a renewal of his Christian faith, which saw suffering as something to be lived through rather than submitted to. For those who strived to live through it, it was creative and redemptive. This insight led him sharply away from the atheistic system he saw as the fertile ground for the dehumanization and tyranny that led to the misery and deaths of millions of his countrymen. For him it was clearly the failure of humankind without the inspiring influence of God, not God, that was the problem.

> **Solzhenitsyn** believed that suffering and adversity brought about spiritual regeneration, but many claim that suffering brings moral despair.
>
> *How far can the view that the benefits of suffering to **some** outweigh its bad effects on **others** be used as a credible theodicy?*

The freewill defence (2): God allows the misuse of freewill and its effects

A second form of the freewill defence was put forward by **Augustine**. Using biblical evidence, he argued that God created the world with the intention

GOD AND EVIL

that it be good in every respect. But two events happened which frustrated God's original plan. First, a rebellion in heaven took place which resulted in the bad angels being expelled with their leader Satan. The keynote of this was the *misuse* of the freewill of the angels, as a result of which they became a source of evil temptation for future generations. Second, there came a similar misuse of freewill by **Adam** and **Eve** when they chose to submit to pride and self-will, and disobeyed God. This resulted in the loss of the goodness and harmony of the world originally intended by God. From this point the world fell into disorder, and both the natural world and human beings became casualties. In the case of humans it meant a descent into decadence and evil.

> *Augustine* God allowed the historic *misuse* of freewill by **Adam** and **Eve** and the bad angels, to be the basis for his plans for the *redemption* of the human race.

Augustine's aim was to show, first, that God was not responsible for the results of the two failures: the initial failure of the bad angels and then that of the first humans. Evil came not from God but from his creatures whom he willed to have freewill. Augustine's second aim was to show, again from biblical evidence, that God did not leave matters as they stood. God intended to bring a

> It was a happy fault, a *felix culpa* (of Adam and Eve), that brought about so great a redeemer.
> St Augustine

greater good from the original evil. To achieve this God intended to compensate for the original sin of our first parents by planning the work of redemption and reconciliation which was successfully carried out through his Son **Jesus Christ** (see box).

Christian theodicy: the understanding of evil in the light of the gospel

A different but related approach to the problem of evil draws specifically on the resources of the Christian faith to provide believers with a compelling reason for trust that God is on the side of the sufferer. Christians in fact see confirmation of God's involvement in suffering, rather than his detachment from it, in the fate of Jesus of Nazareth. **Jürgen Moltmann** believes that no theodicy can leave out of account the event of the crucifixion, the event 'when God died on the cross'. In this event God inspires the world with the hope that suffering and death are not the end, and on the evidence of the resurrection, herald a new future for man in the hereafter. This points to the need for faith in the eschatological message of the New Testament, which speaks of the time when evil and suffering will cease and 'God will wipe away every tear'.

> *Moltmann* Evil and suffering cannot be understood theologically without reference to the way **Jesus**, the Son of God, endured suffering himself, for the sake of human *redemption*.

A variation of this approach to the problem of evil and suffering has been suggested by the Christian thinker, pastor and martyr **Dietrich Bonhoeffer**. In a proposal which again called for trust in God, Bonhoeffer put forward the view that Christians must live in the world 'as if God is not there'. This does not mean that God's existence should be denied, but that God cannot be looked to for divine assistance in coping with the problems of life. Bonhoeffer believes that this is the message of the Cross. Jesus, in whom God was present, went about living an ordinary, unspectacular life which ended with his violent death. The message from this is that Jesus, too, lived in a secular, even godless age, and had to accept that divine assistance was not going to be forthcoming to protect him from his violent fate. In the same way we too must face life in an 'adult' way, which means trusting God, but not looking to him for earthly or miraculous relief.

Christian theodicy
- God allows evil and suffering for a greater good.
- God sees all evil and suffering.
- Evil and suffering can be redemptive.
- Evil and suffering end with death.
- Jesus showed that death is not the end.
- Faith is about trust in God.
- God will reward those who have suffered unjustly.

GOD AND EVIL

> **Bonhoeffer** and **Moltmann** believe that evil and suffering must be accepted, but also fought against, in the way **Jesus** did. For the former this means not expecting miracles from God, but for the latter, the message of the gospel gives hope that where suffering cannot be helped, it will be compensated by God.

Process theodicy: God as a fellow-sufferer with all human beings

Process theology has its roots in process philosophy, which was started by **A. N. Whitehead**, who held that the fundamental characteristic of reality was not its being fixed or static, but having a capacity for development. In other words the basic category of reality was not 'being', as was traditionally thought, but 'becoming'. Although Whitehead as a philosopher did not mention God as such, it was easy for theologians to see his notion of 'fundamental reality' as offering the possibility of a new way of understanding God. This led some theologians, like **Charles Hartshorne,** to see the 'dynamic' God of the Bible as a better model for how God acts in the world than the 'transcendent' God of classical theism, which is all about God's 'fixed' theoretical attributes. In the Bible, God acts like a person, and depends on human beings to co-operate with him to achieve his objectives. Therefore, Hartshorne believes, it is unrealistic to look for an 'omnipotent' God who has the power to deal with evil and suffering.

> ***Classical theism*** Concentrates on God's fixed attributes such as his omnipotence and omniscience. God is omnipotent, but can choose to be 'powerless' for a greater good.
>
> ***Process theodicy*** Concentrates on how God is shown in the Bible as more 'human' than divine. God is essentially 'powerless' without the help of man.
>
> *How far is process theodicy a more, or less, 'comforting' view of evil and suffering than classical theism?*

The views of Hartshorne were later taken up by followers like Schubert Ogden, who saw the story of **Jesus** as confirmation of God's 'dependence', and consequent powerlessness. The result is the apparent 'weakness' of God in the face of evil. Ogden agrees with Hartshorne that God should be defined according to the picture presented in the Bible, not how he is described by classical theism. The biblical picture shows God as a dynamic figure who can interact with human beings as a person, a far cry from the immobile, static, changeless figure of classical thought. In the story of Jesus, the Son of God is revealed as someone who is a fellow victim of evil, thus showing the solidarity of God with all other suffering human beings. However, many theists are unhappy with the idea that God can be thought of as 'powerless', rather than choosing to be so for a greater reason. If God were fundamentally powerless, they point out, he would not be God, and neither would such a 'God' be of much help in offering a solution to evil and suffering.

> ***Process theodicy*** teaches that God ***depends*** on human beings to interact with him to overcome evil. God is 'powerless' to change the world without the help of humans. The example of ***Jesus*** shows that God can be a 'victim' of evil, and in so doing inspires humans to cope with suffering themselves. But mainstream theists disagree with this approach.
>
> *Process theodicy is essentially a religious, and specifically a Christian, view of evil and suffering, stressing the comforting view that God is united with man in his suffering. But what are the strengths and weaknesses of the view that God is 'powerless'?*

Philosophical theodicy: the idea that evil and suffering call for a transcendent solution

While the problem of evil has traditionally been seen to count against the existence of God, there is also the counter view that evil can give rise to a quite different intuition. This is the intuition that a good God could offer a solution to the obvious injustice that evil and suffering normally displays. This is a philosophical defence of the 'idea' of God, rather than a 'defence' of God (theodicy in the normal sense). This is the view that some evils are so overwhelming that nothing less than a transcendent solution appears sat-

GOD AND EVIL

isfactory. In this view evil and suffering do not provide a basis for the non-existence of God, but rather suggest strong grounds for hoping in the possibility of God's existence.

> Philosophical 'theodicy' is an argument in favour of the *idea* of God. It supposes that only a *divine* solution can overcome the human *injustice* of irrational evil and suffering.
>
> *But if something gives rise to the hope for God's existence, how far can the same thing be a basis for claiming God's non-existence?*

The argument depends on the fact that most great evils appear to go unresolved, and to invoke the idea of a righteous God is therefore vulnerable to the charge of wishful thinking. But it is seen by many as offering an approach to evil which is not only compatible with theism, but seen to support it. It can be seen that some of the ideas in this approach can be easily linked to the 'moral vacuum argument' above, p. 47.

> **Summary of the theodicies**
>
> *Irenaeus* God allows evil and suffering for our moral and spiritual development.
>
> *Augustine* God permits, but ultimately redeems, evil and suffering as a result of humankind's fall.
>
> *Leibniz* God allows evil and suffering for a greater good known only to him.
>
> *Christian* God allows evil and suffering, but shares in it for our redemption.
>
> *Process* God cannot alter evil and suffering, but helps us to cope with it.
>
> *Philosophical* Evil and suffering bring injustice, but without God are impossible to understand.

Assessment of theodicy

The strengths and weaknesses of the theodicies

The Irenaean theodicy is acceptable to many Christians because it fits in well with the Christian view of suffering as redemptive. If Jesus' suffering and death led to resurrection, then it is an easy step to see how suffering can be equally redemptive for his followers. The only problem is that for many people suffering can be morally destructive and, in view of this, many would say it is difficult to see how it could be a normal part of God's plan. The Augustinian freewill defence has been successful among many believers because they accept the basis on which it is worked out: the testimony of the Bible, and the traditional Christian understanding of the fall and redemption.

> **Strengths** Theodicies appeal to both faith and reason, and work well for most theists.
>
> **Weaknesses** Theodicies are open to rational challenge, and are unconvincing to non-theists.
>
> *But how far do the weaknesses of theodicy depend on the prior rejection of religious faith?*

Because this approach depends heavily on the acceptance of certain mythological accounts of supposed historical happenings taken from biblical narratives, it is not favoured by many believers who question the traditional interpretation of those narratives. The reasoning of **Leibniz** appears subject to rationalist criticism, because like **Anselm**'s in the ontological argument, his logic is a priori and deductive. As he saw it, logic compels us to believe that a good God could conceivably have reasons for allowing evil, if it led to a greater overall good known only to him. But as sceptics would point out, Leibniz, and other religious thinkers, explain evil by assuming the existence of God, while to them evil is a reason for rejecting it. But many theists would argue that the onus is on sceptics and unbelievers to show why evil and suffering *should* rule out the existence of God, and as we have just seen, this by no means follows.

GOD AND EVIL

> **Non-theism and evil**
>
> Many would claim that the attempt to show that evil disproves the existence of God is done on the basis of **strict empiricism**. Evil, it can be granted, 'appears' to suggest the non-existence of God, but since the empiricist view of truth is limited to what can be empirically verified, its understanding of reality is pre-determined and limited. The empirical approach therefore is inherently paradoxical because it is ultimately based not on empiricism, but on **rationalism**: the view that God's existence is meaningless on grounds that are a priori and **rational**, rather than empirical. Theists claim that there are good religious and philosophically sound reasons for showing that evil does not rule out God, and that **empirically** the matter can no more be decided than the ultimate cause of the Big Bang.

Problems with the non-theist challenge to theodicy

If the rationalist challenge begins with the rejection of the notion of God, evil will inevitably be used to support and confirm that rejection. Granted this, the reasoning of **Leibniz** will be rejected for begging the question of why start with God, if God's existence is the issue. But if the function of theodicy is not to counter *all* objections to God's existence, only the objection that evil and suffering are inconsistent with it, it would be legitimate for a religious thinker to reason in this way. It is therefore not a genuine objection to theodicy to claim that it begs the question of God's existence.

> **Non-theism and theodicy**
>
> *How far is it correct to say that only by ruling out God's existence on other grounds, can non-theists call theodicies meaningless?*

Supporters of the theodicies of **Irenaeus, Augustine** and **Leibniz** can point out that they are simply dealing with how the empirical fact of evil and suffering can be reconciled with an omnipotent and loving God. Their theodicies set out to show, on the basis of biblical and rational evidence, that evil and suffering are not inconsistent with the possible will of a God who is essentially loving, and in sympathy with his suffering creatures. Besides, as we saw above, from a philosophical point of view, there is even a case for seeing evil and suffering making a case *for* God's existence. If these theodicies can claim to be reasonable, is seems unfair of the sceptic to withdraw to the position of saying that because God's existence can be disproved on other grounds, all theodicies are necessarily meaningless *ab initio*.

> If **non-theists** begin by ruling out God's existence, they are logically compelled to reject the theodicies. If **theists** begin by ruling in God's existence, they are logically compelled to engage in theodicy.
>
> *How far therefore can it be said that for non-theists theodicies are logically impossible, and for theists they are logically necessary?*

Finally the theist might point out that the sceptic is above all left facing the indubitable fact that suffering may not be as devastating as it might appear. First, it can be a major element in human spiritual and moral development. Second, it is always set within the context of human finitude. This means that human suffering is always limited by the mercy of death, a limit that may have been set by a loving God. And third, if God exists, he is able to make good the present evil that humans suffer. In the light of these reasons, the argument that evil and suffering count against the existence of God is considerably weakened (see box below).

> Of course it might be argued that all the evil in the world, and God's absence from it, leave little choice but to reject any notion of a beneficent creator, whose existence in these sordid circumstances becomes nonsensical. Yet Christian theology claims precisely that God is not absent from the world, whatever the world thinks, and that God cared so much about creation that he entered it in human form and died within it, in order to identify completely with suffering, death and the general malignancy of the created order. There is little that is overt in secular thought which offers a systematic remedy for the world's ills that is configured in terms of this kind of universal salvation.
>
> Alex Wright
>
> *This is a theistic view of evil, but in what way does it present a challenge to non-theism?*

12 Religion and Science

- Problems with the empirical assumptions in the Bible.
- The discoveries of Copernicus, Galileo and Darwin.
- The question of biblical interpretation.
- Science and the rejection of metaphysics.
- Karl Popper on how science depends on metaphysics.
- Religion and metaphysics.
- Different form of causality.

Problems with the empirical assumptions in the Bible

At the popular level it has become common to hear the claim that 'science has disproved religion'. What is often referred to when such a claim is made is the fact that some *empirical* biblical claims have indeed been disproved, and have had to be revised in the light of scientific discoveries. Theists point out that these apparently mistaken claims or assumptions are quite detachable from the *religious teachings* which are embedded in them. The creation account in Genesis is usually taken as the classic example. Initially, religious leaders were unprepared for discoveries that called for a revision of beliefs that later on were seen as immaterial to the *raison d'être* (purpose) of the Genesis account, namely, its core religious message about God's initial role in bringing creation about.

> ***Empirical assumptions*** That Genesis is historically accurate regarding creation in 'six days', that animals and humans were created 'instantly' and that the earth was 'young', and so forth. Challenged by scientific findings about evolution, etc.
>
> ***Spiritual message*** That the world was ultimately the creation of a personal being, God.

Historic disputes between science and religion

The historic clash between religion and science came to a head as a result of excessive attachment by the Church to the literal truth of the Bible. For instance, both **Copernicus** and, later, **Galileo** made important scientific discoveries about the earth in relation to the universe, and specifically in relation to the sun. They discovered that contrary to accepted belief (both secular and religious) it was the earth that moved around the sun, and not vice versa. This ran into conflict with biblical passages that spoke, for instance, of the oddness of the 'sun standing still' in the heavens. The biblical view that the sun moved and the earth stood still was in keeping with the common-sense view that humankind was the centre of the earth, and the earth the centre of the universe. Up to medieval times this understanding of the world was so established that Venetian mariners had done all their calculations with operational success on the basis of the old belief, wrong though it was!

> The case of the Italian mathematician and astronomer Galileo is a *cause célèbre* which illustrates the mistake of religious leaders defending the Bible over issues of scientific fact. But how far could it be said that this was never the main issue?

The problems created by the discoveries of Darwin and others

Further difficulties arose for religion following discoveries in the fields of biology and palaeontology. Studies of ancient rocks showed that the earth was millions of years old and took ages to arrive at its present state. This

RELIGION AND SCIENCE

conflicted with the long-accepted Genesis account of creation which stated that God created the world in 'six days', an account which suggested that the world was relatively young. It also conveyed the idea that all life forms were created fully formed. This was shown to be false by studies which showed the time-span required for the development of living organisms. In this area, the discoveries of **Charles Darwin** had a particularly devastating effect. Darwin showed that life was a process which needed vast periods of time to take place, and that all animals, humans included, evolved from primitive to more developed stages. On the face of it the human being was continuous with the lower animals, and therefore could not be considered a unique creature, much less one created specially by God.

> *The Bible*   Seen as giving a naive account of physical, astronomical and human processes.
>
> *Darwin*   Showed evidence that animate and inanimate beings evolved over a long timespan.

In the light of these discoveries religious leaders were immediately faced with a dilemma: to agree with the scientific findings might lead to a collapse in the credibility of the Bible. To disagree meant an open war with science. Only gradually did it become apparent that a reconciliation could be achieved. Advances in biblical scholarship eventually paved the way for an understanding of the Bible that would incorporate the latest findings of science. Today most readers of the Bible are unmoved one way or the other about the pre-scientific nature of many of its texts, and are normally directed to see its deeper spiritual and moral message. Earlier conflicts have now been resolved under differences of biblical interpretation (see more, p. 73).

> **The Bible and Science**
> - *Literal* interpretation means taking everything in the Bible at face value, regardless of the findings of science. This is an extreme position mainly held today by *fundamentalists*.
> - *Conservative* interpretation means holding on as far as possible to what the Bible says, but largely accepts the findings of science.
> - *Liberal* interpretation means accepting the views of latest scholarship, and the findings of science, thus separating the spiritual from the material content of biblical texts.

179

The Bible and the notion of personal agency

In the light of scientific studies of rocks, fossils and other remains, it became obvious that the world was much older than the biblical account allowed for. Also, the biblical emphasis on immediate creation by God of all life forms was seriously thrown into question by Darwinian evolution. The response of academic theologians was to see that the Bible was a religious book, and had no pretensions to be scientifically correct. It was seen that the framework of the Bible's message was clearly pre-scientific, but that its fundamental message was religious, and therefore was not susceptible to the changing fortunes brought by scientific updates. Religious scholars see that the biblical writers' aim was to teach a religious truth which, despite the mythical or 'pre-scientific' language in which it was presented, has its own validity as a religious revelation.

> **Fundamentalists** interpret the Bible literally as the 'Word of God'. They believe that its religious and moral message should not be threatened by science. Apparent scientific 'errors' in the Bible are 'tests of faith'. The **Bible** introduces the notion of a ***personal agency*** as responsible for the world. It also introduces the notion of ***personal responsibility*** to that agency on the part of **man**. These are central themes of the Bible's unique message.
>
> *But why do fundamentalists see science as such a threat to the Bible?*

Biblical scholars claim that the essence of the Bible's message is two-fold. First, that the world is in the hands of a *personal agency*. This is an intelligent being, God, who was spiritually present from the start, making possible the contingent physical processes that could never explain themselves, and which eventually led to the arrival of life, and eventually human life. Second, that the existence of God introduces the moral notion of *personal responsibility*, a notion central to the contribution of religion to the significance of human life. Theists would question whether it is this aspect of being held morally responsible before a transcendent being that causes religion to be an unwelcome intrusion into a scientific atheistic world view, but the religious claim as such puts nothing in the way of science, as science, to investigate the world to the limits of empirical truth.

Science and the use of metaphysical theories

Empirical philosophers tended to dismiss metaphysics as too vague and inconclusive to be taken seriously. **Hume** said that all books on metaphysics were pure speculation yielding no real knowledge, and 'should be consigned to the flames'. Yet scientific writing is full of claims that there is nothing at all (that is, no reality) beyond the world of space and time. Many point out that this is of course a metaphysical claim in itself in the form of a denial of such a reality, and as such cannot properly claim to be scientific. This follows from the fact that such a claim cannot be verified or falsified by empirical evidence, as confirmed by both Hume and **Kant**. (See also the verification principle, p. 216.)

> *Scientific* explanation involves laws and previous states of affairs. *Personal* explanation involves persons and purposes. The hypothesis of theism is that the Universe exists because there is a God who keeps it in being and that the laws of nature operate because there is a God who brings it about that they do. The hypothesis is that there is a person who brings about these things for some purpose...So the hypothesis that there is a God, makes the Universe much more to be expected than it would otherwise be, and it is a very simple hypothesis. Hence the arguments from the existence of the Universe and its conformity to simple natural laws are good arguments to an explanation of the phenomena, and provide substantial evidence for the existence of God.
>
> Richard Swinburne

Einstein famously said, 'Religion without science is blind, science without religion is lame.'

What did Einstein mean, and why do scientists challenge this?

The noted Austrian philosopher **Karl Popper**, however, has called attention to the metaphysical grounding of the supposedly *physicalist* enterprise we call science. He believes that if the *negation* of a metaphysical statement is meaningful, then a metaphysical statement is itself meaningful. What he calls the 'arch-metaphysical assertion' that 'there exists an omnipotent, omnipresent, omniscient personal spirit' can be shown to have a 'high degree of probability' in a complicated line of reasoning based on the meaning of probability as understood by scientists. Scientists normally understand probability as near certainty, but base their reasoning on what Popper calls 'confirmability by induction'.

> **Einstein** believed that a world open to scientific investigation raised questions that went beyond science.
>
> *In saying this, how far does Einstein leave room for metaphysical speculation?*

Induction is of course the method of establishing scientific laws on the empirical basis of observation from *particular* instances. Thus if water is observed to boil at 100 degrees centigrade, in a number of particular instances, it leads to a *general law* of physics. At bottom this becomes a *metaphysical assumption* that physical laws can safely be drawn on the basis of experience because 'we can trust experience and learn from it'. Popper points out that it is an assumption, not itself based on experience, that we can *trust* experience to formulate laws that are predictable (on that basis) about how bodies now and in the future will behave. Without this 'a priori metaphysical principle', **Popper** concludes that science would be unable to formulate scientific laws. If Popper is right, it is wrong for scientists to pretend they are above making assumptions not based on experience.

> **Popper** holds that science depends on certain metaphysical assumptions, thus casting doubt on its claims to be strictly empirical in its approach. **Plantinga** also argues that science employs *faith*, as well as reason and experience: the faith that truth can be found, and can be based on experience.
>
> *How far are both right?*

Metaphysical claims about the role of chance

Science claims that the universe began with a Big Bang which happened some sixty billion years ago. This is when time began, and before this there was nothing. Questions about anything outside the physical world are questions

RELIGION AND SCIENCE

that have no validity, according to science. In this respect science accepts the physical world as merely given. If the physical world is contingent (depending for its existence on something else) it cannot be merely accepted as a fundamental given (fact of reality) that raises no other questions. But theists would point out that science in fact is not content to accept the world as merely given. Instead it postulates the notion that everything came to exist in virtue of pure *chance*. But by so doing it introduces a metaphysical theory of reality which is a rival to religion, but one that is, equally, neither verifiable nor falsifiable.

> **Scientists** who rule out religion in favour of naturalism, put forward the ***metaphysical*** theory of ***chance*** as the most likely origin of the universe.

Theists would say that the weakness of this view is how it readily accepts that reality could begin, not by pure chance, but at all. This was a problem that **Aquinas** tried to wrestle with philosophically when he postulated the notion of a divine, or uncaused First Cause. For Aquinas there can be no break in the chain of cause and effect in regard to contingent things, and at some point it is reasonable to suppose that within a limited timespan (that is, ruling out an infinite regress) a non-contingent cause has to be invoked, a cause that cannot be explained in terms of blind chance. It is this contention that really separates science from religion.

> **Swinburne** has pointed out that ***chance*** and ***personal agency*** are the two opposing views about ultimate reality that separate theists from atheists. Empirically many processes, including evolution, appear to be driven by chance, leading some scientists to believe that chance is an ultimate metaphysical fact.
>
> *Theists, by contrast, believe that personal agency lies behind all physical processes, even those subject to chance outcomes, but how far would such a view 'interfere' with science, or the pursuit of scientific truth?*

RELIGION AND THE CHALLENGE OF ATHEISM

The idea that metaphysical questions don't matter much

It could be argued that metaphysical questions do not really engage the ordinary person. **Pascal** said that people were more interested in hunting, fishing and gambling than in such questions. Even at the more serious level of intellectual debate, people can draw a line at questions that they see as impossible to answer. The theory that the material world is all there is is a metaphysical theory, and is commonly known as *materialism* or *naturalism*. **Bertrand Russell** in his refusal to speculate on what might, or might not, lie beyond the material world, clearly implied that this was a 'non-question'. He said 'the world is just there and that's all there is to it'. Russell's refusal to speculate any further made **Frederick Copleston**, his protagonist in their famous BBC radio debate in the early 1950s, to make the droll remark that someone who refused to sit at the chess-table cannot be checkmated!

> More than *homo sapiens* we are *homo quaerens*, the animal that asks, and asks and asks.
>
> George Steiner
>
> *Steiner was talking about metaphysical questions such as 'What is the meaning of life?', but how far are such questions seen as urgent in today's self-absorbed material and secular age?*

At the same time, theists would argue that even the ordinary person frequently asks questions that they consider important, such as, 'How did everything begin?', or 'Is death the end?' or 'Is this life all there is?' or 'Why me?' The scientific view is that if a question is not related to the physical universe then not only has it no answer, but the question itself is nonsensical. Yet a metaphysical question like 'Does life have meaning beyond death?' has, as **Pascal** said, an inescapable urgency, since it is possible that the answer is yes. Questions about the meaning of life and the significance of death, about immortality, and whether the material world is all there is, have engaged the greatest intellects from time immemorial, and continue to be asked by ordinary people. In reality, it seems, they are questions which both can and cannot be ignored.

RELIGION AND SCIENCE

> **Physics** The study and investigation of the natural world, as carried out by science.
>
> **Metaphysics** Speculation about what, if anything, might lie beyond the physical world.
>
> **Religion** The metaphysical view that God lies beyond and behind the physical world.

The central role of metaphysical speculation

However arguable it may be that metaphysical speculation is only for some but not others, modern anti-religious literature put metaphysical claims, such as blind chance being the origin of the universe, at the centre of their agenda. Many would say that it is precisely interest in this claim that explains the popularity of such writings. But theists would offer the counter claim that pure chance is the least credible explanation for the origin of the universe. For a start, many would point out that what **Plato** called the 'big questions' of life are not those answerable by science, but those which belong to the non-material, non-physical, or *spiritual* realm of human existence. This is the realm of the moral (the good, the true), the aesthetic (beauty) and the divine (religion).

> Modern anti-religious writings put *metaphysical* claims at the forefront of their arguments.

These are areas of human life which are central to human existence, but which lie beyond the bounds of science. Many would argue therefore that it is highly presumptuous of science to attempt to describe life without allowing some room for a discussion of its spiritual dimension. Thus an attempt to establish a definitive *negative* metaphysics in the form of 'there is nothing beyond the empirical world of space and time', as typically offered by materialist scientists, would seem to be as open to challenge as other metaphysical claims. Theists would insist that the attempt to limit the human to the material world ignores the spiritual complexity of human nature which, as **Kant** showed, accounted for our capacity to rise above the material aspects of life, and make our own decisive contribution to life by way of free rational and moral choices.

> **Plato** believed that the *big* questions of life were those that went beyond what science could answer, questions to do with truth, goodness, evil, beauty and the like. **Kant** claimed that human life raised questions that necessarily involved metaphysical beliefs of a religious nature.

Religious answers to metaphysical speculation

If metaphysical speculation, despite its admittedly tedious nature, has assumed the importance it has in modern thinking, theists would argue that it is right that the religious viewpoint should be judged on how far it offers a credible answer to rival metaphysical claims. One prominent modern approach is to show how religious conclusions can be drawn from certain facts brought to light by science. One is the fact that the universe had a beginning in time, a fact which brings an end to theories about an 'eternal' universe, or the possibility of an 'infinite regress' of material causes and effects. As we have seen above, the scientist **W. L. Craig** has used this as a challenge to science to accept that the universe (meaning the whole of empirical reality) needed an *explanation* for its coming into existence at all. He believes that the medieval adage came to sum up the essential problem, namely, that 'nothing can come from nothing' (*ex nihilo nihil fit*), even by pure chance! For this reason theists hold that nothing can come from nothing except by the theory of a mysterious personal power called God.

> **Craig** has argued that *infinity* implies no *starting point*, let alone a finishing point. If there could be no starting point either within infinite time or space, then nothing could *begin* without some external reason for its beginning (cf. **Leibniz**).
>
> *But while this is logically compelling, how is it likely to impress, or affect, ordinary people?*

Hence the *Kalam* argument (see above, p. 25) rejected the notion of a so-called infinite regress which supposes that you can go back infinitely far in space and time for the explanation of everything. If this is the case, the idea that particles of matter falling randomly over infinite time could eventually come together to form life, in much the same way as a troupe of monkeys playing long enough with a word processor might eventually produce poetry, or that a Boeing 747 might eventually come together by accident, simply cannot hold water. It follows logically that if particles of matter fall randomly in infinite time, they must have fallen randomly up to now, and there is no reason why they would not do so for ever. In infinite time there can be no starting point, and so, as **W. L. Craig** has pointed out, the Big Bang would have happened infinitely long ago, a notion that is impossible to conceive, and for that matter, has been shown to be factually false.

> **Metaphysics and the meaning of life**
>
> ***Naturalists*** The meaning of life is the meaning that humans give to it.
>
> ***Theists*** The meaning of life comes from beyond life, and depends on the will of God.
>
> *How far is it true that the search for meaning does not need to go beyond a particular 'way of life', and does not need to invoke religion?*

The notion of different causalities

While science and religion are seriously divided on whether life is to be seen as 'purely natural' or the creation of a personal agent, the same division could be represented as a clash between different forms of causality. **Aristotle** distinguished between efficient and final causality. *Efficient* causality is that which explains *how* something happened by way of physical cause and effect. For example, the murder was caused by a gunshot wound. *Final* causality explains the reasons behind the murder (such as revenge), the *why* of the event, the role of personal agency in the event, the role of *purpose*.

In the world of science, causality is part of a natural process in which natural effects follow natural causes. The process takes place according to the established laws of physics. Science does not allow for any exceptions to this system of cause and effect, hence its opposition, for instance, to the concept of *miracle* (see p. 191). But as we have seen in relation to miracle, it

RELIGION AND THE CHALLENGE OF ATHEISM

> **Different causalities**
>
> ***Efficient causality***   The physical reason why something happened, e.g. a fatal injury.
>
> ***Final causality***   The '***purpose-oriented***' reason why something happened, e.g. an act of revenge.
>
> ***Natural causality***   The province of science: explaining events in accordance with ***scientific*** laws.
>
> ***Supernatural causality***   The province of ***religion***: explaining an event as having a supernatural source, while also accepting the relevant scientific explanation. This causality includes the notion of hidden ***purpose***, and the idea of an event having an ultimate ***meaning*** (final causality).
>
> *But how far can science legitimately rule out the notion of a supernatural agency on the basis of scientific theory?*

is possible for believers to see an event both from a *natural* and from a *religious* perspective. The walls of Jericho may have fallen down as the natural result of a fortuitous earthquake, but from a religious perspective the event may have been reported as 'miraculous' because of its timely occurrence and special significance to the Israelites. Here we could have an illustration of two different causalities, what we may call natural and *supernatural* causality, or in terms of efficient and final causality.

> ***Religion*** explains the world in terms of ***final*** causality, suggesting a wider understanding of reality as controlled by a personal intelligence.
>
> ***Science*** explains the world in terms of ***efficient*** causality, the causality of physical cause and effect.

Hence the Big Bang may be seen as a purely natural occurrence by scientists and a natural and a divinely willed (or miraculous) occurrence by believers. This shows that the two causalities need not collide or conflict. It also shows how the religious perspective can fit perfectly well within a scientific universe in which the natural laws of physics are assumed to be the way the world works. For the religious believer the way the world works is the way that God works. Within this perspective religion adds a *new* dimension to a physical event, but does not undermine or deny its physicality, or its place in the scheme of natural causality.

> An *event* (such as the Big Bang) can be seen merely in terms of **efficient** causality by **science**, and in terms of **efficient and final** causality by **faith**.

13 God, Science and Miracles

- Miracles in the Christian tradition.
- The modern challenge to miracles.
- Hume's challenge to miracles.
- Theistic replies to Hume.
- Different views and aspects of miracles.
- Reconciling miracles with natural causality.
- The principle of special-case miracles.

The place of miracles in the Christian tradition

Miracles as events caused by God have occupied an important place in the Christian tradition. The Gospels report various kinds of miracles which collectively have been roughly divided into nature miracles and healing miracles. Nature miracles include the calming of a storm, walking on water, turning water into wine, feeding a large crowd with a small quantity of food and so on. Healing miracles include curing lepers, the sick, the demented, the blind and the lame and so forth. Early church leaders confidently taught that the Christian faith was 'founded on prophecy and miracle'.

This view prevailed for centuries, and was shared by the empiricist **John Locke**. Many regard Locke's defence of miracles to have been the main target of his fellow empiricist **David Hume**, who as we shall see became a major critic of miracles.

GOD, SCIENCE AND MIRACLES

> **Definitions of miracle**
>
> **Aquinas** 'Those things are properly called miracles which are done by divine agency beyond the order commonly observed in nature.'
>
> **Hume** 'A miracle may accurately be defined as a transgression of a law of nature by a particular volition of the deity, or by the interposition of some invisible agent.'
>
> **John Hick** A miracle can be an event perceived as a personal blessing, and credited to the goodness of God, evoking a religious response.
>
> **Popular definition** A miracle is 'an amazing coincidence' or a wondrous event, as when people speak of the 'miracle of science'. However, if an event is seen as *merely* wondrous, or a coincidence, then it is not a miracle in the religious sense.
>
> *The definition given by **Aquinas** may be called **prescriptive**, one that describes the essence of a miracle as involving divine agency. **Hume**'s definition, by contrast, is **descriptive**, an objective definition merely reflecting the commonly accepted way miracles were understood, but framed in philosophical language. **Hick**'s view helps to overcome scientific objections, but how far does it preserve the nature of miracle as the work of God?*

Hume's challenge to miracles

Hume raised doubts about miracles partly on the argument from likelihood based on empirical evidence. For Hume it was always 'more likely' that an event described as a miracle was some sort of illusion to which 'barbarous people' were particularly susceptible. But Hume's challenge to miracles is a little more complex. Hume accepted the standard definition of miracles as happenings that involve the activity of a divine agency usually in breaking a law of nature, such as that the terminally ill should die, or the dead stay dead. **Aquinas** saw no problem about such a possibility since an omnipotent God could if he wished overrule the normal workings of nature, for example restoring the dead to life, or healing the sick (at least in a way impossible under the normal workings of nature). One aspect of Hume's approach, however, is to challenge the possibility of ever *knowing* that a supernatural agent was at work. This is really a 'stand off' position where he raises an *epistemological* objection: we simply could never *know* if an event was the work of a hidden deity. This objection might seem odd to believers, who normally testify to a miracle because they feel *sure* it was caused by God, on the basis of (at least supposed) empirical evidence (like a sudden cure from paralysis).

> **Hume**'s theory of ***causality*** makes him an unlikely critic of miracles. He believed that 'causes' (natural as well as supernatural) were impossible to establish empirically. An effect can only be seen to 'follow' something, not be 'caused' by it. This should have led him to conclude that the divine 'causality' of miracles was theoretically possible if God exists, even if such 'causality' could never be clearly established.

Hume seems not to have ruled out the theoretical possibility of miracles, but he maintained that there could never be any *evidence* to establish the claim of divine causality. Hume did accept the possibility of new and extraordinary happenings, and allowed for events that people had claimed to have witnessed, even though to others they might have been thought impossible. He took the example of an Indian who refused to believe water could turn into ice until he saw it happening. In the same way we must be prepared for 'the extraordinary' to happen, but crucially for Hume the empiricist, we must always await the '*causes*' of their occurrence, which Hume assumed would always be natural, if they were to be called causes at all.

> An understanding of Hume's ***empiricism*** is key to his understanding of miracles. He believes that supernatural agency is empirically impossible to establish. He then suggests that extraordinary events can easily be mistaken for miracles, and assumes that they have been. He then concludes that any reports of miracles will always be suspicious.
>
> *But how far does he (or does he not) leave open the theoretical possibility that miracles could happen?*

To Hume a supernatural cause was no cause at all, since it could never be demonstrated as such. Furthermore, Hume assumed that the laws of nature could be taken as uniform, and therefore the *testimony* of a miracle as something out of the ordinary would always be open to doubt. This latter objection

GOD, SCIENCE AND MIRACLES

> **Summary of Hume on miracles**
> - All events can in principle be explained by natural causes (a priori empiricist principle).
> - All miracles, by religious definition, have at their base a divine cause (religious principle).
> - Divine causality is meaningless because it can never be experienced as such (a priori empiricist principle).
> - Ordinary happenings have ordinary explanations (a posteriori general principle).
> - Extraordinary happenings are not the same as miracles (a posteriori accepted principle).
> - Extraordinary happenings can be expected to be explained naturally (a priori empiricist principle).
> - Testimony of miracles always begs the question (a priori empirical scepticism).
> - Alleged witnesses to miracles are never reliable (a posteriori empirical scepticism).
> - At best miracles are highly unlikely (a priori empirical scepticism).
> - At worst miracles are impossible to establish as miracles (a priori empirical position).
>
> Hume seems to create a jumble of objections going from the ***impossibility*** of miracles to their ***improbability***, and using a mix of a priori empiricist reasoning, as well as a posteriori scepticism about the reliability of witnesses. But how far does Hume overlook the empirical fact that many are convinced that divinely caused events (miracles) have taken place?

is generally regarded as weak, since miracles by definition are extraordinary. It can be seen, however, that since Hume rejects the possibility of knowing if a divine agency was at work, he rejects the possibility that a miracle could ever be claimed to happen. Here Hume is anticipating the logical positivists: if an event cannot be verified or falsified as to its cause, then to claim it happened by some 'invisible agency' is meaningless. It may also be noted that **Kant**, like Hume, also held the view that we could never *know* about any agency working *beyond* the range of phenomena, or what we can experience.

193

RELIGION AND THE CHALLENGE OF ATHEISM

How theists might reply to Hume

Hume's challenge shows that claims to miracles are vulnerable to an empiricist attack. This follows from the empiricist viewpoint that the concept of miracles must be ruled out as *meaningless*, on the grounds that they can never be established (verified) as having taken place. In Hume's view what you see is what you get. At most an apparent violation of a law of nature is merely 'an extraordinary event' which can be expected to have a natural explanation given time. Therefore, if Jesus is claimed to have 'risen from the dead', in Hume's view there must have been some mistake, since people do not 'normally' rise from the dead.

> ***Hume*** Miracles, as acts of divine agency, can never be empirically established to have happened.
>
> ***Theism*** There is usually **some** empirical evidence to justify the **belief** that a specific event was brought about by divine agency, and was therefore a miracle.
>
> Theists would claim that it is normal to interpret events in accordance with one's expectations. This also happens in science, but in religion seeing an event as a miracle takes into account what can be expected if an all-powerful God exists, who occasionally might want to reveal his power for some purpose.

Theists, however, would point out that the whole concept of miracle is based on a specific form of perception that comes from, and only comes from, religious faith. If God does not exist, miracles are logically impossible, but if he does exist they are logically possible. The problem which Hume identifies arises from the distinction between the 'effect' and 'cause'. Theists would accept that the cause of a miracle (God) cannot be established either by verification or by falsification (see more on this in Chapter 14, The Challenge to Religious Language, p. 215). But the alleged effect, or event which represents the outer side of the miracle, can be subjected to either verification or falsification in respect of its 'wondrous' nature.

Admittedly by strict empiricist principles they are impossible to verify as such, but for theists there is usually some evidence to justify a claim of a miracle. However, many find it strange that Hume is not content to rest his

GOD, SCIENCE AND MIRACLES

> **Miracles: cause, effect, interpretation**
>
> *Cause*   For an event to be a miracle it must be caused by God, acting directly or indirectly through the laws of nature. But divine causality, as Hume argued, cannot be empirically established, that is, verified or falsified to be such.
>
> *Effect*   The *outer* side of the miracle. Something with an empirical impact that causes 'wonder' (*mira*). This 'effect' side of a miracle can be verified at least in principle. Some theists argue that the resurrection can be verified by various strands of evidence (see **Pannenberg**, above, p. 157), such as its effect on the apostles, the empty tomb, and so forth, while others are less concerned with its empirical verification. The resurrection would be *falsified* if Jesus was later seen to have strangely 'survived' his crucifixion, or if his body was found. Some alleged miracles in Lourdes have been subjected to strict scrutiny with a view to their verification or falsification.
>
> *Interpretation*   This is the third element in a miracle. Most theists would agree that while God could theoretically 'reveal' his causality, most miracles are seen as such through the way an event is *interpreted*. For this reason a 'natural' event, if interpreted theistically, can be called a miracle (see **Hick** below).

case on miracles being impossible to establish, according to empirical principles. Instead he goes on to impugn the reliability of witnesses. If miracles are impossible to establish there can be no difference between witnesses who are reliable or unreliable: the issue of witnesses is simply irrelevant. Christians believe the resurrection happened despite there being no witnesses at all to its happening! Furthermore, it can be argued that the apostles who later 'bore witness' to the resurrection did, on the empirical evidence of history, prove their collective reliability by suffering martyrdom for their beliefs.

> If Hume rules out the impossibility of claiming a miracle, he is logically committed to consider all who report a miracle to be unreliable. Therefore his argument about (unreliable) witnesses is pointless.

RELIGION AND THE CHALLENGE OF ATHEISM

> **Summary of replies to Hume**
> - If God does not exist miracles are impossible.
> - If God exists miracles are possible.
> - At the empiricist level miracles may be strictly indemonstrable.
> - Yet all miracles by definition have an empirical effect.
> - Not all reports of miracles are reliable.
> - Miracles are impossible to understand without religious faith.
> - Many have testified that miracles have happened.
> - Some miracles have been the foundation of religions.
> - There are therefore good reasons to believe that miracles have happened.

Christians could argue that Hume misunderstood the whole nature of religious perception, which is about faith and belief, and does not depend on empirical verification. In Hume's view if an event is not empirically verifiable it is meaningless, but this has been shown to be a metaphysical principle that is not itself verifiable (see 'logical positivism' below, p. 217). With this principle in hand Hume rules out all claims to revelation, biblical testimony, religious experience, mysticism (see above, p. 65), and along with these the validity of religious belief. It may be for this reason that Hume goes on to impugn the reliability of witnesses. This is a shift from claiming that miracles are 'impossible' because impossible to demonstrate, to claiming that *reports* of miracles, because they depend on the reliability of those who report them, can never be taken seriously. By doing so he muddies the water of his own case by going from saying miracles are *impossible*, to making the much weaker case that reports of a miracle cannot always be believed.

> Miracles are **possible** if God exists, but if Hume makes the reliability of **reporters** of miracles an additional issue, he then goes from making a fair point to having to accept that some reports **might** be reliable. In which case he would have to accept that such reports could have possible credibility. But as we have seen, his impugning of witnesses seems to have been a gratuitous point.

GOD, SCIENCE AND MIRACLES

Miracles as events interpreted as such by faith

The traditional idea that God performed miracles by direct intervention has come under review today for both *religious* and *moral* reasons. Many theists believe that claims of miracles can sometimes bring faith into disrepute. They would agree with Hume that reports of miracles always need to be looked at carefully, especially if they raise questions about God's wisdom and goodness. A related problem is the moral issue raised by the fact that if God can perform miracles, why does he not do so to ward off great evils and the suffering they cause. Both problems are related, since reports of miracles create the impression that God has intervened where he may not have done, at least in the way traditionally understood.

> **Objections to miracles**
>
> ***Religious objection*** Claims for miracles can sometimes reflect badly on God and religion.
>
> ***Moral objection*** If God can perform miracles, why does he not prevent innocent suffering?
>
> ***Atheistic objection*** So-called miracles are merely illusions based on false religious beliefs.
>
> *How could it be argued that the moral objection to miracles is based on a misunderstanding?*

This raises the question whether miracles are meant to be seen as objectively spectacular events, or as events which, though not necessarily spectacular, are subjectively seen as bearing the hand of God. Religious believers down the centuries have testified to miracles happening in their own lives, but such testimony does not necessarily confirm that God was directly involved. Many theists would regard this as a controversial issue, but **John Hick** has suggested that miracles should be seen, not as evidence of God's direct involvement, but as fortuitous enough to the eyes of faith to evoke 'wonder' (Latin, *mira*) and a religious response. He sees many of the Old Testament miracles, such as the crossing of the Red Sea by the Israelites, as an illustration of this. The Israelites perceived the events around them as showing the hand of God working in their favour. The non-believing Egyptians on the other hand would have had a different, non-religious, perception of the same events.

RELIGION AND THE CHALLENGE OF ATHEISM

> A window in Canterbury cathedral shows a series of panels describing how a workman, trapped in a tunnel, is rescued by a passing traveller while his workmates have gone for help. A hand appearing through a cloud indicates the 'miraculous' nature of the event. Here we can see two parallel perspectives on one set of events. One perspective is purely natural, showing a crisis situation of a man in danger, ending with his fortuitous rescue by a passing traveller. Parallel to this is the ***religious*** view set in the context of the cathedral, that the whole thing was not just an amazing coincidence but a ***miracle***, or ***blessing***, the appropriate response to which is to thank God for the miracle of the man's rescue.

What is important in this view is that miracles do not break into the natural *causal chain* which is normally invoked to explain the way events happen in the world. Thus, in this view, God does not intervene in some crude way from outside, but leaves believers free to see fortuitous events as blessings that can ultimately be attributed to God's goodness. A natural event that brings a hoped-for advantage can thus be 'seen as' a miracle through the eyes of faith, where the same event will merely be seen as a 'coincidence' by an unbeliever. An event favourable to a believer will usually evoke a sense of *gratitude*, compelling the believer to 'thank God' for the good fortune brought by the event. For a believer to call it a miracle would therefore be quite understandable, while not necessarily implying that God was directly involved in the event (see the box above).

> **Three views of miracles**
>
> ***Objective view***   God directly caused the Red Sea to part. God raised Jesus from the dead.
>
> ***Subjective view***   My cancer was cured because I had prayed for a cure. I prayed for my daughter's recovery and she became well. I prayed for a safe journey and it was a miracle that we survived a bad car crash.
>
> ***Secular view***   The experience of an 'amazing coincidence', or a 'lucky escape' is often metaphorically described as a 'miracle'. But only within the perspective of religious faith can an event properly be described as a miracle.

GOD, SCIENCE AND MIRACLES

> *In the first case a miracle is seen as the direct act of God, but in the second case a miracle is a way of seeing an extraordinary event in religious terms, something bearing the hand of God, and deserving to be called a miracle. How far does the subjective view meet the moral and religious objections to miracles?*

> Such events as the healing miracles of Jesus had a strong empirical impact, but the hand of God is only visible to faith. Jesus' healings could be seen as examples of miracles, as special events designed to achieve a specific purpose, in this case to show the divine identity of Jesus. The resurrection would be one such miracle. If the Gospel miracles are seen in this light, this may partly explain the relative rarity of such miracles since.

The theistic view that some miracles have a special purpose

The moral and religious objections to miracles are based on the assumption that God continues to 'intervene' in the world in a way similar to how he appeared to intervene in the case of the Gospel miracles. Most religious thinkers today are prepared to accept that this does not normally happen, and see the fact that God does not intervene to stop evil as proof of this. For this reason the non-existence of miracles today is part of *theodicy* (defending God for, say, not stopping the Holocaust). Where miracles are alleged to happen, as for instance in connection with the canonization of saints, theists would argue that it is possible that these are primarily meant to be special signs through which God shows his approval of the saint's life.

> **St John the Evangelist** called Jesus' miracles *signs* performed for a divine purpose. This may also help to explain occasional miracles, such as those 'certified' to have happened in Lourdes.

In the same way Christians believe that some miracles, such as some of those recorded in the Gospels, are *special cases* where miracles are performed by

199

> Above all there is the supreme reported miracle – the Resurrection of Jesus Christ from the dead ... insofar as there is good historical evidence for the physical resurrection of Jesus (as I believe that there is), it is evidence of the occurrence of an event that clearly violates the laws of nature and so calls for an explanation different from the scientific. That is available: God raised Jesus from the dead to signify his acceptance of Christ's atoning sacrifice; to give his stamp of approval to his teaching ...
> *Richard Swinburne*

God for a specific purpose. The raising of Lazarus may be one such, but most would regard the miracle of the resurrection as the classic example. In this case God raised Jesus from the dead for two reasons. First, to put his stamp of approval on the life of Jesus. And second, to show that in raising Jesus from the dead the destiny of all humankind is revealed (see box to left). If this view is taken, then the objection put forward by some (including **Hume**) that miracles belong to the 'distant past' and do not happen today, is answered.

14 Religion and Atheism

- Historical background to modern atheism.
- Theories of religion: economics, psychology and sociology.
- The atheism of Nietzsche.
- Counter arguments to naturalistic theories.
- Counter arguments to religion as illusion.
- Kant's argument against atheism.
- Atheism and human power.

Historical background to modern atheism: God is an imaginary human projection

Atheism (from the Greek *a-theos*) means the rejection of the claim that God exists, and holds that belief in God is either an illusion or a delusion. The early roots of modern atheism may be traceable, with some irony, to **Hegel**, a theology student in Berlin, who had put forward the view that the Absolute, or God, had become 'self-conscious' in man in the course of history. While earlier thinkers like **Aquinas** operated on the assumption that humans and God were separated by different orders of being, Hegel appeared to bring both together so as to make them almost one.

> ***Aquinas*** Man is separated from God as creature to Creator.
>
> ***Hegel*** Man is united to God through his self-consciousness.
>
> ***Feuerbach*** Man's consciousness creates a 'projection' of God.

Hegel claimed he had a precedent. Had not humankind and God come together in the incarnation? For the deep-thinking Hegel the incarnation was a religious illustration of what he was saying in more rationally obtuse philosophic language, that there was an inextricable link between the human and God.

> Hegel laid the seeds of modern atheism by making man the 'bearer' of God. Hegel's ideas were developed in greater detail by later thinkers like Feuerbach, Marx and Freud.

Ludwig Feuerbach, a student of Hegel, argued that since man and God could not be separated, maybe God was a product of the human imagination, and had no independent valid existence at all. Feuerbach dispensed with the whole notion of God, who was simply *'man writ large'*, merely the embodiment of all human hopes and ideals of goodness, power and immortality. God in fact was a 'projection' created by us, onto an imaginary divine figure representing all our own ideal qualities and powers. This paved the way for the idea that God was an illusion.

Economics: the contribution of Marx to modern atheism

Long after **Kant** the onward march of atheism was boosted by powerful thinkers in the fields of politics, sociology, psychology and philology. **Karl Marx** argued that religion was an economic phenomenon. It was both a cause and product of poverty and alienation, first within industry, and ultimately within society at large. Remove poverty, and religion will 'wither away', because people will think less of a future life and concentrate more on this one. Remove religion and the way will be open for us to change society for the better, because the distractions of a comforting, but illusory, belief in a future world of happiness and bliss will eventually give way to a true sense of reality. Marx was later contradicted by **Durkheim** (see below, p. 203), who insisted that religion existed from the earliest societies, and was not dependent on the feelings created by social deprivation.

> **Marx** argued that religion was a product of the social conditions of economic deprivation.

Sociology: religion as a product of humans entering society

The French sociologist **Emile Durkheim** made his own contribution to modern atheism with his view that religion is a product of social forces that went back to primitive times. The supernatural figure of God, who became the focal point of various primitive societies, was in reality an artificial and man-made construct. God had simply usurped the position that should have been occupied by society itself. Human beings' tendency to celebrate their own achievements by looking to a centralizing symbol such as the totem, and later their sense of communal solidarity, led them to 'invent' a God whom they falsely credited with their own human achievements. Because of his acquired position as the father of sociology, Durkheim bequeathed to all later sociologists the standard notion that all religion was false and erroneous.

> **Durkheim** believed that religion could be explained away in terms of primitive social dynamics.

Objections to Durkheim centre on the primitive nature of the evidence he uses, the fact that people are in fact able to distinguish between a religious God and secular forms of human devotion such as patriotic allegiance. There is also the fact that his theories can be neither verified nor falsified. Today his theory has fallen out of favour because it seems to have little bearing on actual religion as it is perceived in the minds of believers. Very few today are prepared to accept that the faith they profess can be traced back, or reduced to, a psychological mistake by primitive tribes.

> **Emile Durkheim**'s theory of religion as a sociological phenomenon is now largely ignored, but at the time it added to the impetus toward explaining religion in naturalistic terms.

RELIGION AND THE CHALLENGE OF ATHEISM

The validity of sociology as explaining particular religious forms and values

Regardless of the shortcomings of Durkheim's analysis, sociological factors have been shown to play a significant part in the particular forms that religion can take in society. The German sociologist **Max Weber** made an important contribution to showing how certain religious beliefs can both influence and be influenced by surrounding social conditions. Weber made no speculations about the truth of religion; he merely pointed out the way religion can be an influential force in society. The so-called Protestant work ethic, for instance, was the product of the Calvinistic teaching on predestination. Those who were influenced by the belief that God had already decided their future fate, either to heaven or hell, turned to the world with a new enthusiasm in the belief that earthly blessings might signal eternal ones as well.

> **Weber** showed how *religion* and *society* have a mutual effect on each other.

Modern examples of how religion can be influenced by social conditions include the way social poverty gave rise to the Liberation Theology movement in Latin America. Such a movement would not so easily arise in conditions of wealth and prosperity. Equally, the example of vibrant religious practice in affluent North America (a phenomenon not allowed for by Marx, who said religion was a product of poverty) could be interpreted either as a sign of awareness of the limitations of material affluence, or the desire to show gratitude to God for material blessings, or a combination of both.

> **Max Weber** took a neutral view of religion, confining his observations to showing how sociological conditions can both affect religion, and be affected by it.

Psychology: the view that religion is an illusion

Sigmund Freud was an Austrian Jew, whose work in solving the problems of neurotic and psychotic subjects led to his fame as the recognized father of

RELIGION AND ATHEISM

psychoanalysis. Framing all his psychological theories within the perspective opened up by **Feuerbach**, he became convinced that religion was an illusory projection based on dreams and wishes, brought in to cover up an otherwise more depressing assessment of human existence. Like Feuerbach he took religion to be a projection of the human imagination, of human hopes and wishes, onto a supernatural figure called God. In doing so Freud added flesh to the bones of Feuerbach's theory by specifying how this projection took hold. Its origin was the Oedipal complex experienced in childhood.

> **Freud** saw religion as an *illusion* meant to alleviate human psychological fears and anxieties.

Humans are not so much influenced by what happens in the economic world of politics and industry, as by what happens much closer to home: during a child's upbringing in his or her own family. It is there that the idea of a father figure arises who is a source of both *comfort* and *unease*. He is a source of comfort as a protector; a source of unease as the enforcer of laws and obligations. From this emerges the idea of a *cosmic father figure* who is an overpowering source of ethical restrictions during life, but who, if *appeased* by religious rituals, also offers the comforts of future immortality. Religion, therefore was a source of wishful thinking and hence an *illusion*. Freud predicted that everyone will eventually shake off religion, and stop practising this 'obsessional neurosis' as they grow towards maturity, and take responsibility for their own lives.

> **Roots of atheism**
>
> ***Hegel*** Man and God are inextricably ***linked*** together.
>
> ***Feuerbach*** God is a ***projectio***n of human powers onto an imaginary God.
>
> ***Marx*** Religion is a false system of belief in another world to ***compensate*** for this one.
>
> ***Durkheim*** Religion is an imaginary ***displacement***, mistaken for society's ideals.
>
> ***Freud*** Religion is an ***illusion*** to allay human fears, and promise wish-fulfilment.

> ***Nietzsche*** Religion is an ***empty*** belief system that holds back human progress.
>
> ***Modern science*** Religion is an ***outdated*** system of trying to explain the world.
>
> *Freud's critique of religion has been highly influential, but his theory of religion as a psychological illusion has serious deficiencies, particularly the fact that it cannot be proved. How might his theory be turned on its head?*

Religion seen as the product of fear and wishful thinking

Freud's more detailed analysis of religion concerned the way it functioned in relation to drives and wishes. He observed two dualisms. The first was between the 'pleasure principle' (wishes for material happiness) and the 'reality principle' (the realization that such wishes often need to be delayed or suspended). The second was between the 'death wish' (aggression) and the 'love wish' (control of aggression through social relationships). Religion functioned in both dualities to offer a 'solution'. The idea of a cosmic *law-giving* father figure helped in the control of human drives such as aggression, and the will to dominate others. A *loving* cosmic father figure satisfied the wish for guaranteed ultimate happiness. This made religion a cure, but it was a 'crooked cure' for human problems, something that appeared real, while it was actually an 'illusion', a false view of reality produced by conflicting drives and wishes.

> Both **Freud** and **Marx** believed religion was ***self-induced***, and so would eventually wither away.

The idea that God is no longer relevant to our future

Friedrich Nietzsche reacted strongly to the idea that God was important for the welfare of humans by boldly declaring the 'death of God'. By this he meant two things. One was what he believed was the conviction of the age, that God was 'dead' as a significant concept in people's minds. Quite simply people had stopped believing in God. The second was a philosophical claim that the notion of an authoritative God was untrue, because it was out of tune with the modern age when people no longer had time for a transcendent authority figure who prevented them from taking responsibility for their own convictions, beliefs and values.

According to **Nietzsche** religion had produced a 'slave morality' dominated by obedience to the authority of God. Such a morality led to the elevation of the poor, the tolerance of the weak, and the forgiveness of the wicked. To overcome the baleful effects of religion over many centuries, Nietzsche argued that man must stand on his own two feet and use his outstanding spiritual possession, his human will, to fully assert himself. He must see through the hypocrisy of the Christian tradition which elevated false values such as kindness, tolerance, humility and love. In its place there must be a new and ruthless project: to replace the weak morality of the past and establish the reign of the strong. Self-assertion must replace humility; aggressive striving for power must replace tolerance of the weak and the mediocre; the supremacy of the strong must replace weak-willed love of neighbour. This, for Nietzsche, was the only route to the creation of the 'superman' in whose hands lay the ultimate salvation of the human race.

> **Nietzsche** believed that religion was belief in a God that was dead. Such a belief was outdated, and a brake on man's striving for supremacy, and his destiny to be the 'superman'.

Nietzsche's realism: his awareness of the provisional need for religion

Despite his arrogance in calling for the overthrow of religion and its supposedly anti-human effects, Nietzsche was keenly aware of its importance in the interim. He was aware of the moral vacuum that **Darwin** threatened to create with his exposure of the apparently blind biological origins of human life. A mechanical world of chance could only lead to such a vacuum. It could also lead to what Nietzsche both feared and advocated, *nihilism*. The nihilism he advocated was the overthrow of traditional morality, but that which he feared was the rejection of all morality in the process. In this light both Darwin and religion posed the same threat: both were enemies of his own project of *moral revival*. But religion would be useful in warding off the danger of a complete moral collapse until such time as its replacement took effect. Many would say that, in the light of history, he was both remarkably shrewd but hopelessly optimistic.

> **Darwin** Humankind is a product of blind evolution, and will have to live with the implications of this.
>
> **Nietzsche** Human origins may be blind, but we have to create our own values now and for the future.

Assessment of atheistic claims

Christian thinkers reply to the charges of Nietzsche

Many of the responses to modern atheism have centred on the claims of Nietzsche that God is (and should be) dead. Religious thinkers have pointed out that Nietzsche, with his view of Christianity as promoting a 'slave morality', has overlooked the power of religion as a dynamic source of significant social and moral change. The Christian philosopher-theologian **Paul Tillich** argued that far from religion being an obstacle to moral progress, it provided a spiritual dynamic that enabled men and women to have the existential 'courage to be' in the best sense. Religion enabled a person to reach beyond himself by its basic principle that God must be the focus of life as our 'ultimate concern'. All other 'concerns' such as wealth, fame or power were trivial (and proved to be trivial) by comparison. Such worldly concerns only lured people towards pursuits that were futile, empty and socially disintegrating, or in biblical terminology, idolatrous. In this way religion helped prevent us from being lured by such false concerns, and revealed to us values that were enduring and ultimate.

> It is as meaningless to assert the non-existence, as to assert the existence of God.
>
> A. J. Ayer

> ***Tillich*** Christianity has the dynamic to promote the highest values for human existence.
>
> ***Chesterton*** Christianity has proved it has the capacity to fight against evil, sometimes physically.
>
> ***Nietzsche*** Humankind is morally degenerate because Christianity created a slave morality of obedience and passivity.

G. K. Chesterton, who wrote of the paradoxes and apparent contradictions of the Christian faith, found Nietzsche oblivious to the other side of the coin: the forceful and aggressive side of Christianity. The monks and saints whom Nietzsche derided for their submissive meekness and humility were the very ones who were criticized for preaching the Crusades, and for their ruthlessness in putting down internal revolts in the Church. Could this be the same Christianity that was accused of a 'slave morality' that took on the Saracens; and was later accused of 'causing wars'; damned for the killing of heretics; and held responsible for being the main cause of social conflicts and divisions? Jesus, he noticed, who spoke on many things, never condemned war, and was always 'nice to Roman soldiers'! Nietzsche was conveniently silent on these matters.

> **Nietzsche's moral claims**
>
> ***Nietzsche*** Moral ideals should not be held captive to belief in a God that was dead.
>
> ***Theists*** Moral ideals are based on reason, revelation and the fear of God.
>
> ***Secularists*** Morality is based on reason, and the general welfare of humanity.
>
> Nietzsche represents the atheistic view that morality should be left to humans. Theists would claim that if morality is left to humans, they might make moral rules that are not fair to all. A regime that recognizes the existence of God is, a priori, more likely to be bound by the laws of such a God, while regimes that reject the existence of God are more likely to create their own rules. They would claim that this has been shown to

> be historically true in the case of atheistic regimes under Hitler, Stalin, Mao, Pol Pot, and atheistic regimes in the USSR up to recent times. In the light of this, theists would say that Nietzsche's bid to 'free' morality from religion is badly misguided.

Reply of theists to the theory of Freud

Theists may draw on a number of responses to atheistic claims that religion is false. With regard to Freud's theory, it may be argued in the first place that an *illusion* is consistent with what *could* be the case, and is not as devastating a critique as might be supposed. Freud was discreet enough not to call religion a *delusion*, which is an impression of what is not the case. A delusion normally denotes a condition in which a person is hopelessly out of touch with reality. An illusion, by contrast, is something that appears to be very much in line with reality. Besides, the lesser claim that religion is an illusion implies not only that it is not a delusion, but grants that it does fit in with how people can legitimately see the world. The appearance of an oasis in the desert may be an illusion or it may be real. It is impossible to know at first sight.

> **Freud** called religion an ***illusion*** rather than a ***delusion***. What was the difference?

When it comes to religion there is no possibility of an immediate confirmation of whether it is an illusion or a reality, but theists would insist that the option to believe that it is the latter rather than the former is the nature of faith. Many see **John Hick**'s proposal of eschatological (afterlife) verification as a provisional answer to Freud's claims, but the question would remain for non-theists whether such future verification might also be illusory. **Pascal** conceded that religion could not be rationally proved true to an unbeliever, for which reason he proposed that a wager on religion being true was the best bet.

> A desert oasis is the classic image of an illusion caused by heat. But an illusion cannot be confirmed at first sight. How far did Freud allow for the possibility, if not the likelihood, that religion was true?

The view that religion comes from revelation, not from the inner psyche

Freud's claim that religion is false was based on his idea that religion emerged from the psyche as a problem-solving device. But many would claim that religion in its major forms comes from *outside* the psyche in the form of experiences variously described as revelatory, numinous or mystical (see above, p. 199). While Freud may be right that humans are psychologically vulnerable to religion, and subject to its attractions, many would argue that his theory fails to take into account the factual nature of religion as it is perceived by followers of the major faiths. It seems beyond dispute that followers of these faiths understand religion as something they are confronted by on the strength of historical events they see as bearing witness to God's existence. In contrast to Freud, his colleague **Jung** saw religion as essentially a product of an experience which dominated the psyche.

Theories of religion

Psychological theory Religion is generated from *within* the psyche under the pressure of psychological forces originating from experiences within the family (Freud).

Alternative theory Religion arises from an experience of the transcendent (Jung).

Revelation theory Religion in its western forms is based on revelatory experiences, and something that comes from *outside* the psyche, and perceived as *confronting* it.

Theists would argue that Freud's theory leads to a form of 'auto-religion', something induced by infantile fears. Such a theory sits uneasily beside the fact that religion, and religious projects, were embraced by people who (sometimes unwillingly) felt themselves confronted by experiences of the supernatural. As a result they felt 'called' to leave their 'comfort zones' and act as spokesmen for God. This was true in the case of **Moses** and many of the prophets. They would also argue that examples from mystics and famous religious converts (like **Paul** and **Augustine**) show that their religious commitment was more likely to have resulted from their experiences of the transcendent, rather

> **The non-existence of God**
> - The *economics* argument: religion is the enemy of social progress (Marx).
> - The *psychological* argument: religion is an illusion based on false wishes (Freud).
> - The *sociological* argument: religion is a mistaken substitute for human society (Durkheim).
> - The *human development* argument: religion prevents proper moral development (Nietzsche).
> - The *evolutionary* argument: things evolved naturally showing no need for God (Darwin).
> - The *modern social* argument: religion is a negative influence in society (Dawkins).
> - The *existence of evil* argument: evil, often caused by religion, disproves the existence of God.

than from some inner drive to solve their emotional problems. **William James** saw that religion can have a galvanizing or integrating effect on the personality, drawing individuals out of themselves, rather than leaving them neurotically impaired. He saw religion as a positive force that gave added dynamism to its recipient, and he saw no evidence that it was linked to a 'degenerative brain', or that it was necessarily linked to emotional maladjustment. If religion functions in this way, then it stands in sharp contrast to a theory which suggests that it will eventually die away when people grow mature enough to see through its illusions.

The possibility that religion is real, not illusory

The alternative to Freud's theory is of course the possibility that what appears an illusion turns out to be real. If religion is so attractive (Freud recognized that it was a 'powerful phenomenon', something he couldn't explain) because it offers to 'solve' so many psychological problems (such as neurotic fears and anxieties about life), why, the theist will ask, is it not possible that it may be true? **Kierkegaard**, we may remember, argued that religion (specifically Christianity) is true because it does exactly this, but not in the way Freud suggested. He believed that religious faith makes it possible to see life, not as meaningless and anxiety-ridden, but as having an ultimate worth. But where Freud saw religion as arising from *within* us, from human fears and wishes, Kierkegaard saw it as coming from *outside* us. It may suit us to have religious faith, but in its Christian form it owed nothing to what humans thought about themselves. Far from being something that could be 'invented' by the human imagination, its source was transcendent. It came from 'beyond' human life as something he called 'unexpected', 'strange', 'paradoxical' and, by the canons of human reasoning, 'absurd'.

> **Freud** We **generate** religious beliefs to solve our emotional problems.
>
> **Kierkegaard** Religion also comes from **historical** events that could never be presumed likely.

Religion seen as an obstacle to the wish for earthly freedom and fulfilment

In response to the Freudian theory of religion, theists have raised the question of who is to decide where the wishful thinking is really going on. Turning back on Freud the notorious ambiguities and ambivalences of the psychology that he exploited so well, perhaps the whole of his religious theory is itself an exercise in wishful thinking. The modern declaration that 'God is dead', it can be argued, is a potentially perfect candidate for wishful thinking, because it fits in so well with the unrestrained character of modern secular liberalism.

> We all have reason to fear the judgements of God, and to wish away the existence of a divine judge.
> *Anthony Kenny*

While Freud opened up important vistas regarding the inner workings of religious faith, and showed how faith can often be driven by narcissistic and unworthy motives, theists could claim that he leaves himself open to the charge of arrogance in selectively applying the terms 'illusion' and 'wishful thinking' to the soft target of religion. Why not argue instead that it is just too much the spirit of the modern age to wish that no God exists who might hold us responsible for the consequences of such wishful thinking (see box above)? If this is true then Freud's theory is turned on its head, and the illusion is not that God exists but that he doesn't!

RELIGION AND THE CHALLENGE OF ATHEISM

Views of religion

- Humans turn away from religion because of selfish pride (Calvin).
- God is dead and religion is false (Nietzsche).
- God is an imaginary (illusory) solution to human problems (Freud).
- It might be desirable that God does not exist since then everything is permitted (Dostoevsky).

*In the light of what **Pascal** said, that most people are more interested in hunting, gambling and having a good time than in religion, how would you assess the relationship of religion to wishful thinking?*

15 The Challenge to Religious Language

- Logical positivism and religious language.
- Verification and falsification.
- The limitations of the positivist view of meaning.
- Language games theory.
- The grammar of religious language.
- Limitations of language games theory.
- Parables and the justification of religious language.

Logical positivism: religious language as meaningless because it cannot be verified

The atheistic challenge to religion, based on the metaphysical theory of *positivism*, was later extended to the domain of *language*. Positivism is a world view in which only empirically testable truth-claims about the world of facts (or facts about the world) are accepted as meaningful. If this is the case, only empirically verifiable truth-claims can be put into words, that is, written or spoken about. This view is called logical positivism, a branch of philosophy which began on the continent but was popularized in England in the 1930s by **A. J. Ayer**. The term positivism derives from the claim that only things which can be shown, or 'posited' as belonging to the world of sense, can be said to exist. Positivism is naturally linked to science which is exclusively concerned with the empirical world of sense experience, and is the classic embodiment of the positivist outlook. Another name for logical positivism could be 'language positivism', since it is about limiting language to the empirical world of material facts (see also the similar challenge to *ethical language* below, p. 259).

> **Auguste Comte** is regarded as the father of positivism, and the grandfather of logical positivism.
>
> ***Positivism*** The view that the only *reality* is what can be empirically experienced.
>
> ***Logical positivism*** The view that the only reality that can be meaningfully *spoken about* is that which can be empirically experienced.

In linguistic philosophy there are only two valid kinds of statement: synthetic and analytic (from synthesis, putting together, and analysis, pulling apart). An analytic statement is true by analysis of terms, for example, 'All spinsters are unmarried women'. More significant is a synthetic statement, one which can be demonstrated to have meaning because its truth can be proved or disproved by the scientific method of observation, experimentation and testing. By this yardstick religious statements are neither analytic nor synthetic, and consequently are *meaningless*. They are meaningless because no scientific test is possible to establish their truth or falsity, that is, no test by which they can be empirically verified. The catchword of the logical positivists was 'verification', and their guiding light was what was called the 'verification principle', the essence of which we have just outlined.

> **A. J. Ayer** formulated the ***verification principle*** by which only those statements are meaningful that are either analytic, or empirically verifiable. Ayer later allowed verification to include statements that could possibly be verified. Historical statements were a problem, but statements of metaphysics and religion can never be verified, and so are meaningless. (See also the falsification principle below.)

Problems with the verification principle

The initial impact of logical positivism appeared to discredit religious language. Any language that expressed truth-claims that could be neither verified nor falsified seemed to incur the ban imposed by the limitations of logical positivism. Religion speaks of 'God existing in heaven', 'God loving us', and claims, 'Jesus is our redeemer and saviour', 'eternal life awaits us'. But such statements all seem immune to events in the world, and appear to remain consistent with whatever happens; and crucially, they cannot be empirically verified or falsified. But theists pointed out that there are some scientific statements that can be neither verified nor falsified and yet are meaningful. For instance, 'the stars continued to shine before human beings existed' is meaningful, even though there could be no way of knowing whether it is true or false.

> According to logical positivists, for a statement to be **meaningful**, it must be possible in principle to show that it is **true** or **false**. Theists could reply that statements about God are at least possibly true, in which case they could claim to be **possibly** meaningful.
>
> *How far does the verification principle allow for possible truth?*

Despite its confident claims about the definition of meaning, the verification principle itself came under scrutiny about its own precise status. It was soon pointed out that if the verification principle itself can neither be verified nor falsified it must be a covert statement of, of all things, metaphysics, since it implied a view about what constitutes (or limits) reality. If reality is limited to what can be empirically experienced, and hence verified or falsified, this would have important implications for certain aspects of human experience. For instance, it would rule out all statements about *aesthetics* and *morality*, both areas of considerable significance to human life. (See more on art above, p. 102, and morality below, p. 259.)

> The verification principle was an expression of confidence in the truth-claims of **science**.
>
> *But how far is it true that the verification principle is really stating a **metaphysical** principle?*

RELIGION AND THE CHALLENGE OF ATHEISM

The verification principle would rule out all statements about *art* and the human experience of beauty. No scientific test is possible, say, to prove or disprove that the *Mona Lisa* is a work of art and an object of aesthetic appreciation, beyond the testimony of people the world over who *say* that it is. And it would also rule out all statements about human *emotions* such as love, hatred, fear, courage, and so on. A declaration of love for one's girlfriend becomes meaningless because there is no decisive evidence that would verify or falsify it. This to most people is patent nonsense. Many declarations of love may be meaningful (and true) even though no empirical evidence can be brought to support them. For example, a soldier who wants to fight for his country may appear not to love his girlfriend, but this does not follow. A parent who disciplines his child may appear not to love him, but in fact may claim that discipline is a manifestation of love.

> Many areas of life have **meaning** to people even though they cannot be empirically verified.
>
> *But how far is it the case that in human relations people are often more likely to rely on* **trust**, *than demand* **verification**, *and why is this?*

Thus it appears that the logical positivists had narrowed down reality so severely that they ruled out important areas of experience that could not be fitted into the straitjacket they had designed. By claiming that only what could be supported by clear empirical evidence was meaningful, they failed to take account of other areas of reality that had important significance for human life. Art and the world of the aesthetic; human relationships and the world of the emotions; human behaviour and the world of morality, were all outside the bounds of the verification principle. In the light of this, theists found new voice in claiming that *religion*, despite being another area of reality that lay outside the verificationist straitjacket, could equally not be dismissed as meaningless.

> **Human concerns**
>
> ***Facts*** Important for knowing about the objective world.
>
> ***Values*** A key aspect of human life, to do with what people see as important.

THE CHALLENGE TO RELIGIOUS LANGUAGE

> ***Opinions*** Play an important role in how people see the world as individuals.
>
> ***Judgements*** Represent the human capacity to assess facts and values.
>
> ***Beliefs*** Convictions and views about things that go beyond experience.
>
> *How far could it be said that the logical positivists were only concerned with what should count as facts, and were dismissive of other areas of human life?*

It appears that the logical positivists had failed to take account of the full complexities of human life. To use the analogy of a swimming pool: the world of provable 'facts' could be said to be the more shallow end of the pool that is human existence. The deep end is that which contains the aspects of life which are not so easily measured by empirical evidence, those that come under the heading of values. Above all, the verificationists seemed to ignore the functioning of trust, something which is frequently used in everyday life as a more normal basis of meaning than strict empirical evidence. **Plato** had said that the more profound aspects of life are to do with *spiritual* things: such as truth, goodness, justice, courage, beauty, and the like. If this is the case, human language can validly speak of realities that are not strictly amenable to empirical testing, as the logical positivists had claimed.

> **Unverifiable but meaningful**
>
> ***Love*** Love between human beings is meaningful but cannot be empirically verified.
>
> ***Beauty*** A meaningful perception than cannot be empirically verified.
>
> ***Morality*** The idea of right or wrong, good or bad, is meaningful but cannot be empirically verified.
>
> ***Religion*** The claim that God's existence is meaningful but cannot be empirically verified.
>
> *How far do the logical positivists give the impression that life could not be lived without adherence to the verification principle?*

RELIGION AND THE CHALLENGE OF ATHEISM

Language games theory in the justification of religious language

Ludwig Wittgenstein was one of the most famous philosophers of the first half of the twentieth century. His ideas triggered the formation of the Vienna Circle in 1920, from which emerged logical positivism. Early in his career he had been largely sympathetic to the ideas of the logical positivists, but later he began to recognize the wider uses of language. He came to see that meaning came from the way language was used in ordinary life, and that it could not be fitted into a pre-formed 'empirical' cast, as he and the positivists had tried to do. In other words you could not begin with a preconceived idea of what was meaningful, and what was not. Many things were meaningful to people even if they could not be empirically verified, as we have just seen.

> **Language games**
>
> People use language in a variety of ways, similar to the way people play a variety of games. In each case the 'rules of the game' are agreed on by those who play that game.
>
> In religion, it is suggested, believers play by rules agreed among themselves concerning their values and beliefs, and therefore the language of religion is meaningful to them.
>
> *But how realistically could theists object that, if God exists, their beliefs are valid also for those who are not 'part of the game'?*

Wittgenstein thus opened the door to the possibility that other areas of life which did not easily fit neatly into the empiricist's framework could still be spoken about meaningfully. The idea hit on Wittgenstein (it is said, during a football match) that as there were many different ball games, there were also many language games. Language games referred to the different uses to which language is put. Language can be used for asking questions, making jokes, stating rules, forming judgements, telling stories, relating facts, and so on. There is scientific language, mythical language, factual language, moral language, poetic language – and religious language. Each language has its own rules of interpretation, and must be understood from within the 'life situation' in which it is used. It would be wrong to interpret one language according to the rules of another. In particular, it was claimed, it would be wrong to interpret religious language according to the rules governing language about empirical realities.

> **Language games theory**
>
> This allows that religion, and religious language, are meaningful *within* the 'form of life' (believing community) of those participating in it. Those outside that form of life cannot criticize the concepts, or the reality, of which it speaks.
>
> *But how far is this view acceptable to theists?*

Religious language as having a special meaning to believers

Another approach to the meaning of religious language was developed by the modern thinker D. Z. Phillips on the strength of Wittgenstein's language games theory. If religious language is taken literally, the impression is given that God is a 'matter of fact', another fact on top of all the facts we come to know about in the world. This would be to misunderstand the nature of God, and the language we use to speak of him. If we ask, for instance, whether this or that physical object exists, we are looking for a factual answer. A deeper question would be, 'What kind of reality is the reality of a physical object?' or 'What does it mean for a physical object to exist?'

> **D. Z. Phillips** warned that religious language could not be understood according to the norms, or rules, of ordinary language. To do so would be to misunderstand its mystical nature, which is not to convey knowledge of ordinary 'facts'.
>
> *But how far is this theory only helpful to theists?*

It is this kind of question, says Phillips, which provides the key to understanding religious language about God. This takes religious language therefore to a deeper and more sophisticated level than ordinary language about empirical facts. For Phillips it is a matter of understanding the *grammar* of religious statements. The key question is, 'What kind of reality is divine reality?' The issue is not whether God exists, but in *what sense* he exists, considering *what kind* of reality he has, or is. It is therefore a logical mistake to speak of (either affirm or deny) God's existence, as if God were part of the vast constellation of facts that we come to know about within the world. Many, however, would say that the problem with this proposal is that it may be helpful to theists in reminding them of the unique nature of religious beliefs, but it fails to show why religious beliefs should claim to be meaningful if they cannot be empirically verified.

> Phillips claimed that religious language had a peculiar 'grammar' compared to empirical statements.
>
> *But while this can be agreed among theists, how far does it beg the question for atheists, and therefore how far does it overcome the problems of religious language being called meaningless because it is not verifiable?*

The limitations of language games theory

Theists would agree that religion stands or falls on whether God exists or not. If God exists religion is true, if not it is untrue. But if language games theory is an exhaustive account of the meaning of God or religion, it would be unacceptable to theists. This is because it attempts to locate these notions exclusively within the subjective minds of religious people. God and religion thus become 'prisoners of the mind'. As a result religion loses its traditional cosmic seriousness, and becomes the product of an agreed 'language game' played by believers. In this view, if people say that God exists, or does not exist, then he does or does not (for them) exist. But for traditional believers God cannot be adequately described as a factor within their subjective awareness. According to revelation God is not only objectively real, but objectively the 'most real' being there is; in medieval terminology, the *ens realissimum*.

> ***Theists*** Religious language is about truths of reality, and cannot be reduced to a subjective language game played by theists among themselves.
>
> ***Atheists*** Religious language is meaningless because it can be neither verified nor falsified.

At the same time theists would have to accept that if by the standards of empiricism religious language is meaningless, this might be at least a provisional solution to how it could be seen as meaningful.

THE FALSIFICATION DEBATE

The later addition of the falsification principle

> **Anthony Flew** borrowed the falsification principle from science, where an hypothesis that cannot in principle be falsified is considered meaningless.

The meaning of religious language was further brought under question by **Anthony Flew**, who went on to introduce the so-called 'falsification principle'. Thus, if a truth-claim could not be falsified, that is, proved false, it could not claim to be meaningful. Thus the statement 'all leopards have spots' is meaningful because it can be tested by experience, and shown to be true as far as we know. The possible discovery one day of a leopard with no spots would falsify the above statement. Indeed all scientific rules and generalizations are always, strictly speaking, provisional, since one day they might be falsified.

> *Verification* An experience, experiment or other test by which a fact, or allegation, is shown to be true. Example: fingerprints or DNA can *verify* that a subject was at the scene of a crime.
>
> *Falsification* An experience, experiment or other test in virtue of which an alleged fact is shown to be false. A proven alibi can *falsify* the allegation that a subject was at the scene of a crime.
>
> **Flew** holds that theists will allow nothing to falsify their belief that God exists. Therefore religious claims are 'mere utterances' and so are meaningless. Responding to Flew, some have pointed out that the experience of life *could theoretically* falsify religious beliefs, but doesn't, while others take the view that religious beliefs will at least be falsified in the *future*, if untrue (see **Wisdom**, **Mitchell** and **Hick** below).

RELIGION AND THE CHALLENGE OF ATHEISM

Flew found that, in this respect, religion contrasted poorly with science, because unlike science it made assertions that can never be falsified. For instance, the assertion 'God exists' can never be shown to be false. No matter what happens in the world, whether good or bad, the believer will still insist that God both 'watches over us' and 'loves us'. Because of this, Flew concluded that religious assertions are no more than 'utterances' and are indeed meaningless. However, religious thinkers have pointed out that the same argument can be used in regard to the non-existence of God. To assert that God does not exist is an assertion that non-theists are not prepared to allow to be falsified, in the same way that theists are alleged not to do regarding their assertions. Like the theist, non-theists use all sorts of qualifications to defend their beliefs. As a result such assertions 'die the death of a thousand qualifications' and are rendered, by Flew's logic, to be also 'mere utterances', and meaningless by empirical standards.

> ***God exists*** This is an assertion that theists are supposed to hold on to despite any evidence that might falsify it (such as the existence of evil).
>
> ***God does not exist*** This is the corresponding assertion made by atheists. But equally they do not allow any evidence to count that might falsify it (such as the existence of religious faith, and the rational and experiential reasons by which it is defended by theists).
>
> *In both cases evidence is selected to defend the assertion (flowers or weeds). But in both cases there is no possibility of falsification, since each interprets the evidence to suit themselves. This highlights the existence of a prior faith in both cases, what Hare called a blik. If this is the case, how far should the falsification theory also be applied to atheistic assertions about religion?*

For some, this verification could be established on the basis of religiously inspired behaviour, something that can be seen by others. For others, it could be established by pointing to empirical factors in the world that can be seen as evidence for God's existence, such as certain features in nature. For others, it could be established by pointing to the way trust operates between human beings, especially when there are reasons both to affirm and to doubt the justification of that trust. For others, religious language could be justified on the basis of trust in its future verification. But we begin by looking at an approach which goes back to the claims of religious experience.

> **Wittgenstein** pointed out that religion can be neither rationally proved nor disproved.

The idea that mystical awareness is a basis for religious language

Wittgenstein himself became aware in the end that there were indeed aspects of life that were very real, but could not be put neatly into words. He believed that life itself had a certain mysterious quality that many people were aware of, and that somehow pointed beyond the fact-based world of science. Wittgenstein called this the mystical. An inkling of what he meant can be obtained from just wondering about the fact that there is 'something rather than nothing', as **Leibniz** had put it. For Wittgenstein it was not 'how the world is, but *that* it is'. This he called 'the mystical'.

> It is not how the world is, but that it is, that is the mystical . . . There are indeed things that cannot be put into words. They make themselves manifest. They are what is mystical.
>
> *Wittgenstein*

The mystical is a sense of awe (the numinous?) which goes with a certain level of awareness about things, but it is an elusive kind of awareness that cannot be pinned down and spoken about in precise terms. Wittgenstein included in the mystical not only the sense of why things should be at all, but certain profound levels of awareness such as those aroused by music, art, memories, and the profound feelings associated with nostalgia. From this it might be suggested that such deep perceptions are very close to the awareness that lies at the root of religion (see also Otto, p. 215). Wittgenstein recognized that when people ask profound questions like 'Why are we here?' or 'How could this happen?' or 'Why me?' they are not asking for causal explanations of the kind that science might provide. They are expressing an awareness of the mystical, an awareness of something that is perceived to be real, but which it is beyond the power of words to express. This implied that reality cannot be limited to what could be 'clearly spoken about' as the logical positivists had maintained.

> **Wittgenstein** called questions like 'Why are we here?' *mystical* questions.
>
> *How far can the legitimacy of such questions be equated with religious questions?*

The use of parables to illustrate how religious faith is falsifiable in theory but not in practice

The problem of showing philosophically whether religious language had meaning continued to engage thinkers in the wake of the falsification challenge. Some thinkers turned to *parables* to show that religious faith is not something which is unfalsifiable. It may be falsifiable in theory, but not in practice, because there is always sufficient evidence to maintain the trust that religious believers rely on. This trust is supported in particular by the ambiguity of many empirical aspects of the world. Such aspects are often open to *interpretation*, and some parables illustrate how faith is an interpretation which looks to certain features of the world that appear to justify it (see human existence, the teleological argument, and miracles). In some cases the aim was to show how faith is able to survive opposing interpretations of the world, and how *trust* can be maintained in spite of doubts. Others have taken a different line, showing that faith is not meaningless despite being unfalsifiable, because its empirical effects can be seen.

> The purpose of the parables is to show that if religious faith can be shown to be a justified interpretation of the world, then it is not meaningless. Hare's 'blik' parable argues that faith is not meaningless because it has empirical effects in terms of people's attitudes and behaviour.

THE CHALLENGE TO RELIGIOUS LANGUAGE

Faith as an inner blik that is unfalsifiable but is still meaningful

The parable is told by **R. M. Hare**, who originally held the view that religious language was meaningless, but came round to believe that it was meaningful to believers because it affected their life and behaviour. (**R. B. Braithwaite** developed this view further by claiming that the meaningfulness of religious language lay in the way religious faith affected people's moral outlook and behaviour, supported by the edifying stories of Scripture.) Hare proposed that faith was a blik, or conviction, that could never be shaken by whatever happens in the world. He told the parable of a university student who was convinced that all dons were out to murder him. Nothing would shake his belief. If the dons were acting suspiciously he was confirmed in his belief; if they were nice to him it was a sign that they were being hypocritical. Belief in God is similar to a blik, argued Hare, not only because it is unshakeable, but because it affects people's lives.

> ***Hare*** Religious faith is set of beliefs (bliks) which, because it affects people's attitudes, feelings and behaviour, is meaningful in that sense.
>
> ***Braithwaite*** Religious faith is meaningful because it is about being committed to a certain way of life. The evidence of this commitment is enough to make religious language meaningful in that sense.

Faith as an outlook that finds patterns in the world that justify it

John Wisdom's parable of the Garden is aimed to show that faith is consistent with patterns found in the world, and is therefore not an irrational world view. The parable is about two people who return to a long-neglected garden to find some plants, together with some weeds. Since the plants are vigorous, one says a gardener must have come to tend them from time to time. The other disagrees, pointing to the weeds as evidence that no gardener comes. The parable is meant to illustrate how the believer looks to patterns in the world which support belief in God, while the non-believer similarly looks to patterns which seem to contradict such belief. The result may be a stalemate, but the parable makes the point that faith is not without regard for some evidence from the world to support its credibility. Crucially, for Wisdom, religious belief may be non-cognitive, but it is such that believers are sufficiently convinced of its truth that it makes a difference to their lives. In this sense it is non-falsifiable but meaningful.

> **The parable of the garden**
>
> ***Wisdom*** The garden is a normal garden, but long-neglected. The plants point to a gardener (God), the weeds point to no gardener. The evidence is ambiguous, but there is *some* evidence for the belief that there is a gardener, and because of this the belief is not falsified in practice. The believer has therefore *reason* for his beliefs, and they become justifiably meaningful to their lives.
>
> ***Flew*** The garden is in a jungle clearing, an unlikely setting for a garden. The evidence is loaded in favour of there being no gardener (God). The believer is therefore not justified in his beliefs because he *refuses* to have them falsified.
>
> In one case the evidence is conclusive, showing that religious belief is not justified, and is therefore meaningless. In the other case the evidence is ambiguous, but justifies religious belief, and by implication religious claims.

Anthony Flew adapted this parable for a different purpose by setting it in a jungle clearing which contains flowers and weeds. Flew's aim is to show that evidence from the world points one way only: to the non-existence of God. A similar debate ensues with one witness claiming that a gardener must come while the other insists there is none. The clearing is then subjected to a test with the placing of watchtowers, barbed-wire fencing and dogs. Still no gardener is seen. But the believer remains unmoved, claiming that the gardener is invisible. In this way, says Hare, faith in God is meaningless, because it is made consistent with all states of affairs. 'What is the difference', he asks, 'between an invisible gardener for which there is no evidence, and no gardener at all?' The believer may reply, however, that Flew takes Wisdom's parable to the point of absurdity. Theists would point out that although the

THE CHALLENGE TO RELIGIOUS LANGUAGE

empirical test for a gardener in such an unlikely place as the jungle can produce predictably negative results, believers see real evidence for God not only in certain aspects of nature (such as its beauty), but in the very mystery that nature exists at all.

> **Flew** believed that faith was meaningless because it allowed nothing to count *against* it. But **Wisdom** argued that believers have reasons for holding that some things count *for* it.

Faith as an option based on trust in its future confirmation

The orientation of faith to the future, and the importance of trust, are the aspects of religious faith which are illustrated by **John Hick**'s parable of the Celestial City, a parable borrowed from **John Bunyan**'s *Pilgrim's Progress*. Two men are on the road to an unknown destination. One believes that the road leads nowhere, the other that it leads to the Celestial City. They both walk the same road but have different expectations; and each has different interpretations of what happens on the road. Hardships on the road are seen by one as misfortunes and bad luck, by the other as trials of worthiness in preparation for the final destination. Only when they reach the end of the road will the truth be finally revealed.

Hick's parable is often used to illustrate the principle of 'eschatological verification', but it can also be used as an illustration of 'eschatological falsification'. This is the claim that one day the truth or otherwise of religious faith will finally be known. The parable is a fair illustration of how faith colours the believer's interpretation of all the stages on the road of life in the here and now, as well as his or her expectation that life leads to an afterlife. It equally illustrates how the believer and the unbeliever differ essentially on how each interprets the same events. There can be no final resolution of the differences between the two travellers until the end of the road is reached. That indeed, the believer would agree, makes the parable a good illustration of the trustful and forward-looking nature of faith.

> **Parable of the two travellers**
>
> ***The theist*** The road leads to the Celestial City. All difficulties on the road are trials and obstacles which the traveller has to endure to become worthy to reach his heavenly destination.
>
> ***The atheist*** There is no evidence that the road leads anywhere. All roads are full of trials and misfortunes which are part of life, and show that there is nothing else.
>
> If the believer can justify his beliefs in the expectation of their future confirmation, then, it is claimed, he can speak meaningfully about them. But the parable can also be used to illustrate how faith can possibly be falsified in the future, if untrue.

Faith as firm trust despite the ambivalence of events

A final parable illustrating how trust is an essential part of faith is told by **Basil Mitchell**. In this parable, set in wartime, a resistance fighter meets a mysterious stranger who comes to visit him and with whom he spends the night in earnest conversation. The stranger tells him he is on the side of the resistance. He must continue to believe this, and trust the stranger, even though at times the stranger will be a double agent, sometimes appearing to help the enemy, at other times appearing on the side of the resistance. The parable illustrates how faith can sometimes be a severe test. Events in the world (like evil) will often appear to undermine the believer's faith, but there is no alternative in the believer's mind but to maintain trust despite what happens.

> **Mitchell** believes that faith is a realistic option that involves a justifiable personal ***trust***, even in the face of reasons that ***could*** undermine that trust, but never ***decisively*** do so.

Mitchell's parable illustrates the fact that events in the world can theoretically falsify a believer's faith, but in practice nothing in the world ever '*counts decisively*' for the believer to give up his faith. This is indeed something that believers can identify with. Their faith may be tested by events in the world, but there is also a buoyancy to faith which comes from the conviction that there are continuing reasons for trust in its truth. Believers might find the parable weak in one respect. The traditional model of faith is not the lonely individual, but the individual immersed in a wider community, the community of faith. Unlike the lonely partisan, the believer is buoyed up by the knowledge that his trust has stood the test of time, and continues to be shared by many millions of fellow believers.

> **The resistance worker**
>
> Like the partisan in the parable who is told to trust the stranger no matter what happens, the believer is committed to ***trust*** in the truth of faith. It is not blind trust, because he has ***reasons*** for maintaining it. While it casts faith as a lonely option, the parable shows that trust in others is an important aspect not only of religious faith, but of life itself. If this is so, then it is meaningful for the believer to defend faith as a justified option in his interpretation of life.

In the end, the challenge to religious language has established that its status is *non-cognitive* if measured against the restrictions imposed by the logical positivists. The non-cognitive nature of religious language has been widely accepted by religious thinkers, but not in the sense that it brings no new knowledge of reality. They would claim that it is cognitive in a deeper sense, and about a deeper level of reality than that which characterizes empirical knowledge, or factual knowledge, and more about convictions, feelings, intuitions, attitudes, and the influence of conscience, in choosing how life is to be understood.

Part 4 Religion and Human Behaviour

16 Religion and Ethics

- Ethics as social conventions or objectively real.
- Religious and secular ethics.
- Kantian ethics.
- Utilitarian ethics.
- Christian ethics.
- Natural law ethics.
- Situation ethics.
- Ethical language.

Ethics as an essential component of all religions

All religions have an ethical code, and believers see this ethical code as an essential element of faith. Christians see the moral life as part of relationship to God, which is the essence of faith. **St Paul** presented the moral life in religious terms by making it an *'ethic of response'* to God in gratitude for the redemption brought about by Jesus Christ through his death and resurrection. From a religious perspective all ethical principles ultimately stand for the will of God, and may be perceived as *divine commands*, although this has to be carefully understood (see below). All this helps to distinguish *religious* ethics from *secular* ethics. Secular ethics is based solely on reason, and morality, as **Hume** held, is that which comes about through *human convention*. In this view morality is a human construct, the

> Ethics is the enquiry into what is valuable, or, into what is really important, or . . . into the meaning of life; or into what makes life worth living.
>
> *Wittgenstein*

235

aim of which is to serve the interests of people through the enactment of moral rules. These are normally enshrined in civil law for the purpose of creating an orderly and just society.

> ***Religious ethics*** Standards or principles of behaviour seen in relation to the will of God. God's will can be found in Scripture (for example, the Decalogue), or deduced from reason (natural law), or both.
>
> ***Secular ethics*** Ethics seen from a rational perspective, and based on reason alone, such as Kantian or utilitarian ethics.
>
> *In practice there is considerable overlap between the **content** of religious and secular ethics, but in what respects are they likely to have considerable differences?*

Secular ethics seen as a matter of social convention

When people speak of right and wrong (or knowing right from wrong), they often are referring to what *society* considers right and wrong. This is technically known as *descriptive ethics*, the kind of things laid down in codes and statutes. Thus 'knowing right from wrong' means learning what the law lays down, similar to learning the highway code. In this way learning 'right from wrong' can become a *prudential* rather than a strictly *moral* matter: it is 'wise' to know what the law says, and 'foolish' to ignore it.

> ***Descriptive ethics*** Ethics seen as ***describing*** what is already established as right and wrong; it involves no judgement about such ethics.
>
> ***Normative ethics*** Ethics seen as what ***should*** constitute right and wrong. Normative ethics is about laying down moral standards or ***norms***, and does, of course, pass judgement on descriptive ethics.

Such a view, however, differs greatly from the understanding of ethics as something much more profound, something that touches on *reality*, rather than resting purely on social convention. Followers of **Kant**, for instance, would see ethics as more to do with an inner sense of *duty* which arises from the dictates of *reason*, and to ignore it is to behave not just in an *anti-social*,

RELIGION AND ETHICS

but in an *immoral* way. The proof of this, some would say, is the fact of our feeling guilty from behaving badly, even when nobody knows we have. In this view morality belongs to our essential worth as human beings; it is something that affects our sense of moral integrity; something that 'pricks our conscience', or in Kantian terms, that makes an inescapable *demand* on us (a categorical imperative). Equally from a *religious* viewpoint ethics have an objective significance, because behaviour is seen as something that will ultimately be judged by God.

> Kant said that **moral** demands are what can be ***universalized***, and bind everyone everywhere. This contrasts with the view of ***ethical relativism***, which holds that ethics are relative to times and cultures.
>
> *But in either case what is distinctive about 'ethical' demands, as opposed to demands like 'keeping the law'?*

The question of how law and morality are related

Morality and law, however, are clearly not the same, since laws are man-made and can be judged to be good or bad. While it can be argued that law is founded on morality rather than the reverse, in a secular age many see the law as prior to morality. In this view morality is defined in practical terms by what the law allows or forbids. This leads to the 'descriptive' view that what is 'good' is what is lawful and what is 'bad' is what is punishable by law. In this view what the law permits (what is legitimate) and what it forbids (what is illegal) become identified as what is right and wrong. This leads to the view that if the law allows something then it must be right, and alternatively if something is illegal it must be wrong. Such an approach to morality is open to criticism, and would be rejected by **Kant**, who saw the moral law as underlying all human law. For him it was the inner moral sense (not a legal agreement) about right and wrong that distinguished humans from the animals, and was the defining mark of a human being (see more on Kantian ethics below).

> ***Law***   The enforcement of ***agreed*** moral principles in society.
>
> ***Morality***   The ***principles*** by which laws are made, codified and enforced.

RELIGION AND HUMAN BEHAVIOUR

SECULAR ETHICS (1): KANT AND THE MORAL LAW, THE CATEGORICAL IMPERATIVE, AND GOODWILL

The two great ethical systems, Kantian ethics and utilitarianism, are strictly non-religious, that is to say, secular. They are both based on rational principles, and make no appeal to religion for their content or motivation. Kantian ethics are based on the principle that there is a categorical imperative, or absolute duty to obey the moral law. The moral law is a universally binding code of behaviour which centres on the just treatment of others. No exception can ever be made for one person over another in matters of law and morality. There can never be a different set of standards binding me from others around me. Morality must embrace all men, and be *universal* in its application. I must always treat others never as a means only but always as an end in themselves. This follows from the unique dignity of human beings, a principle now universally accepted as the rational basis of international justice.

> *Hypothetical imperative* The need to do something *if* I want to achieve an objective. For example, I must have a good moral reputation if I am to work with young people.
>
> *Categorical imperative* I have an absolute duty to obey the moral law. For example, I must never take an innocent human life because it is categorically wrong.

Those who act in the light of reason and obey the moral law by treating others properly, show what Kant called a *good will*. Kant said that there was nothing more perfectly good than a good will. But this gives rise to a problem in Kantian ethics. A good will can never be dependent on objective facts. Ideally a good will should be reflected in good actions, but in reality this may not always be the case. I may act from a good *intention* but do something against the moral law. In extreme cases it is theoretically possible to act from a good intention and do something generally regarded as wrong. For example, dying soldiers were often shot to 'end their misery' on the battlefield because their condition was considered hopeless. In this case an objectively immoral act is

RELIGION AND ETHICS

done for subjectively good reasons. Such an action can be seen to be forgivable (some would say *wrong* but not *evil*) because it can be seen as part of a conflict of duties – the duty to relieve pain against the duty (seen as impossible), to preserve life.

> **Moral law** That which is my moral duty, the **objective** side of the categorical imperative.
>
> **Good will** The *intention* to follow the moral law, the **subjective** side of moral duty.

The importance of good will over the correct calculation of moral duty

The difficulty, therefore, of sometimes knowing where one's real duty lies is something of an unresolved area in Kantian ethics. Kant might respond to this by saying that any action done out of a sense of duty shows good will, and in the fallen state of mankind, such an action always has a high moral value. In fact Kant's Christian upbringing made him keenly aware of the reality of fallen human nature. To this he attributed the way people normally see morality as a constraint rather than as an

> **The categorical imperative**
> - Act in such a way that your action can be a universal law.
> - Never treat others merely as a means, but always as an end.
> - Act so that your actions are part of a community with similar values.

exercise in true freedom. Taking this into consideration Kant conceded that 'a morally worthy act' was one not necessarily in accordance with the moral law, but one done 'for the sake of humanity'. What Kant ranked as morally unworthy were acts done out of *selfishness* or self-interest, which he equated (not convincingly) with acting from the unworthy motive of *'inclination'*.

RELIGION AND HUMAN BEHAVIOUR

The issue of whether the moral law is transcendent or man-made

Critics of Kant object to his understanding of the moral law. According to **Kant** the moral law 'stands to reason' and should be transparently clear to everyone. Kant is often accused of supposing that other people can resolve moral issues as clearly as he can. But anyway, it is objected, there is no fixed 'moral law' laid down in advance to which everyone must conform. Instead morality is, as we have seen above, what people decide is in their best collective interests; or what is necessary for the just running of society; or what has the greatest utility value in promoting happiness and minimizing pain. If this is the case, there is no such thing as an objective moral law and Kant's system collapses. Kant strongly objected to this view, saying that it would put ethics at the service of humanity, not, as it should be, the reverse (see box below). Humanity, for Kant, is always *confronted* with the ethical demands of the moral law. To leave ethics in the hands of human beings would lead in the end to the triumph of expediency over morality, inclination over duty, the interests of the self over the rights of others.

> **Kant** Humanity is the servant of ethics. Human beings ***discover*** ethical rules and principles. Behaving morally is something human beings naturally resist in favour of inclination.
>
> **Hume** Ethics are the servant of humanity. Human beings decide all ethical principles. Behaving morally is something that comes naturally, from an inner sense of sympathy with others.

The problems of ruling out inclination as a motive for action

A further criticism of Kant is the emphasis he places on duty (which is why his ethics is called *deontological*, from the Greek word for duty). When most people do everyday moral actions such as helping out a friend, or paying back a loan given out of generosity, or keeping a serious promise out of a sense of fidelity, they do not necessarily do these things as a matter of 'duty'. In fact many people would feel offended if they knew someone helped them from a sense of duty rather than, say, from friendship, gratitude, love, or indeed *inclination*. Duty might seem to many as an inferior motive for human actions, and implies not only a certain reluctance to do something but also a certain detachment from the person involved. Kant does indeed seem to leave himself little room for manoeuvre on this, since he said that the test of morality is duty rather than inclination. However, the distinction may not be as significant as Kant assumed: he believed that inclination meant the *easy way out*, while acting from *duty* meant acting in a way that involved some kind of *personal sacrifice*. In this he differed from **Hume**, who believed that we are 'naturally' inclined to show sympathy to others and behave accordingly.

> ***Kant*** Inclination panders to selfishness. To do what I am inclined to do leads away from moral duty, and is a poor guide to morality.
>
> ***Hume*** Inclination is the inner impulse to act out of sympathy with others, in virtue of my own humanity, and is a good basis for moral behaviour.
>
> *Hume is optimistic about humanity, while Kant is pessimistic. But in conflict situations where moral dilemmas arise, how far can one view be considered more realistic than the other?*

SECULAR ETHICS (2): UTILITARIANISM AND THE PURSUIT OF HAPPINESS HERE AND NOW

Utilitarian ethics are based on the principle that all human actions should benefit others. This is another way of saying that moral actions are those which have a utility value, that is, they are useful to others. In this view a so-called 'moral' or 'good' action that brings no direct benefit to others is a contradiction in terms. This brought utilitarianism into direct conflict with the idea that a good action, such as the decision to lead a strictly Christian life, might have no immediate utilitarian effects or consequences. The monks and ascetics who sacrificed worldly pleasures for their austere commitments to faith, in the belief that the forgoing of earthly pleasures was worth the wait for future rewards, were regarded by **Bentham** as examples of an ethical waste of time. The principle of utility was therefore inextricably tied to a *naturalistic* moral outlook which equated good with socially useful, and judged actions that had no immediate usefulness as, well, useless.

> **Problems with utility**
>
> For actions to have moral worth they should bring happiness to others. Acts of kindness and charity would be obvious examples, but helping the poor with money dishonestly obtained could also count. In traditional **Christian** and **Kantian ethics** utility is important, but it has its limits. No action can be morally worthy if it violates certain principles of morality, such as those laid down in the Decalogue. But supporters of the principle of utility would argue that if an action brought good consequences to many, it would be justified, even if it meant going against a moral principle. For example, killing innocent citizens in war as a 'legitimate price to pay' for achieving a military objective.

'Useful' means primarily being able to increase the happiness or pleasure of others. In a theistic world view such a purely naturalistic system allows for no consideration of the ultimate welfare of others, something central to a religious perspective. Thus the 'sacrifice' of a human life could be justified, if the overall effect of such a sacrifice was the 'greater' happiness of others (as, for instance, in the case of abortion, euthanasia, or the killing of an innocent citizen to appease a riotous mob). This makes some applications of the utility principle highly controversial.

> *Utility principle*   The end justifies the means. If happiness is the end, or aim, of human behaviour, anything that promotes human happiness is morally justified.
>
> *Christian principle*   The end can never justify the means if the end is morally wrong. Human happiness is a legitimate good, but can never be justified by means that ignore recognized moral principles, such as justice, and the dignity and integrity of the human person, as revealed by God.

RELIGION AND ETHICS

It is generally accepted that the real inspiration of utility ethics was **David Hume**, who argued that morality is a *human* creation devised to make possible social living, in which human, or worldly 'happiness' is the most desirable objective. For Hume the foundation of morals was *within* the world, not something *beyond* the world, derived from either religion or metaphysics. Morals historically emerged as laws of behaviour, and are the result of what people commonly sensed were necessary for harmonious living, and personal fulfilment. Religious ethics, by contrast, allows for a gap between happiness in the short term, and the promise of ultimate fulfilment later. As a result theists would claim that utilitarian ethics is based on a limited and narrow concept of human happiness, and for this reason would be prepared to sanction behaviour incompatible with certain rational and religious principles (see box above).

> ***Bentham***   Happiness determines morality.
>
> ***Kant***   Morality determines happiness.
>
> ***Christianity***   Morality partly determines happiness, but so does God's grace.

Utilitarianism as a reversal of the principle that virtuous action brings happiness

Many would argue that the principle of utility is a case of putting the cart before the horse. **Hume** observed that what people called good or virtuous behaviour was that which actually *did* bring happiness. In this he agreed with **Aristotle**. He saw this happening in two ways. The first was in the form of personal happiness for the agent, and the second, a feeling of happiness in those who witness, or hear about it. Hume gave the example of how saving a drowning person brings deserved fame to the saver, and pride to the community for the good deed done. Here Hume appears to recognize the universal value of virtuous actions, while appearing to claim that their virtue lay in the happiness they brought.

Utilitarianism under **Jeremy Bentham** appears to reverse Hume's reasoning by switching from the end to the means. Instead of saying, with Hume, that virtuous actions were those which brought happiness, Bentham started

RELIGION AND HUMAN BEHAVIOUR

> ***Hume*** Those actions which are generally recognized as morally good, bring happiness to the agent and others. But Hume does not make clear that this is the *reason* why such actions are considered morally good.
>
> ***Bentham*** The aim of morality is to bring happiness. ***Any*** action which brings happiness, or minimizes pain, is for that reason morally good.
>
> Clearly Bentham reverses Hume, by switching from the principle that accepted virtuous actions bring happiness, to working out a new system of how happiness can best be achieved.

from the premise that the pursuit of happiness was important, and then proposed ways to achieve it. Bentham's earlier form of utilitarianism stressed the importance of the *quantity* of pleasure to be produced by human behaviour, regardless of what sort of behaviour it was (see box below and the felicific calculus). The result was a departure from Hume's idea that virtuous behaviour brought happiness, to a preoccupation with what kinds of *actions* would supposedly bring happiness. The result was a departure from virtuous behaviour as traditionally understood, and a preference for any action that brought 'happiness' to others. This led to the question, 'What about actions normally seen as morally questionable?'

> **Bentham's felicific calculus**
>
> Intense, long, certain, speedy, fruitful, pure –
> Such marks in pleasures and in pains endure.
> Such pleasures seek if private be thy end:
> If it be public, wide let them extend
> Such pains avoid whichever be thy view:
> If pains must come let them extend to few
>
> Bentham's calculus describes the qualities of pleasure in the first line, but his main principle is contained in the rest of the verse.

RELIGION AND ETHICS

The shift from quantity to quality of pleasure

In a move back to Hume, **John Stuart Mill** acknowledged that the best actions were in fact those which found approval from others, not only because they brought happiness but because they were good in themselves. This allowed Mill to encourage living by traditional moral rules such as the Decalogue; and the promotion of traditional virtues such as kindness, generosity, tolerance and benevolence. This came to be called *rule utilitarianism*: living by the traditional rules laid down by society because this was seen to be the best way to achieve the utilitarian ideal of happiness for all. Mill also departed from Bentham in respect of the issue of pleasure. He held that some pleasures were more base than others, and therefore all pleasures could not be counted the same. 'Lower' pleasures were those of the senses, and could be properly be called 'animal' pleasures. 'Higher' pleasures were a mark of a cultured person, and were more worthy of pursuit than the lower ones. Hence what was pleasure for a pig would not do for Socrates!

> **Bentham** An action is morally good if it promotes pleasure of any kind.
>
> **Mill** Some actions have a greater moral worth than others if they promote higher rather than lower pleasures. Sensual pleasures cannot be compared to intellectual pleasures, because one elevates humanity, the other lowers it.
>
> *How far can it be said that Mill included other factors in applying the principle of utility?*

Because of its stress on the *effects* of moral actions, many commend utilitarianism for calling attention to an important aspect of morality. Virtuous behaviour may be good in itself, but there are times when the *consequences* of an action are an important guide to its morality. This means that utilitarianism, while not without its defects, is at least a partial guide to what is good and bad. Modern versions of the principle of utility have attempted to overcome some of its earlier deficiencies. It has been argued that some values have an intrinsic importance, like *justice* or *equality*, values which are submerged by classical utilitarianism. Others have proposed an amalgamation with Kantian ethics as the best way to preserve the aims of utility, thus including the treatment of others as 'ends' rather than 'means'.

> Because strict utilitarian principles can sometimes lead to what is morally questionable, many have proposed ***variations*** in the way the principle of utility is applied, such as making ***compromises*** with, say, Kantian ethics (see 'types of utilitarianism' in box below).

The question of whether priority goes to the person or to the action

An important criticism of utilitarianism centres on the question of what makes an action morally worthy: the action itself, or the intention behind it. The answer might also have a bearing on the issue of personal moral fulfilment, one of the driving forces of moral behaviour, the sense of having 'done the right thing'. One of the distinctive aspects of utilitarianism is its elevation of the *action* as the central point of ethical decision-making. This means that a good action done accidentally, or by mistake, or a bad action that happens to benefit others, can gain moral approval. This contrasts sharply with Christian ethics (and indeed with virtue ethics) where the crucial element is the acting *person*, not the action.

> ***Action morality*** Utilitarianism is often accused of stressing the ***action***, in its aim to bring about the best ***consequences***. This might conflict with a sense of 'having done the right thing' and cause problems of conscience.
>
> ***Person morality*** Many would argue that the distinguishing thing in a moral action is the ***intention*** to do the right thing. To ignore this would be to make the consequences come first, thus sacrificing the interests of the ***person***, and reducing the chances of moral ***fulfilment***.

Christian ethics reflects what many people would feel, that it is the good intention of the agent that brings moral approval, especially where a morally dubious action was done by mistake, or as a result of a misjudgement. This does not mean therefore that morality is purely subjective, or that the action

RELIGION AND ETHICS

and its consequences don't matter. In practice it is unlikely that a well intentioned action would be evil, but the priority, it can be argued, should go to the good intention, seeing the agent as deserving praise for the goodwill from which an action is done. This comes close to **Kant**'s understanding of ethical behaviour where personal goodwill is a necessary condition of a good action. It also echoes **Aristotle**'s view that a virtuous action is a product of correct reasoning, but also of what he called *'right desire'*, a necessary condition of *eudemonia*.

> ***Utilitarianism*** Priority goes to the action, not the intention of the agent. A good intention that results in bad consequences is morally bad. The aim must always be to create good consequences.
>
> ***Kant*** No action can be good unless done out of goodwill.
>
> ***Christianity*** God always judges the heart, not the consequences of the action.

Happiness and the question of moral fulfilment

Many would argue that putting the action rather than the person at the centre of ethics must have a bearing on the *happiness of the agent,* something generally regarded as an accompaniment of ethical behaviour. If the person is removed from the centre of ethics it would seem more difficult to achieve the sense of personal fulfilment that **Aristotle** among others considered the *telos* of the virtuous life (see p. 266). In this view happiness is more likely to come from a sense of doing what is good in itself, not something that can later be 'calculated' as good because others have benefited from it. It would apply especially if something was morally approved merely because of the good effects it produced. Violent drug barons, say, who fund neighbourhood projects for the poor come out well in a utilitarian assessment based on consequences, but can they also expect to have a sense of moral satisfaction from doing such things? If conscience has any part to play, the answer would seem to be no (see more on conscience below, p. 276). If this is the case, then the issue of moral fulfilment becomes an important consideration in the assessment of the theory of utility.

> *If a sense of **moral fulfilment** is an important consequence of moral behaviour, could this raise important questions for the **principle of utility**?*
>
> ***Aristotle*** *held that 'virtue brings its own reward', but how likely is this to happen if virtue is merely about acting to achieve the best consequences?*

Utilitarianism as more applicable to social ethics rather than personal ethics

Many see the utilitarian slogan 'the greatest happiness of the greatest number' as a principle of *social* legislation (something Mill was deeply involved with), rather than a principle of personal ethics, a fact which has caused much confusion. This led **Roger Scruton** to say that social legislation was the 'natural home' of utilitarianism. Thus, many would argue, to attempt to solve a personal moral dilemma like abortion by simply 'adding up' the beneficiaries against the loss of the foetus only leads to a superficial view of morality, where issues of personal rights and intrinsic values take second place to the promotion of happiness which could be seen as a selfish objective.

> ***Personal ethics*** Cover issues of personal morality, such as abortion, euthanasia, divorce, sexuality, genetic engineering, cloning, and so forth.
>
> ***Social ethics*** Cover issues about the control of society through laws governing social reforms, welfare assistance, and the legalizing of practices such as divorce, abortion and creation and use of embryos, and so on, all seen as issues bearing on the welfare of society.

In the context of social ethics utilitarianism continues to be a very dominant theory, with its emphasis on 'cost–benefit analysis' and the extension of benefits to the greatest number. This principle is usually seen applied to social dilemmas involving limited resources. The state provision of social aid is usually calculated on the basis of what brings 'the greatest happiness to the greatest number' at the lowest cost. This can be seen for instance in relation to the search for the 'best', meaning most cost-effective, judicial punishments;

and the 'best' use of NHS beds. Many see the principle as having potentially ominous application in relation to moral issues such as euthanasia. The socially 'useless' old and infirm might, with, say, the application of the utility principle, be 'usefully' disposed of to make more beds free for more deserving cases. Whether this should lead to an argument for legalized euthanasia raises important questions for society about whether it is really in people's best interests, to say the least.

> **Types of utilitarianism**
>
> ***Classical utilitarianism*** The theory that the principle of utility (advancing the ***happiness*** of others) is the guiding principle in how I should make moral decisions.
>
> ***Preference utilitarianism*** The theory that the principle of utility is about satisfying the actual ***preferences***, rather than the theoretical happiness, of the people involved.
>
> ***Social utilitarianism*** The application of the principle of utility to social situations such as in the making of laws and ***social reforms*** at a political level. Social utilitarianism is directed to creating 'the greatest happiness for the greatest number' usually in the light of the financial costs involved.
>
> ***Motive utilitarianism*** A modern theory which proposes that the principle or utility is best served by the inculcation of good personal ***motives*** in how we relate to others.
>
> ***Kantian utilitarianism*** A modern theory that the principle of utility is best served by treating as few people as possible as '***means***' and as many as possible as '***ends***'.
>
> ***Theological utilitarianism*** A religious theory based on the principle that God wishes the happiness of his creatures. Hence the theological principle of utility is that all forms of behaviour should advance the happiness of others, but within the limitations of God's will known through reason and revelation. From this it follows that the best means of happiness are virtuous acts, and the ends are not the ***temporary*** happiness of others, but their ***eternal*** happiness. It would thus be wrong to do evil in order to make others happy in the here and now, a view implicit in classic utilitarianism.

> ***Act utilitarianism*** The principle that assessing individual acts is the normal method of showing utility, by working out the consequences of such acts.
>
> ***Rule utilitarianism*** The principle that utility is best served by following traditional moral rules. This is based on the view that fidelity to moral rules brings about the best overall consequences.

RELIGIOUS (CHRISTIAN) ETHICS

Divine commands and the demands of reason

Judaism, Christianity and Islam are properly called *ethical monotheism*, because religious belief is directed towards a God who makes ethical demands on his worshippers. But many would argue that while a religion is typically accompanied by an ethical code, such a code could never command respect unless it was consistent with reason and common sense. This however might seem to be at odds with the religious view that all true ethical obligations must be consistent with the will of God. The result is a dilemma: how should believers decide between the demands of faith and the demands of reason if they conflict? In other words, should the deciding factor in ethics be reason, or the will of God? This is known as the *Euthyphro dilemma* (see box). Many would argue that this is more a theoretical than a practical problem. In practice what are called 'divine commands' are normally seen as conforming to reason (the prohibition against murder, rape, theft, and so on). This means that unless a supposed divine command was seen to conform to reason, it would be unlikely to make a moral demand on rational beings.

> **The Euthyphro dilemma**
>
> Are morally good acts willed by God because they are morally good?
>
> Or
>
> Are acts morally good because they are willed by God?
>
> This is a modern restatement of the dilemma, which asks what comes first, God or morality? If morality comes first, it is alleged, God must

> be bound by it, which diminishes God. If God comes first then, it is alleged, human beings might be subject to irrational commands. But if goodness is God's essence, as Aquinas argued, then the dilemma dissolves: a good God would necessarily have goodwill, which in turn would make irrational commands impossible.

Religious ethics as based on transcendent principles

As we have seen, the distinctive feature of religious ethics is the way moral obligation is seen as ultimately part of a relationship to God. The special nature of Christian ethics may be seen in the way morality is about being 'faithful to God' rather than being faithful to reason, or some rational principle such as the pursuit of happiness. In **St Paul**'s view morality is about understanding the story of redemption, and is ultimately an 'ethic of response' to what God has done for humanity through Jesus Christ. This response means being 'guided by the Spirit', rather than being guided by the lures of the 'flesh'. This means following the Decalogue, but also living the virtuous life through 'kindness, patience, tolerance and agape'. In religious ethics human happiness is subordinate to eternal happiness, the latter gained through moral integrity and the grace of God.

> In ***Christian ethics*** earthly happiness is subordinated to the happiness given by God in the afterlife. This involves the ***sacrifice*** of earthly values for religious ones, and the refusal to be guided by the principle of utility alone.

Christian ethics and the principle of utility

It is therefore not difficult to see that, despite some similarities, there is an important difference between utilitarianism and Christian ethics. Both are clearly concerned to promote happiness and minimize pain. One calls it the principle of utility; the other the principle of the love of neighbour. But while one sees human beings at a *naturalistic*, or *material* level, the other sees human beings within a *spiritual* perspective. Within secular utilitarianism there is no guaranteed protection for the individual, since in this system it is human beings who are the final arbiters of right and wrong, based on the principle that what makes people happy is right, and what doesn't is wrong. Thus when it comes to moral dilemmas the two systems are very far apart. One recognizes the rights and protection of the individual under God, while the other calls for the satisfaction of preferences, which may be granted, if necessary, at the expense of the individual.

> ***Christian ethics*** Certain principles are fixed, such as the will of God, the importance of justice, the dignity of the individual, and the idea that some actions are ***intrinsically*** wrong regardless of any other consideration (murder, rape, serious fraud, and so on). Good will, good intention, good motive are the important factors in morality, locating right and wrong in the ***person***, not the action.
>
> ***Utilitarian ethics*** There are no fixed principles to be adhered to. Morality is determined by how far an ***action*** leads to happiness or to pain. The rights of the individual may have to give way to a greater value: the happiness of the majority. The goodwill of the agent is less important than the good consequences of the action.

The question of happiness seen as temporal or eschatological

If happiness is a common aim of utilitarianism and Christian ethics there is a big difference in how this is conceived in both systems. In utilitarian ethics happiness is limited to the here and now. In Christian ethics happiness in the here and now is recognized as good provided it is achieved through doing good rather than evil. This allows for the pursuit of *eschatological happiness* (happiness in the hereafter), which is seen as the just reward of those who have been judged worthy of it. But while both forms of happiness have their own legitimacy, Christian ethics allows for the renunciation, or sacrifice, of short-term happiness now, for the sake of a higher good such as loyalty to country (patriotism) or love of neighbour (agape), or love of virtue, or love of justice, or truth, and so on. By contrast, utilitarianism seems ready to justify any action on the grounds of its promotion of earthly happiness or the minimization of pain. In one system I can do wrong to make others happy; in the other I cannot.

> **Utilitarianism** Moral behaviour is about creating happiness in the here and now.
>
> **Christianity** Moral behaviour is about doing what is right regardless of earthly happiness.
>
> *How far might this be unfair to both Christian and utilitarian ethics?*

The potential of Christian ethics as a basis for social utility

If Christian ethics incorporate the two main ethical approaches, deontological and consequentialist, it would seem to have major potential for the realization of social utility. Traditionally and historically Christianity has been noted for its sponsorship of social utility. The Good Samaritan has been the model that has driven social Christianity to the service of society. The monastic orders offered the benefits of education and training, teaching the liberal arts to launch careers in all the walks of life; while other agencies were prominent in performing the corporal works of mercy (to educate the young, feed the poor, heal the sick and bury the dead) over centuries. The need for schools, hospitals, clinics, teachers, doctors, nurses, farms, vineyards, food production, hostels for pilgrims, hospices for the dying, was not overlooked by a faith which gave theoretical primacy to the hereafter, and later became vulnerable to the charge of offering 'opium to the people'. But in the end it is eschatological happiness that Christian faith sees as the ultimate goal. As the Stoic **Cicero** put it, 'Can happiness be constituted by any contingent good that is capable of being lost?'

Christian ethics are about acting in response to faith

It would be a mistake to confuse Christian ethics with any of the secular systems we have just seen. Christians are not meant to be directly Kantians, or utilitarians, but followers of **Jesus Christ** and fulfillers of the law of God. In both the Jewish and Christian traditions there is a direct link between ethical obligation and religious faith. For this reason there is a certain logic that the first three commandments of the Decalogue concern duties to God. In

> **Christian ethics**
> - Based on belief in a transcendent God.
> - See ethical obligations in relation to revelation.
> - See the ethical life as a response to Jesus Christ.
> - See the virtuous life as the heart of ethics.
> - See ethics involving personal and social obligations.
> - See ethics as needing to conform to reason.
> - See ethical life as leading to eschatological happiness.
> - See humanity as fallen and needing forgiveness.
> - Stress need for the divine grace for ethical living.
>
> **Secular ethics**
> - Reject belief in a transcendent God.
> - Reject the idea that ethics are transcendent.
> - Reject the idea that ethics are about reality.
> - See ethics as a matter of human convention.
> - See the purpose of ethics as promoting human happiness.
> - See ethical principles as determined by law.
> - See ethical behaviour as determined by legal sanction.

the teaching of Jesus the great commandment to love our neighbour is preceded by the command to love God. For this reason Christian ethics as such concern the moral life as ultimately about obeying 'divine commands', a view that is only made possible within the perspective of faith. A truly Christian ethic, therefore, is not an action done out of duty, or from the desire to promote happiness (although both are often involved), but an action done in the context of a relationship to God. Thus, 'Thou shalt not kill' is not laid down as a fundamental law of civilized society, but is instead a divine command addressed to believers as a fundamental sign of their fidelity to God, who is the creator of human life. To overlook this is to take Christian ethics out of its natural framework and reduce it to just another rational system. Its inherent nature as an ethics belonging within a human–divine relationship is crucial to understanding its essential dynamic.

RELIGION AND ETHICS

NATURAL LAW ETHICS: THE IDEA THAT HOW NATURE WORKS IS A GUIDE TO RIGHT AND WRONG

The concept of natural law goes back to the ancient Greeks, who distinguished between nature (*physis*) and human regulations, customs or conventions (*nomos*). The former pointed to laws that were the same everywhere, whereas the latter could change from place to place. This distinction was later taken up by **Aristotle**, who held that there was a universal law according to nature, and a common law according to convention. Aristotle's understanding of natural law was applied mainly to 'natural rights' but the concept was further developed by the *Stoics*.

The Stoics believed that there was a rational and purposeful order to the universe, and humans were able to detect the correct way to live by seeing how nature operated. The most complete development of natural law was, however, carried out by **Aquinas**. He used the concept of natural law to bridge any theoretical gap there might be thought to be between the perceived law of God (divine law) and the rules of good behaviour as perceived by human *reason* (see also the Euthyphro dilemma above). Natural law has therefore tended to be used to provide a rational basis for divine law, rather than a theory

> We cannot be deterred from its obligations neither by senator nor people.
> *Cicero* (on natural law)

that stands by itself. But many reject the concept of 'natural law' on the grounds that the only sense in which the term can be used is in reference to the 'natural laws' of physics.

Some aspects of natural law have been derived from physical laws, such as the moral injunction against contraception, which appeals to the physical workings of the human reproductive system. According to Aquinas, natural law dictates that no act is morally right if it interferes with the natural working of a human faculty. In the main, though, natural moral law is a working out of man's obligations and entitlements from looking at the needs of a civilized society, a line of thinking not dissimilar to that taken by **Hume**. Thus the Decalogue serves as a summary of natural law principles because it sees divine law as recognizing such basic moral and legal needs as protection from murder, violence against the innocent, stealing, dishonesty, adultery, exploitation of the person, and so on.

> **Aquinas on natural law**
>
> • Natural law is *teleological*: its purpose is to lead to goodness and happiness.
>
> • Natural law *judges* human laws: an unjust law is, in a sense, no law at all.
>
> • The *primary* precept of natural law is to do good and avoid evil.
>
> • The *subsidiary* precepts are: self-preservation, procreation, education of children, living harmoniously in society, and the worship of God.
>
> • To be morally worthy, a moral act must have correct *content* (external) and a good *motive* (internal). In reality a good motive (goodwill) is more important than the content. Because of human weakness God forgives sinners.
>
> Secondary precepts follow from the primary precepts and are more detailed. For example, murder is wrong because it violates the natural right to life. Theft is wrong because it destroys social relations and violates the natural right to possessions. Rape is wrong because it violates the natural right to security of person.
>
> *But how far can the natural law principle of ethics be acceptable to non-theists?*

Natural law and its relation to religious faith

Therefore, according to natural law principles, everyone has certain fundamental rights, while also having corresponding obligations to respect those rights in others. It is perhaps in the area of sexuality, marriage and the family that natural law principles as worked out by **Aquinas** come across more as *moral*, rather than as just *legal* issues. These principles are applied to controversial issues such as the age of consent for sexual practice, sex before marriage, and the ethics of contraception, divorce, homosexuality, abortion, euthanasia and so on. Today natural law is rejected by many as being an out-

RELIGION AND ETHICS

dated concept for the assessment of moral issues, because the meaning of *law* is not something fixed *a priori*, but something devised by *humankind* for the benefit of humans. Besides, natural law is widely perceived as a working out of moral issues within the framework of a religious outlook in which a correspondence between the tendencies of nature, the needs of humans and the will of the Creator are brought into synthesis. While this is indeed the case, the question remains whether the concept of natural law as an approach to ethical dilemmas collapses without a religious foundation, or whether it can survive on the basis of reason alone.

> **Ethical theories**
>
> ***Christian ethics*** A theory of ethics based on the belief that all ethical obligations reflect the will of God.
>
> ***Situation ethics*** A supposedly Christian ethical theory that puts agape as the guiding principle of moral behaviour. Has been criticized for being '***unchristian***' because it attempts to say what agape might mean in different situations, even though it might mean the abandonment of traditional Christian principles.
>
> ***Kantian ethics*** A deontological ethical theory that stresses the duty to obey the moral law.
>
> ***Natural law ethics*** The theory of ethics based on the principle that moral behaviour must be consistent with the laws of nature.
>
> ***Utilitarian ethics*** A theory of ethics based on the principle of utility. Only those acts which have good consequences in terms of utility (promoting happiness and minimizing pain) are morally right.

Situation ethics as an alternative to fixed moral rules

In broad terms all ethical decisions arise from specific situations, and there is general agreement about the adage that 'situations alter cases'. For instance, killing in the particular situation of war seriously alters its morality. Someone who steals a loaf to feed his starving family is not considered blameworthy of theft. A mother who defends her children by using a shotgun would not be judged in the same light as an armed bank robber using the same shotgun. However, what is commonly called *situation ethics* is something quite different. The best-known version is that produced by the American **Joseph Fletcher**, and the term henceforth will refer to his proposal. His ethical theory is fundamentally tied to a *religious* outlook, and his ethics come under religious ethics.

> Fletcher's theory was originally applauded as an ethic for 'man come of age', but critics found it a recipe for ethical chaos.
>
> *What are the reasons for this, and how far is this criticism justified?*

Fletcher claims that his system is an attempt to get beyond fixed, or *absolute*, moral rules in order to put the 'person' at the centre of morality. The supposition here is that moral rules can be prejudicial to the good of the person, a view that would collide say with **Kant**, who saw morality as a matter of following the moral law, and as in the interests of everyone. Fletcher's system would also be at variance with the Christian tradition, which recognizes the centrality of the moral law as laid down in the Decalogue. Above all it would make ethics *relative*, ironically not so much relative to the *situation*, as to the judgement, or perception, of the person in it.

According to Fletcher there is only one fixed absolute principle governing all religious ethics, the principle of agape, or selfless love. While this is in principle the highest ethical ideal, Fletcher allows that it can be used as a reason for choosing forms of behaviour that are inconsistent with recognized moral rules. For instance it may be permissible to commit adultery if in the opinion of the subject more would be *gained* by doing so than not. The word *gain* gives a clue to the utilitarian thrust of his theory, which takes in the notion of 'love being distributed'. The more widely the effects of love are felt, the more meritorious the action. Indeed, one of Fletcher's many adages is that 'justice is love distributed'. Therefore a baby, whose possible cry might give away the whereabouts of a group hiding from the enemy, could permissibly be killed to save the group if no other solution could be found.

> **Situation ethics** has no fixed principles regarding what is morally permissible. It may be right to do **wrong** as traditionally understood, if this is seen as the 'loving' thing to do.
>
> *But what are the drawbacks of this approach?*

RELIGION AND ETHICS

Fletcher appeals to Jesus as an example of one who always 'put people first'. However, critics point out that while Jesus sometimes set aside religious customs in favour of people's more fundamental needs, he never set aside the laws of the Decalogue as a solution to any moral situation. The theory of situation ethics therefore never gained any real following beyond the recognition that agape does indeed represent the highest level of moral endeavour.

Ethical language and the theory of emotivism

We end this chapter by taking a brief look at the problems raised by ethical language. Since ethical statements are neither tautologies nor statements of fact they bear a noticeable similarity to *religious language* (see above, p. 215) and come equally under the logical positivist ban which declares both to be non-cognitive. According to this view ethical claims about what is right or wrong, good or bad express no truths or facts because such statements cannot be verified or falsified (see above, p. 216). Because ethical debate is so pervasive in society, various attempts have been made to give 'meaning' to ethical claims. This has resulted in proposals to give a reduced meaning to ethical language within the constraints of its empirical starting point.

> **Ethical and religious language**
> - Both are seen as non-cognitive
> - Both are seen as unverifiable and unfalsifiable
> - Both are claimed to be meaningless
> - Both are claimed not to deal with reality.
> - Both are claimed only to express personal beliefs and feelings.
>
> *How far can theists justify both languages as dealing with what is real and true?*

The classic proposal is associated with **A. J. Ayer,** who put forward the theory of *emotivism*. This is the view that ethical statements are merely expressions of personal likes, dislikes, emotions, feelings, and so on. Therefore statements like 'murder is wrong' or 'honesty is right' have no cognitive status, that is, they say nothing about what is the case in the real world. They are merely expressions of what could be called *moral taste*. But when understood in the context of the *restricted* account of meaning that Ayer espouses (see logical positivism, p. 215), emotivism can be seen to be equally restrictive, reducing ethical meaning to subjective feeling.

RELIGION AND HUMAN BEHAVIOUR

> ***Emotivism***   Ethical statements or judgements are merely expressions of approval or disapproval of something. Because it is based on empiricist principles, it rejects all claims that right and wrong have either natural basis (Aquinas), a rational basis (Kant), or a religious basis (the Bible).

Theists would, for instance, object to reducing ethical claims to 'emotive utterances' by insisting that fundamental ethical laws (such as those contained in the Decalogue) cannot be reduced to expressions of personal feeling about such things, but are objective statements of truth. In other words some actions are good or bad in themselves (intrinsically good or bad), not because of how we *feel* about them. Besides, theists would say that ethics are about objective *realities*, not subjective feelings, since the assessment of ethical behaviour is subject to the will of God. **Kant** would also object to the reduction of ethics to feelings, because he held that the moral law was *real*, something that was transparent to *reason*.

> ***Emotivism*** allows for no distinction between ***moral*** feelings, and feelings of a more ***trivial*** kind.

Critics of emotivism also point out that ethical beliefs can be shown to go deeper than mere feelings, since they are usually matters that affect our *conscience*, and consequently our inner sense of integrity and moral pride. According to emotivists ethical feelings are similar in kind to our feelings about traffic jams, immigration or high taxes, a view that ignores the peculiar nature of moral judgements as such. And, as we have seen in relation to religious language, the fact that some areas of life are not amenable to verification or falsification doesn't prevent them being claims about reality (such as judgements about duty, or love or beauty). Critics also point out that if everything of moral importance is reduced to how people feel about things, no agreement could ever be reached about the moral seriousness of anything.

> **Terms used in ethics**
>
> ***Divine command theory***   The religious view that ethics are the result of divine commands.
>
> ***Religious ethics***   Ethics as an aspect of religious belief.

> *Secular ethics* Ethics based on reason alone.
>
> *Normative ethics* Ethics seen as those things that are right or wrong.
>
> *Descriptive ethics* Ethics seen as what is laid down in existing ethical codes.
>
> *Absolutism* The view that some things are intrinsically wrong (in themselves).
>
> *Relativism* The view that all moral rules are relative to time and culture.
>
> *Deontology* The system that sees ethics as a matter of duty.
>
> *Consequentialism* The system that judges the morality of acts by their effects.
>
> *Emotivism* The view that ethical statements are only expressions of personal feeling.
>
> *Prescriptivism* The observation that ethical judgements contain a prescription to action.
>
> *Intuitivism* The view that moral goodness can be directly perceived in a thing.
>
> *Naturalism* The view that an ethical term like 'good' can be defined in terms of a natural quality like, say, friendship. Those who disagree call this a fallacy.

The naturalistic fallacy and the is–ought debate

Finally, we take a brief look at the philosophical issue mentioned first by **Hume**, and later known as the *naturalistic fallacy*. The alleged fallacy (mistake) is about whether moral obligations can be derived from *facts* about the world. A simple exposure of the fallacy is when, say, good is defined as 'that which brings peace and harmony to society'. It can then be questioned whether such peace is good (it never is under a tyranny). From this it is supposed to follow that an *'ought'* as in 'I ought to do good' should never follow a specific

RELIGION AND HUMAN BEHAVIOUR

alleged *fact* such as 'peace is good'. Some have argued, however, that this is just logical quibbling.

They argue that the fallacy is not in the connection between *is* and *ought*, or between *fact* and *value*, but in making the wrong connection between them. Clearly some facts logically entail certain obligations, while alleged facts such as 'it is good to be loyal to others' can entail false obligations of loyalty, as in showing loyalty to a terrorist or criminal by concealing their intention to commit murderous crimes. Hume's concern seems to have been about the need for a middle term, or second premise, to make the proper link between the is and the ought. As follows:

> Ethics must somehow be based on an appreciation of human nature – on a sense of what a human being is or might be, or on what a human being might want to have or want to be. If that is naturalism then naturalism is no fallacy. No one could seriously deny that ethics are responsive to such facts about human nature... The fallacy is not naturalism but, rather, any simple-minded attempt to rush from facts to values.
>
> *Daniel Dennett*

Premise 1: L is a religious leader.
Premise 2: Religious leaders should give a good example.
Conclusion: L ought to give a good example.

In practice, however, it is normal to omit the middle premise as unnecessary because it is taken for granted. Obviously it would be nice to put it in to please Hume, but the is–ought debate is seen by many as merely putting an unnecessary logical spanner into the ethical works. The real issue, it could be said, is not being logically correct, but making sound and sensible moral judgements.

Facts and values : the is–ought debate

- I am married, and therefore I ought to be faithful (moral promise).
- A good God exists, therefore his law ought to be obeyed (divine command theory).
- He is a man, therefore he ought to be treated as an end (Kant).

- Men are made to be happy, therefore they ought to be virtuous (Aristotle).
- Natural law comes from God, therefore it ought to be obeyed (Aquinas).

*Note in each case the middle term is left out without any loss to the meaning of what is said. But how true is the claim that the fallacy is not in short-circuiting the **connection** between fact and value, but in making the **wrong** connection between them (as in: 'I am free, therefore I ought to do what I like')?*

17 Religion and Virtue

- Background to the understanding of virtue.
- Aristotle and virtue ethics.
- Aquinas and virtue ethics.
- MacIntyre and virtue ethics.
- Religion and virtue ethics.
- Limitations of virtue ethics.

The virtuous life was highly regarded since ancient times

The word 'virtue' comes from the Latin meaning both *man* and *strength*. Hence the word *virile*, meaning strong. The word virtue implies strength, and specifically strength of *character*. This is clearly a *moral* strength as opposed to physical strength, and the virtuous character usually brings admiration and respect.

> It is not logic that makes men reasonable, nor the science of ethics that makes men good.
> *Oscar Wilde*

Both **Plato** and **Aristotle** esteemed the virtuous life, or *arete*, as that which reflected *phronesis* or moral wisdom on the one hand, and led to a sense of *eudemonia* or personal fulfilment (something more than happiness) on the other. Both agreed with **Pythagoras** that the character of the natural world as an organized harmony (*cosmos*) was the model for the harmony that characterized the virtuous person.

The virtuous person, by acting from *love* and *justice*, points to the perfect harmony possessed only by *'divinity'*. For this reason the virtue approach to

> **Virtue** A quality of character denoting a strength, rather than a weakness.
>
> **Arete** Meaning virtue as moral excellence seen in an individual's character.
>
> **Phronesis** The moral wisdom that leads to an appreciation of virtue.
>
> **Eudemonia** Personal fulfilment and development resulting from the practice of virtue.

ethics centres on the question of what makes a good *person*, rather than on what makes a good *action*. This means a shift away from the approach typical of the ethical theories which stress duties or consequences, and a move towards development of character as the fundamental source of the ethical life. Where the ethical theories are more about 'solving ethical dilemmas' against the background of certain ethical principles (duty, utility, or the will of God) the 'virtue ethics' approach is to create the stable foundations in the development of character that make possible the good life (and its product moral *fulfilment*).

> According to the **Greeks** the virtuous life showed moral wisdom, and led to moral fulfilment. Virtue ethics put personal ***character***, rather than ***rules*** of behaviour at the centre of ethics.

Aristotle and virtue ethics

The tradition of virtue ethics is generally traced to **Aristotle**, who among the ancient Greeks was the one who most clearly worked out their nature and content. He focused particularly on *eudemonia*, a state of being fulfilled, or 'flourishing'. He held this to be an objective condition, as opposed to a subjective one (an idea difficult to grasp, but corresponding to the Christian idea that virtue is a 'state' rather than a 'subjective'

> I saw the Master there of those who know,
> Amid the philosophic family,
> By all admired, and by all revered;
> There Plato too I saw, and Socrates,
> Who stood beside him closer than the rest.
>
> *Dante*, Divine Comedy

sense of fulfilment). Aristotle held that eudemonia is something achieved regardless of the emotional feelings of its subject. It is that which makes a person flourish, or enjoy 'moral health'. In this sense *vice*, the opposite of virtue, creates a condition that could be called 'moral disease' or 'moral disorder'. For Aristotle eudemonia is achieved by a person practising the moral virtues. But this is less likely to be achieved privately, than as part of a wider ethos where virtue and the virtuous life are valued.

> **Virtue** A sign of moral health and personal flourishing.
>
> **Vice** A sign of moral disease, and incompatible with personal flourishing.

For Aristotle, virtue is that which belongs to the nature of a thing, that which enables it to achieve its purpose. A bow must have the virtue of firing an arrow. A good bow does this well, a bad bow does not. The same question can be asked of a human person. What is human life *for*, what is its purpose (or *telos*)? Virtue is that which advances or achieves what a person is for. In Aristotle's view a human person is 'for' using his *reason* correctly, in order to achieve the good life. The good life consists in the practice of the virtues.

> **Aristotle** believed that the ***purpose*** (*telos*) of human life was the practice of virtue.

Among the key virtues were the *cardinal virtues* of prudence (moral wisdom), justice, fortitude and temperance (see below). He argued that each virtue was a mid-point between two vices. This became known as the *golden mean* (see box). Through the golden mean, or moderation, a person lives a 'proper human life' and achieves eudemonia. Not all virtues, however, can easily fit into such a scheme. The virtue of *justice* does not easily fit in, since it involves giving others their proper due, and can hardly have an 'excess'. Neither does *love*, which again cannot easily be divided between deficiency and excess.

The Golden Mean

Deficiency	Moderation	Excess
Cowardice	Courage	Foolhardiness
Meanness	Generosity	Liberality
Arrogance (hubris)	Modesty	Pride
Intolerance	Tolerance	Indulgence
Malevolence	Benevolence	??????????

In setting out moderation as a good working principle to achieve the good life, Aristotle's aim seems to be to equate virtue with what is 'reasonable'. But while theoretically it is possible to divide behaviour between deficiency and excess, how far would the ordinary person see this as a cumbersome intellectual demand?

Virtue as rational and vice as irrational

In this view a good person, armed with a virtuous outlook and attitude, is always likely to do the right, or virtuous, thing in any circumstances, rather than in particular circumstances. A person whose character is directed by a sense of justice towards others is likely to meet every circumstance with goodwill and benevolence, regardless of the ethical decisions he or she may have to make in a particular case. Following **Aristotle**, the Greek view was that virtue (goodness) was the natural product of a *rational* outlook, while its opposite, vice (evil), was essentially *irrational*. Both **Hume** and **Mill** were strong admirers of the virtuous character whom they saw as having an important practical, or utility, value within society. But Christianity later adopted what many would see as a more realistic outlook, made greater allowance for the notion of human weakness (in terms of original sin), and was less optimistic about reason being able to determine ethical behaviour.

RELIGION AND HUMAN BEHAVIOUR

> **The cardinal virtues**
>
> **Prudence** Symbolized holding a mirror, and being attacked by a serpent.
>
> **Justice** Symbolized holding a sword.
>
> **Fortitude** Symbolized with a broken column.
>
> **Temperance** Symbolized mixing water and wine in two jugs.
>
> *These symbols were taken from the tomb of Sir John Holtham, St Mary's Church, South Dalton, but how do they express the meaning of each virtue?*

There were four overlapping virtues held up by **Plato** as fundamental to the pursuit of happiness: *prudence, justice, fortitude* and *temperance*. Prudence was regarded as the first and most fundamental of the virtues because it encompassed both the intellect and the will. A prudent person is likely to have a good sense of what is required in a particular situation, and is able to act on it. Justice is the virtue that makes the 'just man', one who can be trusted to treat others fairly, and with compassion. Fortitude is the virtue which creates the strength of will required to act courageously to do what is morally right. Temperance is the virtue that limits the human tendency towards material excess, by controlling the animal impulses towards sensual pleasures through self-control. The temperate character is he who can control the problem passions like anger, revenge, lust and the desire to put self before others. Aristotle believed that temperance was a key virtue because it enabled the individual to find the elusive *mean* between restraint and indulgence.

The virtuous life as man's highest calling before God

Aquinas agreed with Aristotle about the importance of a virtuous life for achieving happiness, but he saw happiness as eschatological rather than earthly. For Aquinas virtue was important now, but its ultimate aim was the achievement of the 'beatific vision', the state of the blessed in heaven. He accepted the key role of the cardinal virtues, but added the three theological virtues of faith, hope and charity. He believed that human nature needed the inspiration of divine grace to enable it to overcome the downward pull of temptation and sin.

> **The theological virtues: faith, hope, and charity (agape)**
>
> Aquinas added these virtues as grace-based 'strengths' given to believers to achieve their God-oriented destiny. For Aquinas our destiny is to enjoy the ***beatific vision*** in heaven. ***Faith*** is the virtue of believing in God's revelation. ***Hope*** is the virtue which sustains faith. ***Charity*** is the virtue that enables the values of faith to be practised in the world.

Faith is the virtue that makes possible the proper response to God's revelation. It also provides the perspective to see earthly values as transient, compared to the more enduring spiritual values of love, justice, honesty, compassion and so on. For Aquinas the good life lay in the 'imitatio Christi', a way of life which involved *charity*, or agape. But this was no easy task. It required dedication and restraint and therefore *hope*, the grace-aided defence against the natural tendency to withdraw and give up, what the existentialists called *angst*, and perhaps more commonly called despair.

The seven capital virtues	The seven deadly vices (sins)
Chastity (purity)	Lust (sexual exploitation)
Temperance (restraint)	Gluttony (over-indulgence)
Liberality (generosity)	Greed (avarice)
Diligence (care)	Sloth (laziness)
Patience (forbearance/forgiveness)	Wrath (anger/revenge)
Kindness (respect)	Envy (jealousy)
Humility (modesty)	Pride (vanity)

Virtue ethicists today say that virtues are character qualities admired in, and learned from, others. How far are certain social groupings important for the practice of virtue, and how valid is the observation that vice is equally a product of the 'wrong' kinds of association?

The need for group solidarity for initiation into the virtuous life

Aristotle held that the path to the virtuous life began with an understanding of the happiness that virtue brought. Those who were ignorant of this superior form of human happiness, and assumed that happiness came from the immediate pleasures of the senses, were badly informed. Such people merely lived on the level of the animals that were solely driven by such instincts. We also find this idea in **Mill**'s famous remark that what leaves a pig satisfied would not do for Socrates. But it was to the *communal* aspect of virtue that Aristotle gave the most attention. He believed that the virtuous life was impossible to practise by the individual acting alone. It was the product, not of individual effort, but of social solidarity.

> ***Ethos*** Meaning 'inherent spirit'. Often applied in education to mean the overall character, spirit or pervading values, or outlook, of a school. The school's ethos may be claimed to be 'Christian', or 'caring' or 'egalitarian', or a place where every pupil is 'valued'. Unfortunately the actual ethos may fall short of such claims, resulting in a 'negative', 'poor', or 'failing' ethos.

If 'ethics' suggest 'ethos', then the ethical life owes much to being part of the right ethos. The ideal ethos was a community (beginning with family, group, school, neighbourhood) that valued such virtues. This means that a strong secular argument can be made for the morally uplifting effects of belonging to *communities* where strength of character, moral restraint and strength of character are seen as prerequisites for the achievement of virtuous, commendable or noble aims.

Virtue ethics as the best way to modern human fulfilment

Alasdair MacIntyre is the best-known modern exponent of virtue ethics. He believes that the recent history of ethics is dominated by too much concern for the interests of the individual. This focus on the individual has led to concern with 'solving' ethical dilemmas, and has placed undue emphasis on

RELIGION AND VIRTUE

personal opinions, subjective perceptions of right and wrong, and what is the best 'ethical theory' for solving dilemmas. Such an approach, he believes, has led to a forgetting of the real meaning of ethics. Borrowing notably from **Aristotle**, and later **Aquinas**, he believes that ethics are all about enabling a person to achieve his essential purpose, or *telos*.

He agrees with Aristotle that the key ethical project is changing 'man-as-he-is' to 'man-as-he-ought-to be'. Like Aristotle he believes the *practice* of the virtues is what makes possible the formation of the ethical character (the moral wise man). Like Aquinas he believes that ethics is about the formation of the will, which should be directed to those things that help to realize human destiny. This is, in the first instance, happiness and fulfilment, in the second, unity with God. He agrees that this cannot be done by the individual acting alone. Instead the individual must be part of an ethical *community* with the right ethos, in order to learn what the good life means, and be influenced by those who already know.

> Character development should be the focus of morality, rather than working out the best action in particular situations. This is best achieved by living in the right *ethos*.

MacIntyre believes the experience of friendship within a morally sensitive group creates a sense of communal solidarity that has important ethical consequences. This in turn encourages its members to value and strive after the virtues that typify the group's proud tradition. MacIntyre argues that joining with others in a common cause is the best way to combat *selfish* tendencies, because it encourages a sense of respect and care for others within the group. This follows from an appreciation of the heroic tradition of that community, whether it be courage in the face of the enemy, a willingness to sacrifice life for the sake of comrades, or a steadfast dedication to follow the example set by those held in high respect within the group. All this can be seen exemplified in the contexts of army regiments, fire brigades, police forces, religious orders, nursing sisterhoods, lifeboat companies, and among other vocational professions such as priests, doctors, nurses, paramedics, teachers and so on. However, MacIntyre

> You are better being wronged than doing wrong.
> The cause of sin is ignorance of what is better.
> *Democritus*

does not entirely dispense with the need for moral rules. These, he believes, are unavoidable in the practical field of personal and social ethics.

The development of the virtuous life depends on our associations

Hume believed that we are all endowed with *natural sympathy* towards others, enabling us to act towards them out of compassion and benevolence. It appears that Hume's own personal moral character, to his credit, enabled him to hold this conviction. However, a more cynical interpretation of human nature inclines towards the view that human compassion and kindness are more rare, or at least less dependable, than Hume supposed. **Mill** acknowledged that a sense of appreciation for the virtuous life was the mark of a superior person, but it was a 'tender plant' that required a favourable environment for its nurture and growth. This suggests that the great humanitarian virtues of altruism and compassion are not likely to thrive in a climate where these are noticeably absent: where power is valued for its selfish potential, and where physical or sexual abuse, social enmity, lawlessness, drug addiction and crime are seen to be the norm. A more wholesome environment where people learn to live in mutual respect and harmony is more likely to create the soil where virtues such as honesty, compassion, tolerance and love can blossom. It is widely accepted that the right family (and educational) environment provides an important starting point in creating the conditions for such moral development.

Moral communities
- Humanitarian charity organizations.
- Army regiments.
- Fire brigades.
- Lifeboat fraternities.
- Educational establishments.
- Medical units.
- Police forces.
- Sports and athletic clubs.
- Religious communities, orders, churches.

RELIGION AND VIRTUE

> The fraternal dynamism of such organizations has obvious potential to promote virtue and honour, but the same dynamism can be turned in a different direction – among crime syndicates, fraud and extortion rackets, criminal gangs, drugs organizations, people traffickers, and the like.

The potential of religion in developing the virtuous life

It can be claimed that some of the best-known models of exemplary behaviour come from within religious traditions, making religious communities an important resource for encouraging the virtuous life. The Christian elevation of agape-love, for instance, would be unrealistic were it not directly linked to its embodiment in the humanitarian love shown by its founder, with his emphasis on the character virtues of compassion, tolerance, agape and love of neighbour. Jesus did not often specifically target immoral or unethical behaviour (although he sometimes did) such as stealing, lying, murder, rape, adultery, slander and so on. Instead he stressed virtuous behaviour: like being 'peacemakers', 'clean of heart', showing 'hunger and thirst after justice' and, overall, showing a self-sacrificing spirit expressed in selfless concern for others.

> Not everyone who says Lord, Lord will enter the kingdom of heaven.
> *Jesus*

If the distinguishing mark of Christian ethics is its character as an ethic of response to God's revelation, many would argue that this gives it a greater impetus for the adoption of the virtuous life than, say, a purely rational ethic driven by duty or utility. History certainly shows that some of the great religious figures within the Christian tradition (St Paul, St Augustine, St Francis, George Fox, John Wesley, Mother Teresa) have had few equals from within secular systems. In his study of religion, **William James** seemed to confirm this when he said that religious faith had produced *'some of the best fruits that history has to show'*. From an a priori position many would question whether a secular atheistic world view, for instance, which sees life as an accident, and a one-off opportunity to live life to the full, with a consequent preference for material values, could provide the dynamism required for agape, altruism and self-sacrifice, the hallmarks of a truly virtuous life.

RELIGION AND HUMAN BEHAVIOUR

> ***Religion*** may be an important resource for the practice of a virtuous life, but reality shows that many 'fall by the wayside' and fail to live up to the ideals of religious faith. Equally many non-religious people have shown examples of the highest virtue.
>
> *But how far does this reality provide an argument for saying that religion and virtue do not necessarily go together?*

On the other hand there is enough evidence that non-religious people are capable of acts of the highest virtue to make it unnecessary to labour the point. Many would rightly object to the view that religion is necessary to show altruistic concern for others. A parent who runs into a burning building to save a neighbour's child is unlikely to do so for 'religious' or 'non-religious' reasons. The evidence is that those who showed bravery in saving others during the sinking of the Zeebrugge ferry, and other natural disasters, were from all backgrounds. The issue of theoretical motivation simply would not come into play. Many of us act (as **Hume** supposed) out of an instinct for doing the compassionate thing in a crisis situation. As **Karl Rahner** has argued, the capacity of people to live a virtuous life, while in principle it can be aided by religious faith, is not in the end dependent on it (see above, p. 88).

> We all make mistakes, we all make people we love suffer in one way or another – *c'est la vie*, and luckily people don't love us for our virtues or we'd be in a bad way.
>
> Graham Greene

Moral and practical limitations of virtue ethics

While there could be no criticism of virtue as representing what is best in human nature, many have found fault with the modern emphasis on virtue ethics as either too idealistic, or too vague and too general, to be morally significant for most people. One argument is that modern society is not conducive to the practice of virtue. Many argue that too many are exposed to the wrong influences, and are unlikely to appreciate the values of a virtuous life. MacIntyre's reply to this is to say that society needs to learn the value of virtue to bring about the reform that society needs: any other response would be a counsel of despair, accepting the rise of vice and crime as beyond correction. Another criticism appeals to cultural relativism. What are virtues in one society may not be so in another. Virtue ethicists reply to this by saying that right and wrong are universally recognized, and so is the difference between virtue and vice. A final criticism centres on the importance of specific rules, rather than virtues. Without specific rules legislation would be impossible, and people understand the language of rules better than the language of virtue. Again MacIntyre replies to this by holding that rules and laws are indeed important, but emphasis on a change of character is the best way to bring about the moral improvement of society.

> ***Virtue ethics*** Change of character is the best basis for personal and social moral improvement.
>
> ***Rules ethics*** Adherence to rules is the best practical way to ensure moral behaviour.

18 Religion and Conscience

- Definitions of conscience.
- Conscience: subjective and objective aspects.
- Conscience and the demands of reason.
- Conscience and the ethical theories.
- Conscience as the voice of the emotions.
- Conscience as merely psychological.
- Conscience as the voice of God.

Different views of conscience

Conscience has been defined as an inner sense of right and wrong the ignoring of which can bring feelings of shame or remorse. **Aquinas** defined conscience as 'the faculty of reason making moral judgements', and by implication the faculty that makes me aware of my obligations to God. Conscience is seen by some as 'an innate sense of right and wrong', and by others, such as **Freud**, as a humanly conditioned moral reflex caused by the superego, a mental package made up of moral restrictions learned from parents and other authority figures in a child's upbringing. Whatever its origins, Freud recognized its emotional power to cause guilt and shame, which he described as 'fear of a loss of love'. Some might argue that this could be explained as the result of the self-criticism that conscience brings. If I am reproached by my conscience for falling short of my own moral standards, it would not be surprising if I felt less lovable as a result. Conscience can thus be seen from either a religious or a secular perspective, but in either case it seems to have the same disturbing effect on the psyche.

> **Popular expressions about conscience**
>
> I have always acted with a good conscience.
>
> Everyone has to live with a bad conscience.
>
> I did what I thought was right, and I have a clear conscience.
>
> The criminal showed no remorse, and seemed to have no conscience.
>
> People who prey on others cannot be said to have a conscience.
>
> He got off lightly, but he has to live with his conscience.
>
> Everyone should go home and examine their own conscience.
>
> Nobody can escape the pangs of conscience.
>
> I don't know how he could square that with his conscience.

The subjective and objective aspects of conscience

For Aquinas conscience had two aspects: *conscientia* and *synderesis*. *Synderesis* provides the knowledge of what we should do or avoid (a function of the intellect). *Conscientia* is the ability to act on that knowledge (a function of the will). For Aquinas our God-given ability to reason leads to *synderesis*. This is a fundamental awareness, available to all rational beings, not only that we should pursue good and renounce evil, but that certain things are good and certain things evil. Aquinas believed that *synderesis* (or knowledge of the good) includes the primary precepts of natural law (see p. 256), which he believed ultimately represented the will of God. With this wider knowledge of what is right and wrong the individual possesses a truly informed conscience. But many do not have an informed conscience. They rather end up in a state of invincible (excusable) ignorance, but if they follow their conscience with sincerity their actions can be morally excused. Aquinas thus accepted the reality of how conscience operates, sometimes mistaking illusion for reality (Plato) or apparent goods for real goods (see above, p. 287).

RELIGION AND HUMAN BEHAVIOUR

> **Aspects of conscience**
>
> ***Subjective*** The inner ***perception*** of right and wrong, what Aquinas called ***conscientia***. Marked by goodwill, but may be faulty.
>
> ***Objective*** The ***content*** of conscience. An informed conscience (***synderesis***) is the ideal. But morally speaking the ***subjective*** side of conscience is more important than its ***objective*** side (Aquinas).
>
> ***Emotional*** Conscience creates ***feelings*** of guilt and shame if it is ignored (Butler).
>
> ***Rational*** Conscience is directed to what ***reason*** says is right and wrong (Aquinas, Kant).
>
> ***Psychological*** Conscience is that which makes us feel bad when we ignore the ***superego*** (Freud).
>
> ***Secular*** Conscience is a purely ***human*** faculty with no religious significance (Freud).
>
> ***Religious*** Conscience can be seen as the voice of God (Newman).

The need for conscience to respect moral and religious principles

Aquinas held that conscience was an important moral guide, but as a subjective faculty it cannot operate without reference to objective moral norms and, for believers, the demands of Christian ethics. If certain forms of 'conscience' appear to uphold what is generally regarded as morally reprehensible, then most people would say there is something wrong. This means that even at the non-religious, or rational level, conscience cannot be taken seriously if it tries to uphold behaviour that is regarded as socially or morally unacceptable. Eccentric examples have been cases where people have appealed to conscience to, say, kill prostitutes, gays, believers or unbelievers and so on – sometimes with the unconvincing and derisory plea that 'God asked me to do it'! The courts are usually quick to dismiss such appeals as either insane, daft or hypocritical.

RELIGION AND CONSCIENCE

> **Aquinas** was aware of the tendency to appeal to conscience to justify the morally unacceptable.

What might be called the Nazi 'conscience' may be taken as another example of this. Historically it came under universal moral condemnation because the principles it attempted to uphold were declared to be irrational, inhuman and evil. The barbarous treatment of the innocent, the wanton disregard for the individual, the family, the group, the neighbourhood; the flagrant rejection of rights to liberty, property and life itself were officially judged to represent 'gratuitous evil' and 'crimes against humanity', forms of behaviour that could never be squared with reason, human sympathy or conscience as normally understood. All this suggests some objective, indeed universal reference point for conscience, by which it is possible to assess and pass judgement on the behaviour of others.

> ***Macbeth*** couldn't sleep after killing the king, proving that 'conscience doth make cowards of us all'. Those who do evil and act as if they had 'no conscience' are usually considered either to show moral ignorance, or to suffer from a psycho-pathological condition that blocks out moral feelings. Psychopathic behaviour, however, comes at a price: society normally looks for protection from such behaviour regardless of its alleged origins or causes.

In the context of religious faith, if conscience is to be an absolutely true moral guide, this is dependent on how far it takes into account established principles (*synderesis*) of religious ethics. **Aquinas**, while recognizing in practice the value of a sincere conscience, believed something more was required in the form of knowing what was objectively right or wrong. Therefore he made the distinction between an 'erroneous' and an 'informed' conscience. Only an informed conscience can reflect the objective moral insights that make possible a moral action in accordance with what is objectively right (the will of God). This is similar to **Kant**'s view that the goodwill (*conscientia*) of the agent must combine with the objective moral law (*synderesis*) to produce a truly moral act.

> *How far can it be shown that **Aquinas** and **Kant** had similar views about the make-up of conscience?*

However, it can be seen that both Aquinas and Kant were dealing with ideals, and if conscience in the end remains a subjective faculty, it may be asking too much to expect it to be always as informed as it should be. For this reason the Christian Church, in its pastoral practice, has always placed special importance on the recognition of human weakness, and the consequent place of forgiveness. Many would say that the sense of being forgiven for moral failure is something not only of religious significance, but also of serious subjective importance for an individual's personal sense of self-esteem and emotional well-being.

> **The authority of conscience**
>
> If human beings are 'fallen' (prone to evil), as acknowledged by the existentialists (see above, p. 66), it is unlikely that the human faculty of conscience would not also be fallen, making the idea of 'conscience being a sound moral guide' questionable in practice. For **Aquinas**, an erroneous conscience has no real authority, being neither the voice of reason, nor expressing the will of God. But in practice an erroneous conscience may have moral authority for an individual.

Conscience as more an emotional than an intellectual guide

Joseph Butler held that conscience was the inner guide that led to feeling of moral satisfaction or dissatisfaction. But instead of arguing with **Aquinas** or **Kant** that conscience was an intellectual guide to behaviour, he preferred to argue that it was more an emotional guide. Therefore, instead of conscience telling us how we *should* behave, it is more likely to tell us how we *have* behaved. In this view if we feel badly after doing something it is probably a sign that we have acted badly, and vice versa. It can be seen however that these two are not in disagreement about the role of conscience as a moral guide. One merely stresses one aspect, the other another. Butler was in fact quite aware of the moral content of human behaviour, and knew that something else underlay the feelings that conscience created.

For Butler the crucial divide in human behaviour was between selfishness and benevolence, and conscience was always sensitive to this divide. At

> ***Aquinas*** Conscience is an ***intellectual*** guide to moral behaviour. It tells us how we ***should*** behave. But Aquinas would also have known about the emotional side of conscience.
>
> ***Butler*** Conscience is an ***emotional*** guide to moral behaviour. It tells us how we ***have*** behaved. But Butler was also aware of the ***moral content*** of conscience. How we ***feel*** follows from the ***nature*** of our behaviour, whether it was ***self-regarding*** or ***other-regarding***.

one extreme there is self-centred behaviour (*egoistic*), at the other extreme behaviour is other-centred (*altruistic*). Wherever behaviour is driven by selfish interest the effect is dissatisfaction, a sense of something wrong, and at worst a cringing sense of inner guilt. Wherever it is driven by regard for the good of another (through a sense of justice and perhaps agape) the effect is moral fulfilment, a sense of having done the right thing, a feeling of inner pride. But in normal, everyday behaviour there is always a tension between the two, resulting in complex feelings about what was done, or not done, what might have been done, and what should have been done. In the end the authority of conscience cannot be questioned in principle, but, for Butler, it is its emotional effects that provide the best indication of how far we have followed its guidance. If we end up with a 'good conscience' it is likely that we have behaved right, and vice versa.

> For **Joseph Butler** conscience always alerts us to how ***egoistic*** we are when deciding on moral issues. But he believed that the guidance of conscience also lay in what ***feelings*** it gave us about how we have acted. Good or bad ***feelings*** were a sign of a good or bad conscience.

Conscience as merely a psychological conditioned phenomenon

> *Freud reduced conscience to a socio-cultural phenomenon. How far can this view be defended, and how does it compare and contrast with other views of conscience?*

We end this chapter with a look at conscience as merely an emotional phenomenon that can result in neurotic feelings of anxiety and guilt. **Freud** claimed that conscience was a psychological signalling mechanism that alerted the individual to his or her perceived moral shortcomings. These shortcomings were merely socially conditioned; they were related to the failure to live up to the demands of the superego (a sense of what others expect). Once the superego is seen for what it is, a socially or family conditioned sense of moral awareness, the individual can become free from its effects and experience release from guilt and anxiety. Therefore, if Freud is correct, conscience is not related to morality in any transcendent sense (as theists would argue), but is merely a reflection of humanly imposed rules of behaviour perceived to come from parents or other socially positioned authority figures. In this view conscience is reduced to a humanly conditioned moral reflex mechanism that can eventually be seen for the illusion that it is.

> *Aquinas* Conscience touches on what is objectively right or wrong in the eyes of God.
>
> *Kant* Conscience reflects what reason can see as the objective moral law.
>
> *Butler* Conscience tells us how selfish or benevolent we have been.
>
> *Freud* Conscience is the result of how we are brought up, and can be changed.

Those who do not see it for what it is are classed as emotionally immature, and subject to irrational forms of fear, anxiety and guilt. Those who come to realize their immature state can, said Freud, grow up sufficiently to escape its restricting demands. But many would point out that there is little evidence that conscience can be so easily escaped from. Most people testify to a deep-seated awareness of demands of a moral (rather than social) nature, that seem to have an inescapable demand even when we 'get away' with something. In other words people are able to distinguish social rules from moral rules. The latter have an inescapable universal validity, and have a compelling hold on the individual because of their perceived seriousness. Conscience, it seems, continues to 'make cowards of us all' long after the superego has been exposed for what it is. This would certainly be in line with Kant's view of morality, something open to reason, resulting in a categorical imperative that cannot

RELIGION AND CONSCIENCE

be reduced to human conditioning. Kant as we know (see p. 46) went on to argue that moral reason pointed to the existence of a rewarder and punisher, who would ensure the *summum bonum* for those who kept the moral law with goodwill. In this way Kant argued that conscience properly understood leads to the intuition of God's existence.

> **Conscience and the ethical theories**
>
> *A Christian conscience*   Influenced by the demands of the Christian faith.
>
> *A Kantian conscience*   Influenced by the moral law and the need for goodwill.
>
> *A utilitarian conscience*   Influenced by the need to create happiness and minimize pain.
>
> *A situationist conscience*   Influenced by the need to show agape.
>
> *In view of the fact that situationism allows for the breaking of traditional principles if the situation demands it, what problems of conscience might a situationist have to deal with?*

The idea that conscience is a compelling moral voice that points to God

When **Freud** maintained that guilt was rooted in the fear of a 'loss of love' he was merely referring to the loss of love of those who represented the superego (parents, society). This, however, raises questions about why conscience should have this effect. If, as many argue, conscience is a moral voice which alerts us to what we deep down perceive as universally binding moral principles (not mere social restrictions), it appears odd to link its effects with fear of just losing the love of other human beings. Besides, many would argue that this view hardly accounts for why we feel guilt over something even if nobody knows about it. **Aquinas**, who believed that evil meant the loss of the love of God, argued that while conscience was also related to revelation, it was primarily the voice of *reason* in moral matters. But if the ignoring of conscience leads to the sense of a 'loss of love', there are grounds for saying that this is about more that losing the love of others.

RELIGION AND HUMAN BEHAVIOUR

> **Freud** held that conscience was about *guilt*, and guilt was rooted in the *fear* of losing the love of *others*. But many have pointed out that this does not explain why we can feel guilty over something known only to *ourselves*.
>
> *How far could this point to a transcendent aspect of conscience?*

John Henry Newman took up this point when he held that conscience, while it directly signalled approval or disapproval in regard to one's moral obligations, was indirectly the voice of God. Obviously influenced by **Aquinas** and **Kant**, he pointed out that moral obligation had a rational compulsion that demanded our attention, but he did not think this was the complete picture. As **Freud** had suggested, the real 'pangs' of conscience come not from breaking a moral or social rule, but from a sense of offending the *people* we love, and who love us. Conscience therefore had a personal dimension: the moral law points to a law-giver, a hidden personal source we call God. But obviously this view is highly conditional. It could only apply to a conscience that was sincere and backed by goodwill on the one hand, and was well informed and consistent with reason and revelation on the other. Newman was aware that if conscience 'permits' what is widely seen as immoral or irrational then it loses its claim to be a moral guide, much less the voice of God.

> Newman believed conscience was an inner source of moral guidance that *could* be the voice of God, provided it was both sincere and well informed. An ill-informed or selfish conscience would be the voice of the person, not the voice of God.
>
> *How far could it be argued that Newman's view is more idealistic and theoretical, rather than having practical significance?*

> **Views of conscience**
>
> **Aquinas** Conscience is the voice of *reason* in making moral judgements. But conscience can also be selfish, erroneous, unreasonable and misleading.

RELIGION AND CONSCIENCE

Kant Conscience is the voice of ***reason*** which tells us our moral duties. But when we perceive our duty wrongly, our moral reason, or conscience, becomes misleading.

Butler Conscience is the voice of ***the inner self*** telling us whether we have acted selfishly or altruistically. A good conscience brings satisfaction, a bad conscience guilt.

Newman Conscience is the voice of ***God***, revealing his will. But if it is ill-informed it is neither the voice of reason nor the voice of God.

Freud Conscience is the human voice of ***society*** whose approval we need. Once we achieve moral maturity we can lessen its impact, and escape from guilt and anxiety.

*The Christian view of conscience is that it is both the voice of reason and the voice of God, but how far can this view be said to take into account the **reality** of how conscience works in practice?*

19 Religion and Freewill

- The implications of freewill and determinism.
- How knowledge or ignorance affects behaviour.
- The problem of real and apparent goods.
- Religious implications of soft determinism.
- Philosophical arguments against hard determinism.
- The implications of hard determinism.
- Determinism and legal justice.
- Reconciling freewill and God's foreknowledge.

The implications of freewill and determinism

The problem of freewill has engaged philosophers for thousands of years. Are we really free or are we subject to outside forces that determine how we behave. If our actions are determined by, as some claim, the physical forces of cause and effect then there can be no morality, since morality is based on the assumption that we are free, that is, that we could have acted otherwise than we did. If morality is impossible, there can be no room for the concepts of praise and blame. There can be no courage and no cowardice, and the commonly accepted notions that some people deserve honours for valour, like the Victoria Cross, would lose their meaning. This issue also has important implications for religious faith and behaviour. Only on the basis that we are free can we be held responsible by God for how we act, and consequently be punished or rewarded for our actions, a notion central to all western religions.

The notion of freewill has also been an issue in relation to the omniscience

RELIGION AND FREEWILL

of God, which also includes his foreknowledge. If God knows everything in advance, then he knows all our actions in advance. If he does, how can we be free? We return to this question at the end of the section.

How knowledge or ignorance affects behaviour

Plato held that our knowledge of the good was enough to make us follow it. But was Plato referring to what people *thought* was good, or what was *really* good? As we know from his allegory of the Cave (see p. 105) Plato was a realist, and knew that people were often taken in by illusions about what is good and what is real. If this is true Plato would have been aware of the difference between what is thought to be good, and what is really so. **Aquinas** recognized this distinction when he pointed out the difference between real and apparent goods.

> He who knows the good will follow the good.
>
> *Plato*

Mill showed a similar awareness of these distinctions when he recognized that people often had a restricted vision about what was good. Just as there were higher and lower pleasures, there were higher and lower goods (see p. 245). But people might often choose a lower pleasure because the capacity to appreciate a higher one was beyond them. What might look really good to a pig would not look the same to Socrates! If this is true, then it is possible that people can be 'victims of ignorance' and 'not know any better', which in turn has implications for their capacity to exercise full freedom when faced with moral choices. This implies that ignorance can restrict moral freedom, but only within certain limits.

> A good man is free though he be a slave, an evil man is a slave though he be a king
>
> *St Augustine*
>
> *Augustine, following Plato and Aristotle, believed the proper use of freedom was limited by moral ignorance. To be enlightened is to see virtue as the highest moral good, to be unenlightened is to choose evil and be a 'slave'. But how far might this view let criminals 'off the hook' by excusing their actions on the grounds of ignorance?*

RELIGION AND HUMAN BEHAVIOUR
The religious understanding of moral freedom

The notion of personal responsibility is central to Christian ethics. This presupposes the freedom of the individual to make moral choices based on the knowledge of good and evil. The concept of the Last Judgement incorporates the notions of reward and punishment, notions which would make no sense without the presupposition of freewill. In religious terminology humans are free because they can rise to the heights of virtue, or fall into the depths of sin. This, however, is not the full picture. Equally central to the Christian tradition is the doctrine of original sin, which means that human beings are 'fallen' and their moral capacities weakened. Factors that can accentuate this are generally recognized to include such things as inheritance, genetic predispositions, character formation and the impact of social or environmental conditioning.

> ***Soft determinism*** is the view that human actions are sometimes subject to mitigating factors.

All these factors are seen to contribute to what is called 'the weakness of the will', something however that cannot be reduced to moral 'ignorance'. While a knowledge of the good may be impaired, this does not excuse by itself actions that are clearly wrong by universal standards. Original sin is about the human tendency to go against what we *know* to be wrong, and still do it.

But if there is a reason for saying that we may be influenced (although not compelled) to act in certain ways then our freedom is not absolute, but in some way subject to circumstances. This is known as 'soft determinism', a view that allows for freewill, but also allows for extenuating circumstances that might impair the full use of that freewill.

> **Factors in soft determinism**
> - Ignorance of the good (Plato).
> - Mistaking apparent goods for real goods (Aquinas).
> - Fallen character of human beings (Heidegger).
> - Weakness of the will (Luther).
> - Effects of original sin (Christian).

RELIGION AND FREEWILL

> *Circumstances such as poverty, upbringing, drugs, alcohol, passion, education and the rest can affect will power, but how far can these factors totally excuse certain forms of behaviour?*

The absolute inability to act freely is known as hard determinism

So-called 'hard' determinism is the view that all our actions can be explained as being the result of the influence of inexorable physical laws. In this view human beings are seen as part of the physical chain of cause and effect and all human actions can be explained in terms of mechanical inevitability. Determinists hold that all exercises of the human will are predetermined by biological or psychological forces and can be completely explained in terms of the physiological make-up of the human organism.

> Philosophers have pointed out that there is one serious problem with hard determinism. Those that hold it are already determined to do so.

Philosophical arguments against hard determinism

Hume did not believe in determinism because he denied that causes could ever be fully established beyond the experience that one thing is only seen to follow another. This undermines the concept of determinism, which holds that things follow in causal sequences, that is, the claim that I act as I do because I am causally programmed (determined) to do so. For Hume such a claim could never be experienced to be true, and is therefore meaningless. **Kant** rejected hard determinism and held that the freedom of the will was an absolute given, in view of the categorical imperative. If man has an absolute obligation to follow the moral law then he must be free since, as he famously put it, 'ought' implies 'can'. Besides, to imply that we have no real freewill would undermine our dignity as human beings who are distinguished, as Kant pointed out, by our ability to follow the moral law through the dictates of reason and conscience. To overstate determinism would mean renouncing

RELIGION AND HUMAN BEHAVIOUR

our entitlement to praise and blame, normally seen as necessary aspects of human behaviour. It would mean I could never be credited for living a virtuous life, or be discredited for not doing so.

> ***Hume*** We could never know about being determined by physical laws, even if we were.
>
> ***Kant*** Without freedom of the will, we would lose our human dignity.
>
> ***Boethius*** Human beings behave too unpredictably to be determined.
>
> ***Honderich*** Nature is too unpredictable to be a basis for determinism.
>
> ***Christian*** Human beings are subject to original sin, but have sufficient freedom to act properly.

Hard determinism was rejected by **Boethius** among others. He saw life as a conflict between the fixed spiritual realities of goodness and truth against the transitory realities attached to the material side of life. In dealing with this conflict human beings behave in unpredictable ways, and therefore human behaviour can never be explained by a theory of determinism. Instead, life was best imagined not as a fixed or determined series of events but like a random 'wheel of fortune' on which everyone is fated to turn, some to good luck and some to misfortune. But he believed that it remains for everyone to do what they can to ensure that the wheel turns to their advantage!

> Boethius believed that life was too dependent on fortune to be credibly seen as determined, but it remains for everyone to act in such a way that the wheel turns to their advantage.

The contemporary philosopher **Ted Honderich** rejects the notion of physical determinism on the grounds that nature contains too much unpredictability and novelty to be a strict basis for any kind of determinism. He takes the example of how a breeze affects the leaves of a tree. Here it becomes impossible to predict how the breeze will move the leaves. In the same way human decisions cannot be determined if natural forces are unpredictable. He agreed that such a view would reduce us to playthings of nature, and undermine our value as free moral agents. However, physical determinism was already firmly undermined by **Heisenberg**'s *uncertainty principle*. In quantum physics a quantum of light can interfere with either the position or velocity of a particle, making the behaviour of either completely unpredictable, thus undermining the credibility of extreme physical determinism.

> ***Hard determinism*** I could not have acted other than I did because I was completely determined.
>
> ***Soft determinism*** I could ideally have acted other than I did, but I was constrained by a number of factors (ignorance, poverty, weakness, etc.) to act as I did.

Hard determinism not accepted in legal justice

The view that we do not possess freewill is not the commonsense view, and is not acceptable in the common estimation of society. While we can allow for the fact that by upbringing, environment and genetic predisposition we are subject to forces that might appear to impair our freewill, this does not let us off the hook of personal responsibility. In other words although by nature we may be predisposed to lean towards egoism and self-interest, we are still accountable for our actions before every court of law. In the context of legal justice it means that in the common opinion of reasonable people we are, as a norm, to be held accountable for our actions. This is because we are deemed to be able to act otherwise than how our impulses tempt us to act.

> When we obey moral laws we are autonomous and free. Because we are imperfectly rational, and subject to desire and selfishness, we see morality as constraint, as duty.
> *Kant*

Quite simply it means that we are held to be free enough for our actions to be judged as worthy of approval or disapproval. Indeed, any other view would make the ordinary running of society impossible because it would undermine the whole concept of personal responsibility, which in turn would undermine all national and international law. If I am never to be held responsible for what I do (allowing for recognized extenuating circumstances) then

I can never be punished for what I do, and the concept of deterrence would collapse. But the reality is that I am held responsible, on the grounds that I am considered to be free enough to obey the law or violate it. The hard determinist view is also contrary to the basic beliefs of the Christian tradition which holds that, even allowing for human weakness, we are responsible to God for the things we do.

> The Nazis who were tried for war crimes were held fully responsible for their actions, showing the established rejection of determinism as a theory of behaviour.

Soft determinism is accepted in legal justice

A variant form of determinism was espoused by the American lawyer **Clarence Darrow**, who held that no client of his could ever be held fully responsible for their crimes, and therefore could never be fully blamed for their actions. This was because he saw all behaviour explicable in terms of pre-existing influences. Critics of Darrow pointed out the 'buck-passing' implications of explaining criminal behaviour as the result of 'what others had done to them'. If this is true, they claim, an endless chain begins backwards in which nobody is responsible for their behaviour since each individual in the chain can appeal to prior influences to excuse their behaviour. Darrow himself, it is said, was not beyond feeling that he was denied praise for his success as a defence lawyer, thus revealing an inconsistency in his position. However, in practice he was successful in getting many of his clients reduced sentences because of his eloquence in convincing juries that they were not 'fully' responsible for their crimes.

> **A summary of terms**
>
> ***Hard determinism*** The view that we are completely determined by physical laws and are therefore not morally free.
>
> ***Soft determinism*** The recognition that we are morally free but are subject to influences that reduce our freedom.

> ***Compatibilism*** The view that determinism is ***compatible*** with freewill. Held by the Stoics, Hume and Hobbes and central to the Christian and other religious traditions. The will may be influenced by prior causal factors, but no individual is ***forced*** to make specific choices. Hence acts are always free unless the agent is compelled to act by the influence of another ***person***. **Hume** believed that the only way we are determined is by our beliefs, desires and character, but that these are not determined by physical laws. In this view it is a ***category mistake*** to credit the ***laws of nature*** with the ability to undermine an agent's freewill. **William James** believed that determinism led to an unacceptable ***pessimism*** about ourselves and our capacity to make moral choices. Compatibilists are also known as ***soft determinists***.
>
> ***Incompatibilism*** The view that determinism is ***incompatible*** with freewill. It follows from the theory of ***hard determinism***, which holds that all our actions are causally determined by the physical laws of the universe. It sees freewill as a 'metaphysical' concept which ignores the fact that we are all part of the physical universe.
>
> ***Libertarianism*** The view that no determining factors exist to influence our behaviour, and that we are consequently completely free in making moral and other choices. Libertarians believe that the history of the world is dependent on the free choices of individuals and groups, not on some supposed deterministic scheme of inevitable happenings.
>
> ***Behaviourism*** The view that behaviour can be determined or controlled by the impact of certain psychological forces, and the effect of mental associations.

The problem of human freedom in relation to God's omniscience

We end this chapter on human freedom by considering the question of how God's omniscience (which includes his foreknowledge) can be reconciled with genuine human freedom. The argument states that if God already knows how I am going to act, then it becomes impossible for me to act otherwise. From this it follows that I can never be free. The corollary of this is if God does not know how I am going to act then my freedom is confirmed, but God cannot be omniscient. At the secular level *logicians* have shown that such reasoning is based on fallacy. The standard expression of the problem states that if something is foreknown to happen then it '*must*' happen. This is known as epistemic determinism, that is, determinism related to someone supposedly already knowing how things will happen. But some logicians point out that such a view of determinism is mistaken. Nothing 'must' happen for the event to be theoretically foreknown. What is foreknown is what *did* happen, not what must happen (see box).

God's omniscience and human freedom

- Logical answer. Nothing **mus**t happen. God only foresees what ***did*** happen.

- Religious answer (1). God only foresees how I ***used*** my freedom to act.

- Religious answer (2). God can ***choose*** not to know how free creatures will behave.

- Religious answer (3). God ***logically*** cannot know how free creatures will behave.

Applied to the problem of freedom and God's foreknowledge, the same logic would apply. The fallacy lies in the claim that if God already knows how I am going to act, then I *must* act in that way because the matter is already decided. But, as some claim, God does not foresee how I must act, he only foresees how I acted. God can only foresee how I *actually* used my freedom to act. If this is the case, it is a fallacy to argue that God's foreknowledge already determines my actions and so undermines my freedom. How I freely decided to act, and what moral choices I made, is what God foresees. This view, held by **Boethius**, is that God's omniscience is fully compatible with human freewill.

> God is like a spectator at a chariot race; he watches the actions the charioteers perform, but this does not cause them.
>
> *Boethius*

Another solution to this problem is to argue that God cannot know how free creatures will behave because (a) he deliberately chooses to deny himself such knowledge, and (b) human freedom is beyond what God can know. Those who hold the former view claim that it is perfectly feasible for God to do this without prejudice to his omniscience. Those who take the latter view say that it is similar to faulting God's omnipotence because he cannot make a round square. In both cases, it is claimed, God cannot be held responsible for not being able to do or know what is logically impossible to do, or know.

> If God had absolute foreknowledge he would know *if* a nuclear war was going to happen, and if so **when** it would happen.
>
> *How far would theists feel that this would lessen their obligation to make sure that it didn't?*

Profiles of Key Names Mentioned in the Text

Al Ghazali (1058–1111) Persian Islamic philosopher and mystical thinker. He wrote extensively on law, philosophy, theology and mysticism. He is associated with the Kalam argument for God's existence.

Al Kindi (801–73) Pioneering Islamic philosopher, scientist, mathematician and religious thinker. He believed in the compatibility of philosophy (reason) and theology. His ideas on the nature of God and the soul influenced other Arab thinkers who came later. He worked mainly in Baghdad.

Anselm, St (1033–1109) As one-time Archbishop of Canterbury he probably came into contact with people who denied the existence of God. It was this that made him analyse the meaning of God, and show that God was only denied by those who failed to understand what God meant. Thus was born the ontological proof.

Aquinas, St Thomas (1224–74) Generally regarded as the greatest Christian thinker of the medieval period, Aquinas was not only concerned to defend religion against rationalist attacks, but also to work out the implications of faith for believers. His theory of natural law is an attempt to align the will of God with the requirements of reason in regard to morality.

Aristotle (384–322 BC) Generally regarded as one of the outstanding figures in western thought, no study of any area of philosophy can be done without reference to him. His ideas on metaphysics and ethics were highly influential in the medieval period, particularly in the thought of St Thomas Aquinas. In an age of material and efficient causality, his notion of final causality is an important concept in the theistic world view.

Augustine, St (354–430) Famous for his conversion to Christianity from

PROFILES OF KEY NAMES

various pagan systems, he became renowned as an academic of high ability, gaining university posts in Milan and Rome. His Christian leadership led to his appointment as a bishop in the north of what is today Algeria. His writing output was enormous, but he is often remembered for the theodicy which bears his name.

Ayer, A. J. (1910–80) Crusading champion of logical positivism in England, he strongly supported the verification principle, but was later compelled to 'lower the bar' and admit that verification was not as clear-cut as he originally thought. Always remaining an empiricist, he is also remembered for his theory of emotivism as an account of ethical meaning.

Barth, K. (1886–1978) Noted for his opposition to the idea that God could be derived from human needs, he firmly defended the absolute transcendence of God over man. To understand God, human beings had to submit to his Word in the Bible and the Church. Barth's uncompromising religious ideas were not unrelated to his experiences in the Great War, and later to his experience of 'man becoming his own god' in the Third Reich.

Bentham, J. (1748–1832) Widely regarded as the father of modern utilitarianism, Bentham was an intellectual genius who wanted to see a more liberal social regime than that influenced by the established church. He believed actions should be judged on their consequences, rather than on how they conformed to traditional principles. The aim of action should be the maximization of pleasure and the minimization of pain. He believed that lifestyles which had no social effects were a waste of time, but many have seen this as a theoretical point rather than one that was true in reality.

Boethius, A. (480–524) Christian philosopher born in Rome to an aristocratic family. His most famous work is *The Consolation of Philosophy*, a book that reveals his debt to Plato, with its denigration of earthly things compared to the enduring values of the spirit. He believed true happiness came through the spiritual pursuit of the good, not through earthly attachments. He also recognized that life was uncertain, a 'wheel of fortune' on which everyone turns. He believed God's foreknowledge did not impede human freewill.

Bonhoeffer, D. (1906–45) German pastor, martyred for his faith under the Nazis. A devout Christian, he felt sympathy with those outside the official sphere of the Church, and proposed that faith could be practised in a 'non-religious', or secular way.

Bowker, J. Important religious thinker, especially on the relationship between reason and faith. He rejects the modern allegation that faith is some kind of 'virus', arguing instead that the tendency towards religious faith is rooted in human neuropsychological makeup, and has emerged in different forms throughout the history of religion.

Braithwaite, R. B. (1900–90) Distinguished British philosopher who worked in philosophy of science, ethics and philosophy of religion. Held that religious faith had an empirical aspect in respect of its moral implications for promoting an 'agapeistic way of life'. In this respect religious language could qualify for being meaningful. Theists argue that faith is about more than this, and that religious language is meaningful in itself without reference to empirical effects.

Buber, M. (1868–1965) A Jew born in Austria, he was removed by the Nazis from his teaching post in Frankfurt before settling in the Hebrew University in Jerusalem. In his famous and influential book *I and Thou* he argued that God could never without loss be reduced to an object, even an object of study. Divine reality can only be apprehended in a personal relationship, where God is addressed as *Thou*. In this sense he echoes Pascal, who criticized the cold objectified God of the Philosophers as a misleading shadow of the living God of the Bible. Buber also shows the influence of Kierkegaard, whose understanding of faith as a personal decision, as opposed to an object of philosophical speculation, bears many similarities with his own relational view.

Bultmann, R. (1884–1976) German New Testament scholar and a major contributor to Christian existentialism. He held that the Bible needed to be 'demythologized' to reveal its religious message about the meaning of human existence. In a direct riposte to Heidegger he believed that the questions raised by human existence were answered only by the insights of religious faith.

Burke, E. (1729–87) Famous Irish statesman and political philosopher, he was decried by Marx as a 'vulgar bourgeois' for his opposition to the French Revolution, and lauded by Churchill for his defence of liberty, and his attack on tyranny and political corruption. Famous for his aphorisms, he is remembered for phrases like 'the only thing necessary for the triumph of evil is for good men to do nothing.'

Butler, J. (1692–1752) Born in Wantage in England, Butler became a distinguished bishop and religious thinker. His interest in moral psychology led to his views on the emotional significance of conscience. Torn between the opposing attractions of self-love and benevolence, the human mind is always caught in a moral dilemma. Conscience, operating under the guidance of reason, is the faculty which helps to ensure the dominance of unselfish attitudes and actions over our natural tendency towards self-love. But conscience can also function through its emotional effects. An uneasy conscience was a sign that something was wrong, while a good conscience signalled the opposite. In this way nature equips us with an in-built guide on how we live.

Calvin, J. (1509–64) French Protestant theologian, and one of the leading Reformers. His theory of predestination was seen by Max Weber as a significant factor in the rise of capitalism, and the drive for wealth was later seen as the 'Protestant work ethic'. Calvin also held that belief in God was innate, but was widely suppressed by sin and 'unrighteousness'.

Chesterton, G. K. (1874–1936) Born in London, he became one of the best-known figures of his time for his witty writing and his profound observations on humankind and the world. He was also a strong religious (Catholic) apologist, and wrote, as he might have said, unapologetically about his convictions. Like Oscar Wilde he is remembered for his quotable quotes, such as, 'If there was no God there would be no atheists', and, 'He who does not believe in God will believe in anything.'

Cicero, M. (106–43 BC) A Stoic philosopher and regarded as one of the most versatile minds of his time, he introduced the Romans to the chief schools of Greek thought through his massive writing output. Although he declared himself a sceptic, claiming that no philosophy can be conclusively true, he embraced Stoicism as the one that he believed made the greatest contribution to the welfare of society. He believed that laws were sacred because they came from the gods and were made available to humans through reason. He believed therefore that the laws of nature were a good indication of how we should live, and that justice was above all else the hallmark of the virtuous person.

Copernicus, N. (1473–1543) Regarded as the first astronomer to detect the errors in the Ptolemaic cosmology which had made the earth the centre of the solar system. His ideas were first attacked by the Protestant Reformers, then by his own Catholic Church. But only with the arrival of Galileo was his work fully recognized.

Copleston, F. (1907–94) Jesuit priest and authority on St Thomas Aquinas, he is especially remembered for his mammoth and highly regarded *History of Philosophy*. He is also remembered for his participation in public radio debates with Bertrand Russell and A. J. Ayer. A man of gentle disposition, he made many friends both inside and outside academic circles,

PROFILES OF KEY NAMES

and remained greatly respected for his wide learning and keen intellect. He held that Aquinas was concerned to emphasize that God was not just a First Cause, but the continuing and omnipresent *ontological* cause of everything that exists.

Craig, W. L. (1949–) Research Professor of Philosophy at Talbot School of Theology in California, USA, he studied at some of Europe's leading universities including Munich and Louvain. He is well known for his examination of the Big Bang theory, and for what he sees as the religious implications of a beginning of the universe. He follows the Kalam argument in ruling out an infinite regress as inconceivable, and holds that only a personal God could create the universe *ex nihilo*. His views however have been challenged by the atheist Quentin Smith, who argues on the basis of a complicated *quantum cosmology* that the universe needs no cause. Craig is clearly at odds with those who hold that religion cannot realistically rest its case on issues that bring it into conflict with science, but he believes the implications of the cosmological argument cannot be ignored.

Cupitt, D. (1934–) Controversial Anglican divine and former Dean of Emmanuel College, Cambridge. He founded the *Sea of faith* movement dedicated to making religion more acceptable to the modern age. Its hallmark is non-realism. By this is meant its rejection of traditional Christian beliefs about Christ or God, which they see as unwarranted in the secular age. Instead they believe in the ethical standards and spiritual practices associated with traditional Christianity.

Darwin, C. (1809–82) Famed biologist and the founder of evolutionary theory, his ideas were to have a massive impact on religious belief, especially the understanding of the Bible. Originally impressed by Paley's teleological argument, he later had a crisis of faith when he saw the apparently random nature of natural selection: to all appearances nature showed no evidence of a divine 'guiding hand'. It is this idea that has provoked religious thinkers to defend what they see as the key notion of biblical theology, the existence of a personal God. Some philosophers admit that, despite the ambiguity of the empirical evidence, a personal creator is not an unlikely explanation compared with its alternative, blind chance.

Dawkins, R. (1941–) Oxford professor and reputed biologist, he has recently come to prominence with his anti-religious views strongly expressed in his book *The God Delusion* (2007). High sales of the book testify not only to the author's popular appeal, but perhaps as much to the popularity of its subject matter. Neither an established philosopher nor an objective religious thinker, his ideas have not been taken seriously by fellow academics, and have come in for much criticism from fellow atheists not just for the inappropriate manner in which they are expressed. To some (see Plantinga, p. 40) he is an emperor without clothes for his espousal of atheistic naturalism, which, on inspection, provides no sound basis for any objective truth-claims. If evolution is unguided, as he claims, it seems that its product (intellectual enquiry, say, and all scientific truth-claims) would have to be seen as unreliable, since there would be no reason to trust that it is reliable. This leads to the paradox that to rant against God one must first believe that one lives in a dependable universe.

Descartes, R. (1596–1650) Called the 'father of modern philosophy', his ideas have provided food for thought for philosophers for over five centuries. As a religious thinker he is remembered for his version of the ontological proof. But he is also being rediscovered for his claim that only God could guarantee the evidence of the senses. Without the assurances of believing in a good God who couldn't deceive, it would be impossible, he claimed, to trust our experience. This idea has recently been invoked to discredit naturalism, the view that our cognitive powers are merely a product of blind evolution.

Donoghue, D. (1928–) Irish academic and literary critic, he was elected Chair of the American Academy of Arts and Sciences. He currently teaches at New York University. His ideas on art, literature and poetry have particular influence. He is an authority on T. S. Eliot.

Dostoevsky, F. (1821–81) Born in Moscow, he became one of the most influential thinkers of his time and is generally regarded as one of Russia's greatest writers. His thoughts on humanity and religion were expressed in his many novels, some of which document his own sufferings. Before becoming a writer he joined the army but found himself sentenced to death for holding unacceptable liberal views. This was commuted to exile in Siberia, where he experienced the isolation and human anguish for which it became a by-word. He described his imprisonment as 'living in unendurable cold, packed like fish in a barrel'. Although a strong apologist for the Christian faith, he had a shrewd knowledge of human nature, and the motives that drive men both towards and away from religion. On his tombstone are the words of Jesus: 'unless the grain of wheat falls into the earth and dies it remains only a single grain; but if it dies it yields a rich harvest' (John 12.24).

Durkheim, E. (1858–1917) Regarded as the father of sociology, his main interest was in how social groups began to form, and how religion arises as a mistaken interpretation of the dynamics of social forces. He identified religion with what society holds most dear, and claimed that 'religion was society writ large'. His ideas opened up a new understanding of how religion can be influenced by social factors, but his theory of the origin of religion, based as it is on a narrow shelf of evidence, is not taken seriously today.

Feuerbach, L. (1804–72) Originally a follower of Hegel in Berlin, he later abandoned the study of religion, believing that Hegel was right about man and God being so intimately related. From this he went on to argue that religion was really a projection of humans' essential qualities onto an imaginary God. His ideas later influenced Marx, Nietzsche and Freud.

Fletcher, J. (1905–91) An American professor who established the ethical theory of *situation ethics*. While the theory advocates the unfaultable exercise of love of neighbour (agape) as the dominant factor in ethical decision-making, in Fletcher's hands it became complex and controversial. For instance he himself became the judge of what was 'the most loving thing to do' in particular situations. This led to his supporting a range of controversial ethical practices such as abortion, euthanasia and cloning. Today his situation ethics is largely seen as an ideal.

Flew, A. (1923–) Former Oxford academic who became involved in the falsification debate. He was generally derisory about the arguments for God's existence, but more recently he has had problems with accepting a naturalist account of human beginnings as expounded by Dawkins and others. He is said to be no longer an atheist, but his exact religious beliefs continue to be held secret. In 2005 he caused a major stir with a new book entitled *There Is a God: How the World's Most Notorious Atheist Changed His Mind*.

Freud, S. (1856–1939) Known as the father of psychoanalysis, Freud used his psychological theories to argue that God was an illusion based on imaginary wishes developed during childhood. His ideas were highly influential in the rise of modern atheism, and continue to be cited by those who see religion as no more than a purely human phenomenon, devised by humankind for illusory comforts.

Galileo (1564–1642) Renowned Italian astronomer, he is famous for confirming the theories of Copernicus that the world is heliocentric rather than geocentric. His discoveries brought him into conflict with the Church at a time when the Bible was understood literally. He remains an historic exam-

PROFILES OF KEY NAMES

ple of how not to challenge science in the field of empirical fact-finding.

Haldane, J. (1954–) Professor of Moral Philosophy at St Andrews University, Scotland. He has argued that the 'quiet desperation' of many humans poses questions that philosophy is obliged to face. This, he suggests, calls for a Philosophy of Spirituality which should examine the implications of how a religious world view differs from a non-religious one. If there is a difference it may hold the key to something that all people desire, the best way to cope with life, a secret which he believes may ultimately be described as peace of soul.

Hare, R. M. (1919–) Well-known British philosopher in the logical positivist tradition, he added to the emotive theory of ethical meaning by the observation that ethical claims are 'prescriptive' rather than merely 'descriptive' of a state of mind. Thus when someone says 'murder is wrong' they are not just expressing a negative feeling about murder, but are also implying that such a practice should be avoided, thereby 'prescribing' a course of action. He was also a strong defender of the principle of utility as the key theory of ethics.

Hartshorne, C. (1897–2000) A well-known American philosopher and religious thinker, he is widely associated with process theology. He rejected classical theism for holding an image of God that was too *static*. Instead he saw God as having a *dynamic* relationship with the world and human beings. He believed that God suffers through events in the world, and needs the world in order to 'surpass himself'. His ideas came to be used as part of a solution to the problem of evil. The main criticism of his proposal was his failure to show how such a 'dependent' deity could be worthy of adoration and worship. At the same time he has probably shown that traditional concepts of God create philosophical problems that cannot be resolved without reference to the questions raised by human existence.

Hegel, G. W. F. (1770–1831) Famous German philosopher of 'idealism'. His ideas about humanity being a reflection of God were taken up by others to argue that God is really a mythical reality created by the human imagination. He is therefore seen, contrary to his intention, as one of the founding fathers of modern atheism.

Heidegger, M. (1889–1976) Renowned and intellectually complex German philosopher of human existence, he is noted for his sharp analysis of what it means to 'be' human in the world. His secular ideas about 'Being' as some quasi-mystical reality which enables 'beings' to 'be' were used by some Christian thinkers to argue that God was really the Being he was trying to describe. They held that his view of human life only raised questions that religious faith could answer. Many saw his lofty ideas about human existence as rather too cerebral, something they saw confirmed when he found nothing amiss about becoming a member of the Nazi party.

Heisenberg, W. (1901–76) Renowned German physicist and Nobel laureate, he was one of the founders of *quantum mechanics*. His famous *uncertainty principle* is the result of the discovery that the location and momentum of quantum particles of light have an unavoidable uncertainty. Some theist writers have seen this discovery as a blow to the claim that science 'knows everything'.

Hick, J. (1922–) Contemporary British philosopher and religious thinker, Hick is well known for his contribution to the understanding of the Christian faith in the face of the rationalist challenge. He is credited with bringing to light the Irenaean theodicy, and the view that human life is meant to be a 'vale of soul making'. He is also remembered for his understanding of miracles, and his theory of 'eschatological verification'.

Honderich, E. R. (1933–) Canadian philosopher who has since moved to England and become a British citizen. Noted for his views on science and causality and his rejection of causal determinism.

Hume, D. (1711–76) Outstanding Scottish empiricist who challenged religious claims such as miracles, and the theological conclusions drawn from the teleological argument. He is also highly influential in showing that ethics are merely a human construct to enable human beings to live in society.

Irenaeus (c. 140–200) Ranked as one of the leading Fathers of the Church, he later became bishop of Lyons, where he established himself as a strong defender of the faith against the Gnostics, an influential pseudo-religious group. Irenaeus believed that Jesus set the pattern for salvation by showing the importance of accepting suffering and adversity. The Gnostics taught that salvation was a mystical prize that came by way of secret knowledge, and involved little in the way of moral input. Irenaeus, by contrast, taught that suffering and evil were a central challenge to human life, but could be defended as part of God's plan for human religious development, and ultimately our eternal salvation.

James, W. (1842–1910) American philosopher and psychologist, he is remembered for his objective and sympathetic study of religious experience. He said it 'bore the best fruits history has to show' but its truth from an objective standpoint was impossible to establish. Nevertheless its effects

PROFILES OF KEY NAMES

were so impressive that the phenomenon of religion could not easily be ignored.

Jung, C. G. (1875–1961) One-time pupil of Freud, he developed his own ideas about religion, seeing it as a more positive influence on the human psyche than did his famous colleague. Contrary to Freud he believed religion was the result of mystical experiences, not something explicable in terms of human drives or wishes. He believed that spiritual experience was crucial to the development of the Self, and was closely related to a perception of the divine.

Kant, I. (1724–1804) One of the most outstanding philosophers of all time, Kant rarely travelled from his home town of Konigsberg in the old East Germany. He became famous for working out how the mind contributes to the organization of experience, and for his conclusion that anything beyond experience could not be truly known. However, he believed that if God could not be known by reason, neither could his existence be ruled out by it either. In the end the question remained as to which made the most sense for the moral life of humankind. In this way Kant proposed that belief in God was most in keeping with our ultimate welfare, regardless of the limitations laid down by the methods of pure reason.

Kierkegaard, S. (1813–55) Kierkegaard's daring, and indeed demanding approach to religious faith is still heard today long since his untimely death on the streets of Copenhagen in 1855. Far from the eccentric he was earlier presumed to be, he has become one of the most provocative voices on the subject of life and faith. While others still feel that he has been too cavalier in his dismissal of more rational or experiential approaches, there remains a certain element of reason in is own complex vision. His understanding of faith as a leap made in the face of easier options has been based on a realistic, if grim, assessment of life in general. The belief that there is a God whose existence and revelation throws a new light on life, giving it a meaning that could not be arrived at by purely human reasoning, continues to find a resonance among those who find life, as he did, unable to deliver humans from angst and despair. His thoughts on the lonely individual are generally recognized to be the forerunners of what later came to be called existentialism.

Laplace, P. (1749–1827) A French mathematician and astronomer, he is remembered for his legendary reply to Napoleon, who asked him why he had not mentioned God in his astronomical theories. 'I have no need of that hypothesis,' he said. But his critics have claimed that he misunderstood the

PROFILES OF KEY NAMES

nature of God, who is not a *scientific* hypothesis as Laplace assumed.

Leibniz, G. W. (1646–1717) Renowned German philosopher and religious thinker, he made a large contribution to *theodicy* (a word he coined) by arguing that since God 'created the best of all possible worlds' the existence of evil and suffering is necessary for the overall good of the whole. Because only God can see the whole, and we can only see the part, it is impossible to know the real meaning of evil and suffering from God's point of view. He is also famous for contributing to the cosmological argument by posing the need for a *sufficient reason* to account for the existence of anything, including the world. His question *why is there something and not nothing* was named by Wittgenstein as the fundamental metaphysical question.

Lewis, C. S. (1898–1963) Born in Belfast, he became an Oxford academic and a prolific writer of both religious and non-religious books. After returning from atheism to the faith of his upbringing he became a noted apologist for Christian beliefs and values. For many he is best remembered for his internationally renowned *Chronicles of Narnia*.

Locke, J. (1673–1704) British empiricist whose views on the Christian religion as 'founded on miracle and prophecy' led his fellow empiricist Hume to challenge the basis of such claims. However, Hume merely showed that the alleged divine source of miracles could not be verified, leaving them only convictions of faith. In this sense Locke was right.

Luther, M. (1483–1546) Leading figure of the Reformation, Luther raised important questions about the importance of Scripture and the nature of faith, questions that led him to part company with the Catholic Church. A noted critic of the arrogance of 'natural man', he coined the 'Protestant principle' of salvation: it could only be gained by 'grace alone', 'faith alone', and 'scripture alone'.

MacIntyre, A. (1929–) An important figure in the promotion of virtue ethics, he believed that recent preoccupation with the 'ethical theories' had deflected interest away from the pursuit of a more human and worthwhile approach to ethical development.

Marx, K. (1818–83) Remembered for his observation on religion as 'the sigh of the oppressed creature, the heart of a heartless world, and the soul of soulless conditions . . . the opium of the people'. While this was partly true, any such theory purporting to explain religion as exclusively a response to intolerable social conditions has since been disproved.

Mill, J. S. (1806–73) Leading figure in the popularity of utilitarianism, he moved away from Bentham's concern with pleasure as such, and promoted

PROFILES OF KEY NAMES

the idea that the higher pleasures that defined culture were the most worth pursuing. He believed that the virtuous life was the best means for achieving the utilitarian ideal of widespread happiness in society.

Mitchell, B. (1917–) Fellow and Tutor in Philosophy at Oxford (1947–67). Professor of the Philosophy of the Christian Religion there (1968–84). Fellow of the British Academy (1983). A highly esteemed and widely travelled academic, he is remembered for his parable of the Resistance Worker as an illustration of how religious faith can survive on the basis of human trust, and as such could not be faulted just because it was impossible to falsify in practice.

Moltmann, J. (1926–) German Protestant theologian who was born into a secular background. He was drafted into the army and later became a prisoner of war. His knowledge and experience of his own country's atrocities led him to take an interest in theology. He was a strong advocate of the need for human involvement in the remaking of the post-war world, and rejected blaming God or waiting for miracles. Much of his writings centred on the theology of hope. He believed the presence of God could be perceived in mankind's spiritual capacity to rise above all evil and suffering. This he saw expressed in the widespread drive against injustice, and for peace and reconciliation.

Muggeridge, M. (1903–90) Author, satirist and Christian thinker, he was prominent for his public ridicule of modern materialism and the cult of instant gratification. He was famous for his scathing remarks on the youth culture of the 1960s, comparing its members to the Gadarene swine, 'high on sex and drugs and embarking on LSD trips over the hills and far away'. Passing through an atheistic phase, he finally became disillusioned with communism, and set out to expose its essential hypocrisy in having one law for its rulers and another for their unfortunate subjects. In his latter years he returned to the Christianity of his upbringing although, finally, as a Catholic, and was always a firm apologist for spiritual values.

Müller, M. (1823–1900) A German religious thinker who specialized in comparative religion through his extensive studies of eastern religions. He strongly opposed the use of Darwin's evolutionary theory to explain anything more that human physical development. When it came to culture and religion it was inapplicable because, he said, 'language places an insuperable barrier between man and beast'. He believed however that all religions needed constant purification and reform.

Newman, J. H. (1801–90) Renowned English religious thinker and preacher, his interest in the philosophy of knowledge led to his view that conscience, provided it was consistent with rational principles, was fundamentally the voice of God. He believed that the sense it created was of offending a person rather than an inanimate thing such as a law, and that for believers the ultimate source of all moral obligation was a personal God. Other views of conscience were a challenge to this, but for believers it remains largely true.

Nietzsche, F. (1844–1900) A self-confessed atheist, his attack on Christianity as a 'slave religion' was sharply rejected by religious thinkers who believed he had greatly misunderstood its true moral dynamic. His appeal, for many, lay in his twin aims of wanting a new human-centred morality devoid of traditional restraints, and the elimination of religion as its precondition. Unfortunately history has shown that both have since been tried, one with results Europe at least would not have wished for.

Otto, R. (1869–1937) German philosopher who made a major contribution to religious thought with his view of the numinous as a mystical factor in the rise of major religions.

Paley, W. (1743–1805) One-time Cambridge lecturer, and later archbishop of Carlisle. He is remembered for his teleological argument, which was greatly weakened by the discovery of evolution and natural selection. However, the questions he raised have returned in a new guise. Whether naturalistic answers are sufficient to explain the emergence of human life continues to be at the forefront of philosophical debate.

Pannenberg, W. (1928–) Contemporary German philosopher and theologian, his claim that the resurrection of Jesus can be established as an historical fact is a challenge that has gained serious attention.

Parmenides (550–420 BC) An important Presocratic philosopher who wrestled with the notions of truth, reality and change. He held that truth could not be reached by so unreliable a method as sense perception. He also held that nothing could come from nothing and therefore matter must be eternal. This view was countered by the medieval philosophers, like Aquinas, who held that God could create from nothing (*ex nihilo*) and that matter was ontologically dependent on God.

Pascal, B. (1623–62) French genius, religious thinker, mystic and renowned mathematician, he is famous for his rejection of religious philosophy because of the inadequate understanding of God that it produces. His one-time association with freethinkers and men of the world led to his proposal of the famous Wager that bears his name.

PROFILES OF KEY NAMES

Paul, St (c. 10–67) Born as a Jew in Tarsus in modern Turkey, his mystical experience on the road to Damascus led to his conversion to Christianity. He became a travelling missionary whose theological and ethical letters were to form not only a significant part of the New Testament, but its earliest written documents. His teachings on the death and resurrection of Christ were to be definitive for the understanding of the Christian faith. In Athens he tried to combine philosophical ideas with religious truth, but the main thrust of his writings was to show that his message was purely religious, something that he called a 'scandal' from a human, rational or philosophical viewpoint. His method was to target large cities (like Antioch, Athens, Corinth, Caesarea, Rome) and form centres of faith which would inspire others to see the truth of the incarnation, and readjust their lives in response to the crucified and risen Christ. He died as a martyr in Rome around AD 60.

Phillips, D. Z. (1934–2006) Former Welsh philosopher at the University of Swansea, he made his own contribution to the understanding of religious language by separating it completely from the language of science. Where other thinkers had either dismissed religion as meaningless, or tried to give it a rational or experiential basis, Phillips took a different view. Following Wittgenstein's inspiration he saw religion as belonging to a different realm of reality, with its language having a distinctly different 'grammar' to that of ordinary language. Thus God is not another 'truth' or 'fact' whose existence can be challenged, but a being whose reality is incomparable to anything in the world. But by removing religion away from the challenge of science in this way, many have felt he left more questions behind than answers.

Plantinga, A. (1932–) American philosopher and religious thinker who has taken a special interest in the relationship between science and religion. He has contributed to the ontological proof, and believes that without the existence of God the pursuit of truth, including scientific truth, has ultimately no trustworthy foundation.

Plato (428–348 BC) One of the most outstanding figures in the history of philosophy, his ideas combined with those of Aristotle to lay the foundation of western culture. In his writings he uses the person of Socrates, who held that the philosopher was like a doctor. While the doctor's task is to cure disease, the philosopher's task is to cure the mind of its worst complaint, ignorance. In his allegory of the 'cave of ignorance' he illustrated how earthly knowledge is a shadow of true reality, while real knowledge in 'the light of the sun' is about ideal realities beyond the material world. His ideas had particular influence on Christian thinkers, who used them to distinguish the spiritual world of God from the inferior material world of the senses.

Plotinus (205–70) Colourful and influential philosopher, generally credited with reviving Plato's ideas about the superiority of the spiritual realm as the key to humankind's true destiny. He held that happiness (*eudemonia*) resided in human consciousness, and was ultimately a spiritual capacity of the soul. It was beyond anything material, physical or corporeal, and could not be determined by either human fortune or misfortune. Happiness came from the contemplation of what was best in the universe, and lay in the pursuit of the Good. His ideas had particular influence on St Augustine, and were seen by many as laying the seeds of the mystical tradition which stressed union with the divine.

Polkinghorne, J. (1930–) Anglican priest, particle physicist and theologian, he made a major contribution to the science–religion debate through his lectures and writings. He argued for a 'moderate' anthropic principle, suggesting that the existence of God was a better explanation for the 'fine tuning' required to produce conscious life than pure chance.

Popper, K. (1902–94) Born in Vienna, one of the most influential and controversial figures of the twentieth century. Some of his more interesting ideas concerned the relationship between science and metaphysics. He rejected the verification principle as too narrow, confining meaning, as it did, to statements about the world. He believed science concealed its own metaphysical assumptions based on theories such as the reliability of induction, for which there could be no empirical warrant. Because laws of science could be formulated now, there was no empirical evidence to guarantee that one day they might not be overturned. Hence they were based on a priori metaphysical assumptions. Popper also contrasted the Greek concept of rationality with its modern counterpart. For the Greeks rationality led to an approximation of the truth because it was the work of humans: only the gods knew absolute truth. Today everyone claims to possess absolute truth.

Rahner, K. (1904–84) Born in Freiburg in Germany Rahner became a distinguished Catholic philosopher and theologian, but his ideas were influential across denominational boundaries. Influenced by Aquinas, his outstanding contribution to religious philosophy has been his theory of *transcendence* in relation to human knowing and loving. Rahner drew significance from the fact that human beings have a spiritual, but often unconscious, awareness of all human limitations on the one hand, and of the need to go beyond those limitations on the other. In regard to knowledge a point is never reached when the human mind is satisfied. In regard to love the object of affection is always beyond what can bring ultimate human fulfilment. In both respects man is faced with a horizon which can never be reached within the framework of human resources alone. This, for Rahner, was a pointer to the existence of an ultimate fulfilment of human spiritual striving, what we call God. This enabled him to hold that those who showed earnestness in knowing and loving, regardless of whether they were even explicitly atheistic or agnostic, were implicitly oriented towards God, and were entitled to be called *anonymous* believers in virtue of their moral integrity.

Ramsey, I. (1915–72)   Oxford Professor of Philosophy of Religion and later bishop of Durham. He opposed the logical positivist dismissal of religious language as meaningless, arguing that ordinary people saw religion as a source of 'disclosure' about the transcendent. He held that religion was empirically significant and was more about living and doing than mere thinking. He suggested the use of 'models' drawn from ordinary experience (such as power, wisdom, love) which when 'qualified' (by words like almighty, infinite, etc.) expressed for the believer what God was like.

Richmond, J. (1931–)   Former lecturer in Philosophy at Nottingham University and later Professor of Philosophical Theology at Lancaster. He combined philosophy and theology to defend a vision of the world which was thoroughly Christian. He believed that the word 'cognitive' had been understood too narrowly to exclude the moral, the historical, the existential and the religious. As a result he held that religious language was cognitive in the fullest sense because it yielded true knowledge of reality.

Rublev, A. (1360–1430)   Famous Russian icon and fresco painter. His best-known work is the *Trinity*, a work of remarkable power based on the visit to Abraham of three angels.

Russell, B. (1872–1970)   Famous British philosopher noted for his staunch atheism. Engaged in friendly but learned debates with the Jesuit priest Frederick Copleston on BBC radio. When he declared the universe to be a 'brute fact' he was told that this was not an intelligent answer to a major question of metaphysics. As Copleston told him 'he who leaves the chess table cannot be checkmated'! His answer however revealed the perception that such metaphysical questions could forever be put off.

PROFILES OF KEY NAMES

Schleiermacher, F. (1768–1834)   Recognized as one of the major figures in the history of religious thought, his analysis of religion as the 'feeling of absolute dependence' put a new focus on religious experience as the key to religious faith. He was later criticized for making religion too dependent on human factors, and thus creating the impression that God is in some way 'dependent' on humankind. His legacy was to shift attention away from rational approaches to God's existence in favour of a new approach, that of religious experience. Most subsequent writers on religious experience have recognized their debt to Schleiermacher.

Scruton, R. (1944–)   Former Professor of Aesthetics at Birkbeck College, University of London. Prolific author, and frequent contributor to newspapers, radio and television, he is widely regarded as a leading and authoritative thinker on philosophical, moral and religious issues. In his writings he frequently makes reference to the transcendent aspect of life, and shows little sympathy for the view that science either knows all the questions or has all the answers.

Socrates (470–399 BC)   Famous Greek philosopher but whose ideas and writings are often difficult to distinguish from those of Plato. He believed that the soul pre-existed the body and once lived in the realm of 'pure ideas', where it learned everything before birth. Thus truth is a matter of 'recollection' rather than of discovery. He popularized the 'Socratic method' of evincing answers to graded questions by way of dialogue, until the pupil sees the answer for himself. For this reason Socrates considered himself merely a conduit of truth, a 'midwife' who enables the birth of knowledge in others. He believed the pursuit of the Good was the highest calling, and 'virtue was the greatest human possession'.

Solzhenitsyn, A. (1918–)   Nobel Prize for Literature (1970), Solzhenitsyn became one of Russia's most famous modern writers. After serving in the army with distinction he was suddenly arrested and imprisoned for his criticism of Stalin. His harsh experience of prison made him resolved to reveal and record the injustices and sufferings endured by his fellow prisoners. He aimed as far as possible to record the exact names of those who had suffered in the camps, to offset official attempts to reduce everyone to the anonymity of a number, and for some not even that. He became an outspoken advocate of spiritual values which he believed were needed to counter the empty materialism and its attendant inhumanity that had been the hallmark of the regimes under which he lived. Emerging from prison he became a prophetic figure, seeing religion, and specifically Christianity,

PROFILES OF KEY NAMES

as the necessary bulwark against the pervading atheism that led to his and others' degradation in the camp-islands that he famously called the 'gulag archipelago'.

Steiner, G. (1929–) Highly decorated and renowned French academic who specialized in comparative literature. Noted for his colourful expressions and his wide range of learning, Steiner always argued for a greater vision of life than that provided by science. He believed that art was an important source for such a vision since it penetrated beyond the purely material. He is known for throwaway lines like 'the ordinary man casts a shadow in a way we don't understand, but the genius always throws light'.

Swinburne, R. (1934–) Eminent British university professor and philosopher, with special interest in religion and science. He recognizes his debt to Aquinas in his belief in the systematic rationality of belief in God and Christianity. He is associated with arguments in support of God's existence, religious experience, the possibility of miracles, and the plausibility of the belief that the world most likely came about through personal agency rather than by blind chance.

Tertullian (160–235) One of the earliest Christian writers and a vigorous defender of the Church. He wrote extensively on matters of faith and doctrine and strongly supported the *apostolic succession* as the key to the Church's authority. His distinction between *vera religio* and 'superstition' was a major theme in his writings.

Tillich, P. (1883–1965) Born in Germany but moved to America and became renowned as a Christian philosopher of existentialism. He tried to reconcile religion and modern culture arguing that the existentialist vision was inadequate for the full understanding of human existence. He held (like Schleiermacher) that our sense of finitude provided an insight into the reality of an infinite God, a reality that could only be expressed through symbols. He agreed with Aquinas that revelation was consistent with reason and human experience: it was the answer to what the existentialists failed to recognize, that no finite solution can be found to the mystery of existence. In reply to the existentialists, he held that God, the 'Ground of our being' is the only answer to the question of 'human being', and the only solution to the angst we experience from the threat of 'non-being', or death.

Vergote, A. (1921–) Professor Emeritus of the University of Louvain where he founded the Centre for Psychology of Religion. He has written extensively on religion as a psychic phenomenon, while holding to its validity as something coming from beyond the human. As a Christian priest and practising psychoanalyst, he is regarded as one of the most authoritative figures in the modern study of the psychology of religion.

Weber, M. (1864–1920)   German sociologist who made observations about the mutual effect of religious beliefs on social movements and tendencies. Calvinistic belief about predestination was a big factor in the rise of capitalism, which in turn had an effect on religious beliefs. On a wider front he observed the influence of religion on culture and civilization. In the West religion helped in the elimination of magic, and freed science to explore the empirical world. Unlike Marx or Durkheim he made no judgements on the truth of religion, confining his studies to its social impact.

Whitehead, A. (1861–1927)   English mathematician who went on to found *process philosophy*. In his book *Process and Reality*, he argued that change was an essential feature of all reality, including God. His ideas influenced later thinkers like Charles Hartshorne to develop his understanding of theism into what came to be called *process theology*.

Wisdom, J. (1904–1993)   Professor at Cambridge with special interest in language. He believed that religious language was non-cognitive because it could not be verified, but it could not be definitely falsified either, so the believer had reasons for persisting with it. He illustrated this in the parable of the invisible gardener.

Wittgenstein, L. (1889–1951)   One of the most profound and thought-provoking philosophers of modern times, he is widely regarded as one of the academic giants of the twentieth century. Initially he saw language as only valid for expressing empirically verifiable facts, but later held that its meaning should be extended to include its use for expressing insights and activities belonging to various *forms of life*. He saw religion as a complex form of life related to what he called the *mystical*, which gave rise to the need for expressing beliefs that could not be empirically verified. His ideas led some to adopt new methods for expressing religious truths. These included a *non-realist* understanding of transcendent realities, a method based on how such realities impinge on human understanding, activities and interests. Although notably secular in his approach, he differed from other philosophers of language in having a life-long interest in religion as something which arouses fascination but defies normal expression. He claimed his two favourite books were St Augustine's *Confessions*, and William James's *Varieties of Religious Experience*.

Glossary

Absolutism   In ethics the view that there are moral standards against which moral questions can be judged, and that some things are objectively good or evil, regardless of the context of the act.

Agape   Term taken from Greek philosophy, and used in the scriptures to mean the selfless care of others. It is also seen as the highest form of love.

Agnosticism   From the Greek *a gnosis*, not to know. The word is usually associated with religion; and an *agnostic* is one who refuses to accept religious claims because they cannot be known with certainty.

Analytic   Statements are said to be analytic if their meaning is already contained in the terms used, e.g. a wife is a married woman. Such statements provide no new information about the world, and so are said to be meaningful but trivial. (See *synthetic*.)

Anxiety (German, *angst*)   A major aspect of human existence in existentialist writings, it referred to the fundamental disturbance caused by the human awareness of 'finitude' or the 'threat of non-being' or more simply, death. Christian thinkers have used the concept to argue that it reveals a flaw in existence that justifies belief in God.

A posteriori   A form of reasoning or argument based, and dependent, on experience, or evidence. For example, a watch provides a posteriori evidence of the work of a watchmaker.

A priori   A form of reasoning or argument independent of, or 'prior' to, experience. In the ontological proof Anselm argued a priori that God must be 'that than which nothing greater can be conceived' and therefore must exist in reality. A priori reasoning is familiar in mathematics. (See *argument*.)

Argument   An argument is a form of reasoning involving premises leading to a conclusion. A *deductive* (or *a priori*) argument logically draws a nec-

GLOSSARY

essary conclusion from given premises, and claims to be a proof (the ontological proof is an example). But if the premises are challenged the conclusion becomes uncertain. An *inductive* argument is the kind typically used in science, and proceeds from observations of particular phenomena to a conclusion about all similar phenomena (all water tested can freeze, therefore all water can freeze). Aquinas and Paley used the method of induction in their cosmological and teleological arguments respectively. If all the things we see need a cause of their existence, there must have been a first 'uncaused' cause, for without such a concept existing things would never have come about. If this object (e.g. a watch) suggests a maker, all objects with similar characteristics also suggest a maker. Even in science it is generally accepted that inductive proof only leads to probability, not certainty.

Art The term is often used in opposition to science, because the latter is about empirical and factual accuracy, and art is of the imagination. Art comprises the visual arts (painting, drawing and sculpture); the harmonious arts (music); the dramatic arts (drama, opera, ballet), and the literary arts (poetry and literature). Every religion has attempted to find expression through art in one form or another. Pictorial art lent itself easily to a religion such as Christianity which was rooted in historical events and persons. Christian art therefore became important for illustrating key religious events such as the birth, death and resurrection of Christ. The great European cathedrals were seen as works of religious art in themselves, as well as locations for specific religious imagery in the form stained glass, painting and sculpture. But whether art in the wider, more secular, sense can work in the reverse direction, and give rise to emotions and intuitions that suggest some sense of the transcendent, is claimed by some, but is not found to be true for everyone.

Atheism Historically a movement claiming the non-existence of gods or God. Atheistic arguments are usually based on the belief that only material things exist (materialism), and that no evidence can be found to justify belief in anything beyond the material world.

Canon (of Scripture) The official list of books recognized by Christians as 'inspired' and belonging to the Bible. The canon was officially agreed by the early Church, but at the Reformation some Old Testament books were rejected as 'apocryphal'. The canon was reaffirmed for Roman Catholics by the Council of Trent in 1546. Today there is little controversy about the canon of Scripture: most Bibles on sale in bookshops include the agreed canon.

GLOSSARY

Causality The theory (challenged by Hume) that things follow others in a relation of cause to effect. An *efficient* cause is one that adequately explains how some effect is brought about. A *final* cause is that which explains the aim or purpose of an action, and always presupposes personal agency. Religious thinkers make use of this distinction to highlight the contrasting causalities operating in science and religion. The former deals with efficient, the latter with final, causality.

Cognitive From the Latin for 'knowledge'. Statements of religion are said to be 'non-cognitive' because they cannot be verified empirically. Theists would argue that they are cognitive within the perspective of faith, because they contain beliefs which touch on reality. But such cognition is gained through other faculties such as intuition, the sense of the numinous, mystical awareness, and the experience of conscience, rather than through empirical methods.

Consequentialism An ethical theory which holds that actions should be judged primarily by their consequences. Acts are good insofar as they create happiness, bad insofar as they increase pain. The classic example of consequentialism is utilitarianism.

Deism A religious movement that developed in seventeenth-century Europe, including Britain, in reaction to the religious conflicts among the churches. Deists turned to the fundamentals of religion, claiming that reason was enough to live by. They accepted the existence of God on rational grounds, but rejected all biblical claims and church teachings. They held that God was the 'architect' of the world and allowed it to run by itself according to natural laws. They accepted morality based on reason, but believed that the good would be rewarded in the afterlife, and the evil punished.

Delusion To claim that someone is under a delusion often amounts to saying they are mentally ill. The essence of delusions (unlike illusions) is their persistence in spite of evidence that they are wrong. Pathological delusions are normally associated with schizophrenia and related mental disorders (e.g. thinking I am someone else). Religious beliefs have never historically been seen as delusions because, for one thing, there is no conclusive evidence to show that they are wrong. To use the word delusion of deeply held religious beliefs is generally felt to show a misunderstanding of their essential nature, and a lack of respect for those who hold them.

Deontology An ethical theory which holds that the material content of ethics is moral rules, but the real essence of ethical behaviour is acting from a sense of duty to obey those rules. The classic deontological ethical theory is that of Immanuel Kant.

Dualism The term dualism is employed in opposition to monism to signify the ordinary view that the universe is composed of two different kinds of reality, matter and spirit, body and mind. Dualism is rejected by materialists who deny that this duality has any meaning. If the whole substance of the universe is material, there is no room for dualistic distinctions. Therefore there is no such thing as a soul, and the concept of spirit has no application apart from its material connections. Therefore the notion of a human spirit underlying the personality is simply explicable in terms of functions of the human body (brain, nerves, etc.). Dualism is central to religious beliefs which presuppose that body and soul, matter and spirit are valid distinctions. Theism, the belief that God is a spirit and separate from the material world, implies dualism. The distinction between good and evil is another key area of controversy between monists and dualists.

Education A process of learning which historically began with the teaching of the *seven liberal arts*. These were divided into the *trivium* (grammar, rhetoric and dialectic); and the *quadrivium* (arithmetic, geometry, astronomy and music). For our purpose education may be divided into secular and religious. Secular education refers to the study of secular subjects, which form the main content of the normal school syllabus. Religious education can mean education *of* or *into* a particular faith; or education *about* religion as a social phenomenon, and may also include the study of different religions. Philosophically it is argued that only education *about* religion should have a place in an educational setting, because only such a study can be objective, and fit the requirements of academic impartiality. While others see education into religion as an important component of human development, and part of education in the widest sense, the subject continues to raise many controversies.

Empiricism A theory of knowledge based on experience. The knowledge produced by science is called empirical knowledge, and is typically ascertained by the 'scientific method' of experimentation, testing and the pursuit of verifiable evidence. Empiricists reject the notion of innate ideas on the grounds that they cannot be based on experience, but rationalists hold that such ideas derive from the intellect, and are more certain than empirical knowledge.

Epistemology From the Greek *episteme*, 'knowledge'. The branch of philosophy concerned with knowledge, what it means, and how it is acquired. Historically it focused on the claims of the rationalists and empiricists as to which was the best path to truth and knowledge. Descartes represented the first, Hume the second. Theists hold that faith is a valid path to knowledge while atheists deny this. Plato held that knowledge extended beyond what was clearly true, to include that which was reliably believed. Some thinkers have claimed that an 'epistemic distance' separates man from God, and is part of the challenge of faith.

Eschatology From the Greek *eschaton*, meaning 'end', the term refers to the Christian doctrine of the 'four last things': death, judgement, heaven and hell. Eschatology sometimes includes the idea of an *apocalyptic* ending of the world by way of a cosmic catastrophe. While this is not taken literally by all Christians, the belief in the temporary nature of the world is widely accepted. Eschatology is directly opposed to *naturalistic* world views, and is central to belief in an afterlife. Hence the distinction between *eschatological happiness* and earthly happiness.

Ethics The study of human behaviour, or the study of what should constitute the best behaviour of human beings. Leads to ethical theories, laws, principles. Religious ethics is distinguished from secular ethics by its concept of God as the supreme ethical law-giver.

Fallacy A supposedly false line of reasoning. The 'naturalistic fallacy' is supposed to lie in the mistake of defining 'good' through its relation to specific 'goods'. G. E. Moore held that good was indefinable, and was something that could only be visible to intuition (like the colour yellow).

Falsification The falsification debate about religious language hinged on the claim that religious statements can never be falsified (disproven). It led to the claim that for this reason they were meaningless. Falsification is the negative side of verification. That religious beliefs cannot be falsified is both an alleged theoretical principle, and a fact of religious faith. The latter means that religious beliefs are not falsifiable in fact, because believers see nothing about the world to decisively make them so.

Fideism A term in theology to denote that faith stands by itself, and does not need the support of reason. Luther is generally regarded as the classic exponent of fideism.

Genetic fallacy The mistake of understanding the reality of something on the basis of how it came about. In connection with religion it appears in the claim that if religion, or a religious experience, began through psychological influences, its reality remains purely psychological. This is known as reductionism, and is seen by theists as an example of the genetic fallacy.

Hedonism The view that pleasure is the greatest good, and that all human endeavour should aim at the creation and enjoyment of pleasure, is the popular understanding of the term. Hedonism is in fact much more complicated. Epicurus, one of its founders, believed that the pursuit of pleasure and happiness must always allow for the same objectives to apply to others. Thus my desire for pleasure must not impede another's similar desire. The result is a much more ethically balanced life than might be supposed. Utilitarianism is generally regarded as a form of 'ethical hedonism', the view that the pleasure of all *should* be the aim of human behaviour.

Humanism   A word difficult to define because of the many meanings it has acquired. At its widest it means the sum total of all human ideals and sympathies that make people truly human. When used in a religious context it means those human ideals that are supported by a particular faith. Hence it is possible to speak of *Christian humanism*, which centres on the love of neighbour for the sake of the love of God. Supporters of Christian humanism argue that religion is needed to provide the spiritual inspiration that is necessary to reach all human ethical ideals. The term is also used in an anti-religious sense meaning the defence of human ideals purely from a rational (i.e. from an anthropological, personal and social) point of view. This is called *secular humanism*. Humanists of this category insist that morality has nothing to do with religion; and tend to campaign, for instance, for the removal of religion from schools, and its replacement with 'humanist' ideals based on the ideals of reason, and the perceived good of society. There is an inevitable friction between religious and secular humanists because one claims that a religious connection is important for the ethical life, while the other insists that reason and human sympathy alone are sufficient.

Hypothesis   Empirical hypotheses are suppositions pending final proof leading to the establishment of scientific laws. A logical hypothesis is one that leads to a logical conclusion (as in mathematics). A religious hypothesis goes beyond, but does not contradict, all possible scientific ones, to postulate a personal agency (God) as the ultimate origin of all things. A hypothesis can also be a proposition accepted for the sake of argument, in which case the conclusion will depend on the truth of the hypothesis. Hypothetical statements are characterized by the use of the word 'if', e.g. 'If this is gold it will not tarnish.'

Idealism   A complex philosophical position about what constitutes reality. It centres on the distinction between the 'external' world of objects, and the ideas of those objects in the mind. Some thinkers (like Descartes) have held that only what exists in consciousness is real, everything else can be doubted (*cogito ergo sum*). In the ontological proof, Anselm appears to adopt an idealist stance, arguing that God's reality can best be perceived in the mind.

Idolatry   Traditionally the worship of false gods. Idolatry in the Bible is seen in placing trust in a being who is at enmity with the true God. Hence 'the evil of idolatry' lies in turning to gods who do not subscribe to the ethical standards of the true God, the God of the Decalogue.

Illusion   Mistaken deception or belief which has to be revised when the truth is revealed. A mirage in the desert may turn out to be merely an illusion. People tend to be aware of the possibility of illusions, and often disclaim that they are 'under no illusion'. Freud held that religious beliefs were an illusion because they were based on feelings and wishes that he saw as having psychological origins. He was struck by the similarities between childhood beliefs in an almighty father, and religious beliefs in God as an almighty father. He believed the similarities included the feelings of guilt, the need the for appeasement of an offended superior, and the wish for security and salvation. According to Freud a young girl who wishes to grow up and marry a prince is under an illusion even though it turns out to be true. Freud's theory therefore leaves open the possibility that God exists, but he was completely convinced of its illusory possibilities. He was polite enough never to call religion a delusion, because this has other implications (see *delusion*).

Incarnation   The term which refers to the Christian belief that Jesus was the Christ, the Son of God who became 'incarnate' for the guidance of man, and by his death, for the salvation of humanity.

Infinite regress   The term refers to an infinite series of causes and effects going back through infinite time. While some say the past can be divided into a time era, and a pre-time era of prime matter (when nothing changed), many claim that it is difficult to imagine *timelessness* since it is one of the organizing categories of the human mind. Therefore the notion of endless time into the past is theoretically unintelligible. Or is it? Aristotle said that infinite time *cannot be traversed* since it has no starting point. Hence the view that Big Bang could never be dated, for the same reason. It would have happened infinitely long ago, and be infinitely distant from us. The idea of an event happening infinitely long ago is considered an absurdity, and science confirms that the Big Bang can indeed be dated. But it can only be dated from us, and the question arises how it arose in the first place.

GLOSSARY

Inspiration (of Scripture)   The view that the scriptures (Old and New Testaments) are not merely human documents, but were the product of both human and divine influences. Traditionally they have been seen as the work of the Holy Spirit, who 'breathed on', or 'inspired', the sacred writers who were the human instruments of God in bearing witness to his revelation. Some views of inspiration take more account of the human elements in the scriptural writings, leading to more liberal (sometimes symbolic or mythical) interpretation of these writings, while others take more account of the divine elements, leading to a more strict (sometimes literal) interpretation of them.

Intrinsic   Refers to what has value in itself, as opposed to its 'extrinsic' value. A gold key is intrinsically valuable, while an ordinary key is extrinsically valuable for opening a door. In ethics some actions are claimed to be intrinsically wrong, such as deliberate murder or rape. In this sense such actions cannot be justified by appeal to extrinsic (or, say, consequential) reasons. The extent to which any action can be called intrinsically wrong is debated by some ethical thinkers.

Kalam   The term means 'discussion', and refers in Islam to the 'religious sciences'. A follower of Kalam is one who relies on dialectic (reasoned argument) in religious discussion. The so-called Kalam argument is based on the principle that everything that exists needs a cause of its existence outside of itself. Only God does not need such a cause – because he is divine, and because he is a personal agent who can move himself.

Kantian ethics   The ethical system of Kant which puts duty to obey the moral law as the fundamental principle of ethical behaviour. At the subjective level the willingness to do one's duty is the sign of a good will, an essential precondition of ethical behaviour.

Materialism   A metaphysical theory that reality is confined to the material world, and that all living organisms, including human beings, are ultimately material substances. It underlies the belief that the object of life is to satisfy legitimate human desires, and to achieve happiness and success either through material possessions or spiritually through a respect for duty and honour. It is opposed to a religious outlook which looks beyond the material world and recognizes a transcendent Being (God) in the light of whose existence all material actions and values are judged and put in perspective.

Metaphysics   The term means 'beyond physics' and fell into disrepute after Hume called for all books on it to be 'consigned to the flames'. Metaphysics

GLOSSARY

is about all questions that can be raised about reality, including what constitutes reality itself. Hence experimental and scientific methods are not appropriate for metaphysical knowledge, which goes beyond the physical and the empirical. The central topic of metaphysics is the question of Being (ontology). Under this heading are a host of questions about what really *is*. Metaphysical thinking is a purely rational activity and examines questions that lie behind notions such as being, existence, the world, reality and God. Those who challenge metaphysical claims, such as the existence of God, already enter metaphysical debate, often holding contrasting metaphysical theories, such as the ultimacy of matter. This leads many to argue that if scientists stick to science, there would be less conflict with religion. Metaphysical speculation is difficult to rule out since it is natural to ask with Leibniz, 'Why is there something and not nothing?'

Modal Pertaining to 'modes' of being or existence (*de re*), or of propositions (*de dicto*) as necessary, or possible. Both 'necessity' and 'possibility' are modes of being of a thing, or of a proposition. *Modal logic* is a special form of logic that analyses modes of existence such as necessary, possible or contingent. Modal logic has been applied especially to the ontological proof for the existence of God, and is associated with the work of Hartshorne and Plantinga.

Monism This is the philosophical theory that the universe is composed of one substance, matter. Monism denies the existence of spirit, and rejects the distinction between body and soul, and good and evil. All reality is reducible to material substances and all events can be explained in terms of material or psychological forces.

Naturalism An important concept in the debate between religion and science. It is the view that ultimate reality is *natural*. It is opposed to the view that what is ultimate goes beyond (transcends) what is natural. It therefore stands as an atheistic theory which rejects the existence of a transcendent realm and with it the existence of God. Devastating critiques of naturalism have been produced by thinkers like Plantinga, who point out that if naturalism entails, as it does, the view that everything has evolved by accident (unguided evolution), then no absolute claim can be made for the reliability of either sense perceptions, or supposed rational thinking. Under a naturalist world view we may all (as Descartes said) be living in a dream world under the control of an evil demon.

Natural theology A branch of theology which uses reason alone to establish religious claims such as the existence of God. The traditional arguments for theism are classic examples of natural theology.

Numinous A term borrowed from Kant, who distinguished between '*phenomenon*' and '*noumenon*'. The former can be directly experienced but the latter 'lay behind' experience. The term was popularized by Rudolf Otto, to denote a hidden reality, or 'mystery', that can be sensed in certain situations. The numinous is that which evokes awe and wonder, a mystical awareness from which a sense of the 'holy' can be detected. Otto believed the numinous lay behind all great religious experience.

Ontology The science of being. Ontology examines all questions about the meaning of reality and is therefore the fundamental subject matter of metaphysics. The ontological proof of Anselm is about the 'being' of God.

Original sin A religious concept, meaning a tendency towards evil innate in human nature derived from the 'original' sin of Adam and Eve. The truth of the concept has been recognized by existentialist thinkers like Heidegger, who spoke of the 'fallenness' of human nature, something that makes us prone to temptation, and prevents the attainment of 'authentic existence'.

Paradox A term used by Kierkegaard to refer to the rational impossibility of revelation. From a rational viewpoint revelation was a 'paradox'. A paradox is an apparent contradiction.

Philosophy Literally, 'the love of wisdom'. A system dedicated to the acquisition of knowledge about reality using reason alone. There are many branches of philosophy. Philosophy of religion examines all aspects of religious belief, and aims to make rational judgements about its claims for credibility or coherence.

Pragmatism A movement in philosophy, especially in America, which stressed the importance of making truth 'work'. The measure of truth was its pragmatic effects. Seen in this light the truth of religious beliefs is not in their abstract correctness, but in how far they help in understanding reality, and in advancing the good of the believer. In a sense they believed that 'truth was known by its fruits'. Pragmatists had little time for philosophical arguments about the meaning of 'concepts' and what they saw as various forms of philosophical 'hair-splitting'.

Probability Distinguished from proof, because the conclusion is only likely rather than certain. In religious arguments, many believe that conclusions lead to probability rather than proof, but Aquinas and Anselm would be unlikely to accept this.

Proof The demonstration by argument or some practical means that something is certainly the case. It is questioned whether the word proof can always be used in an empirical sense, since empirical facts are at best only 'beyond reasonable doubt', and things may not be the same in the future. The term is completely acceptable in mathematics and formal logic.

Rationalism A theory based on the claim that reason is the surest path to knowledge. It is generally opposed to empiricism, although both systems rely to some extent on each other. Descartes held that what he knew by reason was superior to what he knew from experience, since the latter is often mistaken or misleading.

Realism The theory that what is real is what can be directly experienced, and is usually identified with 'facts'. If something is 'unreal' it is untrue. Recently the issue has been seen to be more complex. Some things are only real by convention. The equator is not an objective fact, but a 'reality', a guiding principle decided on by human convention. It exists as a reality, but its reality is not real in the ordinary sense as, say, Everest is real. In the same way, it is claimed, the concept of God can be understood in a 'non-realist' way as part of a *language game*. This happens if God is seen as representing what people hold most dear, a symbol of what they are prepared to honour and worship above all else. If realism begins from the top down, seeing God as objectively the Highest Being, non-realism begins from the bottom up, seeing God as that which represents what humans have idealized as most valuable and most true.

Reason In its widest sense reason is the faculty by which we make judgements about truth leading to knowledge. Kant distinguished between *theoretical* reason and *practical* reason. Theoretical, or *pure*, reason leads to knowledge of facts about the world. Practical reason leads to knowledge of how we should act, and the knowledge implied in why we should act. This leads in turn to a knowledge of God. Other faculties such as feeling and intuition give rise to questions which reason is employed to examine and pass judgement on. Faith is sometimes contrasted with reason because it relies on data that cannot be ascertained by reason alone, i.e. revelation.

Hence philosophy is contrasted with theology, which, although using reason, draws on data not available from human knowledge alone. *Rationalists*, who rely on reason alone, argue that faith is outside reason and cannot lead to rational convictions. Thus faith is often deemed to be *irrational*. Believers would say this hardly holds water, for two reasons. One, religious beliefs are generally seen to be possessed by reasonable people. Two, because faith can be claimed to be a reasonable interpretation of the world

GLOSSARY

of facts, is consistent with many aspects of human experience, and is not unrelated to genuine feelings and intuitions.

Reductionism The tendency to conclude that if something like a religious experience can be explained in terms of natural, or psychological causes, then there is no justification to claim any further cause. This is to 'reduce' the significance of something seen as 'religious' to purely natural components. Empiricists (like Hume) argue that alleged supernatural causes can never be demonstrated, and therefore such claims are meaningless. Theists often allow for the operation of natural causes in an alleged religious event (such as a miracle), but would see reductionism as a predictable function of an atheistic starting point.

Relativism An ethical theory which holds that there are no absolute principles which are binding on everyone everywhere. Instead all ethical principles are relative to times, places and cultures. Relativism is a complex view, since to state it is already to support some form of absolutism. Relativism in ethics is strongly opposed by Christian ethicists because it implies that ethical principles are ultimately decided by man, not God. At the same time religious ethicists allow for the relative influence of changing human perceptions.

Religion A system of belief in the existence of a supernatural being, or beings. An exception may be made for Buddhism which is called a religion despite having no belief in the supernatural. Religions generally have distinctive features such as a body of beliefs centring on the supernatural (God), ritual customs, special buildings for worship, and a system of values derived from their beliefs.

Religious A term used in opposition to secular. A religious viewpoint is one that assumes the existence of God, and so on. Religious ethics are generally understood as comprising those principles contained in Scripture, and focus on motives related to specific religious beliefs, such as the incarnation.

Revealed theology The branch of theology dealing with the truths revealed by God in the Bible. The later working out of the meaning of the revealed truths of faith, such as the identity of Jesus as the Son of God, and the doctrine of the Trinity, are classic examples of revealed theology.

Revelation A fundamental term used in religion to denote the disclosure by God of truths about himself and his relationship with humanity. The beliefs of the Christian faith, for instance, are seen as the 'truths of revelation'. How the concept stands up to rational analysis is the task of philosophy. What it means in itself, and its implications for human life and values, is the task of theology.

Scientism The view that all truths are ultimately scientific. Scientism rejects all truth-claims that are not supported by empirical evidence. In this category is put religion and metaphysics.

Scripture The name commonly used by Christians for the writings of the Bible. The question of the interpretation of Scripture is a major area of controversy within Christianity, stretching from the conservative or fundamentalist 'literal' interpretation, to more 'liberal' interpretations favoured by many thinkers and scholars.

Secular A term meaning non-religious, as in 'secular ethics' or 'secular values'. Secularism as a movement is anti-religious, and is based on the belief that all principles of living should rest on human reason alone.

Situationism The view that situations permit the overthrow of ethical obligations based on traditional moral laws. So called 'situation ethics' is a Christian theory in which traditional moral laws can be overridden by love of neighbour (agape), if the situation requires. It has been rejected by traditional Christian ethicists on the grounds that theoretically it promotes relativism, and in practice encourages a dangerous disregard for traditional moral rules and obligations.

Spirituality In its widest sense the word refers to the capacity of human beings to go beyond the bodily and the instinctive, and seek fulfilment in what is noble and spiritual. In a religious context spirituality refers to the awareness of the transcendent, and the capacity to rise above material temptations in the pursuit of spiritual and moral values. While spirituality is something that can be developed by all human beings, its development has always been the special concern of religion.

Superstition Superstition is distinguished from religion insofar as it rules out any belief in personal morality. While religion is based on an ethical relationship with the supernatural (God), superstition attempts to gain favour from the gods by the detached use of material things such as charms, horoscopes, lucky omens, spells or rituals. Superstition can sometimes take the form of belief in the occult and the demonic, but in ordinary usage it is generally seen as relatively harmless. Religion itself can become a form of superstition, especially if it is used naively for selfish advantage, and without regard for inner conversion or repentance.

Symbols Conventional ways of expressing truths, ideas or beliefs by way of icons, logos, signs, etc. Christian symbols are valued for their power to

GLOSSARY

focus attention on key aspects of faith, especially in the context of religious buildings, or in surroundings of emotional significance such as graveyards, tombs, gravestones, gardens of remembrance, etc.

Synthetic To call a statement synthetic is another way of saying that it is about something in the real world. Such a statement 'synthesizes' or brings together a subject and a predicate (e.g. the weather is good), and is normally able to be verified or falsified as to its truth. (See *analytic*.)

Theism From the Greek *theos* (God), it means the belief in one God. It is opposed by *pantheism* which identifies God with the world; *polytheism* which stands for belief in many gods: and *atheism* which denies the reality of any God. 'Believers' and 'theists' are usually synonymous.

Theology The philosophical enterprise carried out by believers into the meaning and implications of their religious beliefs. A theologian can be a philosopher, but a philosopher is not necessarily a theologian. The classic function of the theologian is to engage in the task of understanding the nature and significance of faith (*fides quaerens intellectum*), a function which normally presupposes its prior acceptance.

Truth A fundamental concept usually meaning 'what is the case'. Empiricists limit what is the case to what can be proved to be so by empirical methods. Theists hold that truth extends beyond the empirical, to include morality and religion. The common-sense view of truth is that which corresponds to reality. In this view reality is that which is objectively true as 'a matter of fact'. Classical theism was based on the assumption that God exists as a real Being (in fact the 'most real' Being, the *ens realissimum)*. Non-realism is the product of what is called the *coherence* view of truth. In this view truth is not a matter of objective facts, but a matter of what people decide is true for them. Some see the coherence between religious beliefs and the possibility of their being true, as an example of this theory of truth (see also *realism*).

Verification A key word in the debate about the meaning of religious language. The word is used as shorthand for 'empirical verification' as in the 'verification principle'. It is argued that because religious claims cannot be empirically verified they are meaningless. The fact that other claims to truth (verities) such as moral, aesthetic or emotional claims, can also not be verified undermined the authority of the principle as an absolute test of truth.

Select Bibliography

Audi, R. (ed.). (1995) *The Cambridge Dictionary of Philosophy*, Cambridge: Cambridge University Press.

Bowker, J. (1991) *The Meanings of Death*, Cambridge: Cambridge University Press.

Buber, M. (1923) *I and Thou*, Edinburgh: T&T Clark (1960 edition).

Copleston, F. C. (1946–75) *A History of Philosophy*, 12 vols, London: Continuum (2003 edition).

Craig, E. (ed.) (1998) *The Routledge Encyclopedia of Philosophy*, 10 vols, London: Routledge.

Craig, W. L. and Smith, Q. (1995) *Theism, Atheism and Big Bang Cosmology*, Oxford: Clarendon Press.

Freud, S. (1927) *The Future of an Illusion*, London: Hogarth (1962 edition).

Gilbey, T. (ed.) (1951) *Aquinas, Philosophical Texts*, London: Oxford University Press.

Gilbey, T (ed.) (1955) *Aquinas, Theological Texts*, London: Oxford University Press.

Goodman, R. B. (2002) *Wittgenstein and William James*, Cambridge: Cambridge University Press.

Haring, B. (1954–63) *The Law of Christ*, Cork: Mercier Press.

Hick, J. (1968) *Evil and the God of Love*, London: Macmillan.

Hooker, B. (2001) *Morality, Rules and Consequences*, Edinburgh: Edinburgh University Press.

Hume, D. (1746) *Dialogues Concerning Natural Religion*, in *Hume Selections*, ed. Charles W. Hendel, New York: Scribner (1955 edition).

James, W. (1902) *The Varieties of Religious Experience*. London: Longman (1945 edition).

Jung, C. G. (1933) *Modern Man in Search of a Soul*. London and New York: Routledge (2001 edition).

Kant, I. (1788) *The Critique of Practical Reason*, London: Routledge (1961 edition).

Kenny, A. (2004) *Ancient Philosophy*, vol. 1, Oxford: Clarendon Press.

SELECT BIBLIOGRAPHY

Kierkegaard, S. (1846) *Philosophical Fragments*, Princeton: Princeton University Press (1962 edition).
McGinn, B. (1992) The Foundations of Mysticism. London: SCM Press.
McGrath A. E. (ed.) (1993) *The Blackwell Encyclopedia of Modern Christian Thought*, Oxford: Blackwell.
MacIntyre, A. (1981) *After Virtue: A Study in Moral Theory*. London: Duckworth.
Macquarrie, J. and Childress, J. (eds) (1990) *A New Dictionary of Christian Ethics*, London: SCM Press.
Russell, B. (1946) *A History of Western Philosophy*, London: Unwin (1984 edition).
Pannenberg, W. (1964) *Jesus: God and Man*, Philadelphia: Westminster Press.
Pascal, B. (1670) *Pensées*, Harmondsworth: Penguin Classics (1966 edition).
Pateman, T. (1991) *Key Concepts: A Guide to Aesthetics*, London: Falmer Press.
Polkinghorne, J. (1991) *Reason and Reality*, London: SPCK.
Popper, K. (1963) *Conjectures and Refutations*, London: Routledge & Kegan Paul.
Schleiermacher, F. (1799) *On Religion: Speeches to its Cultured Despisers*, New York: Harper & Row (1958 edition).
Scruton, R. (1998) *An Intelligent Person's Guide to Modern Culture*, London: Duckworth.
Steiner, G. (2001) *Grammars of Creation*, London: Faber & Faber.
Wakefield, G. S. (ed.) (1983) *A Dictionary of Spirituality*, London: SCM Press.
Wikipedia Internet Encyclopedia (2008).
Wittgenstein, L. (1953) *Philosophical Investigations*, Oxford: Blackwell.
Wright, A. (2002) *Why Bother with Theology?*, London: Darton Longman & Todd.

Index

anthropic principle 35
argument
  kinds of 7–8
art
  and religion 102–103
atheism
  arguments for 205–208
  Christian responses to 208–214
  history of 201–208
  historical roots of 205–206

basic beliefs 84
Bible
  empirical assumptions in 177–178
  interpretation of 73–76
  morality and 74–75
  personal agency and 180–181
  symbols in 96
  see also scripture
big bang theory 29, 35, 182, 186–189
big crunch 158
blind chance 43, 182–183, 185
  Swinburne on 183
brute fact universe 27–29, 35
  Russell and 184

causality
  different causalities 187–189
  religion and science 188
Christianity 3–4
  ethics and 250–254
  modern culture and 116–118
  revelation in 62–63
  science and 177–179
  see also churches
Church and churches
  and scripture 72
  as human phenomenon 113
  as social organisation 115
  authority of 85–88
  classical theism
  cultural contribution of 115–118
  meaning of 53–56
  philosophical problems with 57
  religious problems with 58
conscience
  Aquinas and 278–279
  aspects of 278
  Butler and 280–281
  different views of 276–277, 284–285
  ethical theories and 283

331

INDEX

Freud and 281–282
Newman and 283–284
popular expressions about 277
cosmological argument
  Aquinas' version 23–24
  Copleston's version 27–28
  criticisms of 28–29
  Kalam version 24–25
  origins in Plato and Aristotle 23
  religious faith and 31

death of God 206, 213
Darwinism 178–179, 208
  see also evolution
determinism
  hard and soft 288–292
  summary of terms 292–293
  views about 289–293
  see also freewill

eschatology
  Christian 153
  happiness and 252–253
  in ethics 150–151
eschatological verification 229–230
ethical language 259–263
ethical terms 260–261
ethical theories
  survey of 238–261
  summary of 257
ethics
  Bentham and Mill 245
  Christian ethics 250–254
  Kantian ethics 238–240
  natural law ethics 255–257
  religious and secular ethics 235–237
  religious ethics 250–254

situation ethics 257–259
social convention and 236
utilitarian ethics 241–244
see also virtue ethics
evil and suffering
  Augustine and 168–169
  Irenaeus and 167–168
  non-theism and 175–176
  responses to 166
  theodicy and 166–167
  see also theodicy
evolution 37, 41, 178–179
  see also Darwinism

faith
  as an I-Thou relationship 79–80
  aspects of 78
  different views on 107
  evidence and 81–83
  idea of implicit faith 88–89
  Kierkegaard and 108
  moral values and 80–81
  nature of 77–79
  personal fulfilment and 84–85
  relation to reason 83–84
  religious authority and 85–86
  trust and 78
falsification debate
  outline of 223–224
  theistic responses to 225–231
  see also parables
fideism 105, 107–108
fundamentalism 180
freewill
  God's omniscience and 293–295
  determinism and 286–292
  religion and 288–289
  summary of terms 292–293

INDEX

see also determinism
freewill defence 167–169

God
  arguments for 8–48
  assessment of arguments
    for 49–51
  classical theism 53–56
  Judeo-Christian concept of 52–53
  language about 93
  non-existence of 212
  non-realist approach to 59–60
god of the gaps 42
genetic fallacy 132

idolatry 64
infinite regress 22, 27, 186
is–ought debate 261–263

knowledge
  academic 7
  a priori 8
  a posteriori 8

language games theory
  outline of 220–222
  problems with 222–223
life after death (afterlife)
  challenges to 154
  coherence of 151–153
  eastern religions and 159–160
  evidence for 155–158
  God's existence and 145–146
  history and 155–158
  Kant and 149–150
  Plato and 147–149
  religion and 145–146
  resurrection of Jesus and 155–158

symbols of 99–100
see also resurrection, soul
logical positivism 215–216
see also religious language

meaning and verification 219, 227–231
metaphors 101
metaphysics
  defence of 184–185
  religion and 186–187
  science and 181–183
miracles
  as more subjective than objective 197
  as amazing coincidences 199
  defence of 194–200
  different views of 197–198
  definitions of 191
  God's intervention and 197
  Hume and 191–193
  in Christian tradition 190
  meaning of 197–198
  natural causality and 198
  objections to 197
  special purpose kinds 199–200
  summary of Hume on 193
moral arguments
  Kant's moral argument 43–47
  moral vacuum argument 47–48
morality
  philosophical views on 138
  see also ethics
mysticism
  assessment of 133
  examples of 129
  historical significance of 126–129
  place in Christianity 134–135

333

INDEX

problems with 129–133
see also religious experience

near death experiences 160–161
natural law
  Aquinas on 256
  philosophical background to 255
  relation to religion 256
  Stoics and 255
naturalistic fallacy 261–262

ontological proof
  Anselm's version 10–13
  Descartes version 13, 14, 15, 18
  Kant's objections to 15–17
  modern formulations: Hartshorne and Platinga on 19–21
  relation to faith 21–22

parables
  in defence of religious language 226–231
Pascal's wager 108–110
personal agency 180
philosophy
  Christianity and 3–4
Plato's allegory of the cave 105–106
positivism 215–216
process theodicy 171, 172
proof and probability 8

quantum mechanics
  Heisenberg and 291, 304

reason
  and faith 104–108
  different views on 107–108

revelation, faith and 64
religion
  cultural values and 115
  Durkheim and 203
  Freud and 204
  Marx and 202
  meaning of 113–114
  modern culture and 116–118
  Neitzsche and 206
  personal agency and 180
  philosophy of 1
  roots of 124–125
  society and 115–117
  theories of 211
  views of 212
religions
  common features of 114
  origins of 63
  religious experience and 126
  revelation and 62
  society and 115, 118
religious authorities 88
religious authority
  Church and 86–87
  exercise of today 87
  mediators of 86
  significance of 85–86
religious and ethical language 259
religious ethics 250–254
religious experience
  authority of 126–127, 135
  existence of God and 135
  feeling and 121–122
  kinds of 116, 119–120
  mysticism and 127–129
  numinous and 124–126
  problems with 123, 125–129
  religious founders and 126–127

334

INDEX

Schleiermacher and 122–123
verification of 129–130
see also mysticism
religious language
  analogy, symbol, myth 92–95
  language games and 220–221
  logical positivism and 215–216
  problems and use of 91–92
resurrection
  objections to 158
  Pannenberg and 155–159
  views about 156
revelation
  different beliefs about 62–63
  faith, reason and 68
  fundamental concept 61–62
  philosophical issues and 65–68
  possibility of 66
  propositional and
    non-propositional 69–71
  relation to scripture 71–76
  sources of 71–73, 12

science
  Bible and 179–180
  causality in 187–189
  challenge to religion 178–179
  metaphysics and 181–183
  religion and 178
scripture
  authority of 72–75
  canon of 72
  interpretation of 73–74
  relation to tradition 73
  revelation and 71
  source of morality 74
  see also Bible
situation ethics 257–259

soul
  immortality of 146–147, 149
  Plato and Aristotle and 146–148
  powers of 149
  problems with 152–154
  see also life after death
spirituality
  aspect of human
    development 137–139
  morality and 139
  philosophy and 143
  religion and 141–142
symbols
  Christian 98
  function in religion 95–98
  of life after death 99–100
  problems with 100–101
  science and 100
  Tillich and 96–97

teleological argument
  anthropic argument 35
  Aquinas and 33
  challenges to 37, 43
  Paley and 33–34
  Swinburne and 36–37, 181
theodicy
  assessment of 174–176
  Augustine and 168–169
  Christian theodicy 170
  Irenaeus and 167–168
  Leibniz and 167
  philosophical theodicy 172
  process theodicy 172–173
  summary of theodicies 173
  see also evil and suffering

Utilitarianism
  action centred 246

INDEX

Christianity and 251–253
moral fulfilment and 248
social ethics and 248
types of 249

verification
  principle 216
  problems with 217–219
  religious experience and 129–133
virtue ethics
  Aquinas and 268–269
  Aristotle and 265–267
  background to 264–265
  cardinal virtues 268
  limitations of 274–275
  MacIntyre and 270–272
  religion and 273–274

world views 3
why believe 90